Who Cares for Them?

Recent Titles in
Contributions to the Study of Aging

Old Age in a Bureaucratic Society: The Elderly, the Experts, and the State in American History
David Van Tassel and Peter N. Stearns, editors

The Aged in Rural America
John A. Krout

Public Policy Opinion and the Elderly, 1952-1978
John E. Tropman

The Mirror of Time: Images of Aging and Dying
Joan M. Boyle and James E. Morriss

North American Elders: United States and Canadian Perspectives
Eloise Rathbone-McCuan and Betty Havens, editors

Hispanic Elderly in Transition: Theory, Research, Policy and Practice
Steven R. Applewhite, editor

Religion, Health, and Aging: A Review and Theoretical Integration
Harold George Koenig, Mona Smiley, and Jo Ann Ploch Gonzales

Philanthropy and Gerontology: The Role of American Foundations
Ann H. L. Sontz

Perceptions of Aging in Literature: A Cross-Cultural Study
Prisca von Dorotka Bagnell and Patricia Spencer Soper, editors

Residential Care for the Elderly: Critical Issues in Public Policy
Sharon A. Baggett

Senior Centers in America
John A. Krout

Shared Housing for the Elderly
Dale J. Jaffe, editor

WHO CARES FOR THEM?

Workers in the Home Care Industry

Penny Hollander Feldman
with
Alice M. Sapienza
and
Nancy M. Kane

Contributions to the Study of Aging, Number 16
Erdman B. Palmore, Series Adviser

GREENWOOD PRESS

New York • Westport, Connecticut • London

Library of Congress Cataloging-in-Publication Data

Feldman, Penny Hollander.
Who cares for them? : workers in the home care industry / Penny Hollander Feldman with Alice M. Sapienza and Nancy M. Kane.
p. cm. — (Contributions to the study of aging, ISSN 0732-085X ; no. 16)
Includes bibliographical references.
ISBN 0-313-26837-1 (lib. bdg. : alk. paper)
1. Home health aides—United States. 2. Visiting housekeepers—United States. 3. Home care services—United States.
I. Sapienza, Alice M. II. Kane, Nancy M. III. Title. IV. Series.
RA645.35.F45 1990
362.6′3—dc20 89-17234

British Library Cataloguing in Publication Data is available.

Library of Congress Catalog Card Number: 89-17234
ISBN: 0-313-26837-1
ISSN: 0732-085X

First published in 1990

Greenwood Press, Inc.
88 Post Road West, Westport, Connecticut 06881

Printed in the United States of America

The paper used in this book complies with the Permanent Paper Standard issued by the National Information Standards Organization (Z39.48-1984).

10 9 8 7 6 5 4 3 2 1

Contents

Figures and Tables ix

Acknowledgments xiii

PART I. The Labor Market, the Work Force, and Industry Conditions

1. Providing Home Aide Services: The Challenge 3
Introduction 3
The Growing Demand for Home Care 4
Numbers of Providers and Workers 7
The Problem: Work Life Issues for the Home Aide Work Force 8
Management Concerns 10
Work Life Programs 13

2. The Home Care Labor Market 17
Labor Market Trends Affecting the Home Care Industry 17
Characteristics of the Home Aide Work Force 23
Summary and Implications 26

3. The Job of the Home Aide 29
A Day in the Life of a Home Aide 30
The Practice of Home Care 34
Sources of Job Satisfaction and Motivation 39

4. Understanding Job Satisfaction and Turnover 41
The Rationale for Examining Worker Attitudes 41
Worker Attitudes toward the Job 42

Explaining Job Satisfaction and Turnover 43
Summary and Implications 52

5. Financial Conditions in the Home Care Industry 55
Demand Characteristics of the Industry 56
Supply Characteristics of the Industry 56
Overview of the Home Care Market 58
Performance of Publicly Held For-Profit Home Health Service Companies Providing Primary Services 61
Implications 65

PART II. Case Studies of the Work Life Demonstrations

6. Introduction to the Case Studies 71
Underlying Assumptions 71
Site Selection 72
Main Characteristics of the Demonstration Sites 73
Key Actors 74
Characteristics of the Work Force 76

7. Remedy Home and Health Care, Inc., San Diego 79
Introduction 79
Agency and Corporate Management 80
The Union 80
Employment, Labor Market Conditions, and Work Life Issues 82
Components of the Demonstration 85
Program Implementation 85
Program Costs 92
Program Effects 92
Program Postscript 99

8. Independent Living and Long Life Home Care Services, New York 103
Introduction 103
The Home Attendant's Job 104
The Unions 105
Worker Attitudes 106
The Work Life Demonstration at Long Life and Independent Living 106
Program Implementation 109
Program Costs 112
Program Effects 112
Program Postscript 117

9. Quality Care: Syracuse and Milwaukee 123
Introduction 123
Agency and Corporate Management 124

Working Conditions 125
Worker Attitudes and Job Satisfaction 126
The Work Life Demonstrations at Quality Care 128
Program Implementation 129
Program Costs 136
Program Effects 136
Program Postscript 142

PART III. Overview of Work Life Programs

10. Overview: Adopting and Implementing Work Life Changes 149
Motives for Adopting Work Life Improvements 149
Factors Affecting Implementation 154
Implications 160

11. Overview: Worker Participation, Turnover, and Continuity of Care 165
Worker Participation in the Work Life Programs 166
Program Dropouts 168
The Impact of Work Life Changes on Turnover and Continuity of Care 172
Target Groups and Program Components 177

PART IV. Recommendations and Policy Implications

12. Summary 185
Major Findings 185

13. Management Strategies and Policy Options for Ensuring a Sufficient and Reliable Home Aide Work Force 193
Recommendations for Home Care Employers and Managers 194
Policy Options 204
Expansion of Third-Party Financing and Development of Innovative Delivery Systems 207

Methodological Appendix 211

Glossary of Names and Abbreviations 219

References 221

Index 229

Figures and Tables

FIGURES

4.1	Causal Model	45
4.2	Causal Model: Satisfaction and Intent to Leave	47
4.3	Causal Model: Satisfaction and Intent to Leave, Public Client Agencies	49
4.4	Causal Model: Satisfaction and Intent to Leave, Mixed Client Agencies	51

TABLES

2.1	Income Differentials Between Males and Females, Selected Health Occupations	22
2.2	Typology of Industry Characteristics	24
2.3	Characteristics of Survey Respondents	25
4.1	Attitudes of Survey Respondents, 17 Sites	43
4.2	Results of the Regression Analysis	47
4.3	Regression Results—Public Client Agencies	50
4.4	Regression Results—Mixed Client Agencies	51
5.1	Segments of Medical Home Care Market	58
5.2	Home Health Care Services—Publicly Held For-Profit Companies and Subsidiaries	62
5.3	Profitability by Nonfinancial Evidence	63

5.4	Evidence Regarding Profitability of Companies with Financial Statements or Prospectuses that Identify Home Health Sector Profitability	64
5.5	Average Hourly Earnings, Nonsupervisory Workers in Selected Occupations: United States	66
6.1	Characteristics of Demonstration Sites	73
6.2	Actors Involved in Adoption and Implementation	75
6.3	Characteristics of Home Attendants: Demonstration Agencies	77
7.1	Attitudes of Remedy Homemakers	84
7.2	Proportion of Remedy Homemakers Successfully Contacted	87
7.3	Proportion of Contacted Remedy Homemakers Who Agreed to Participate	88
7.4	Remedy Homemakers' Reasons for Declining to Participate	89
7.5	Remedy Homemakers: Completion of Training	90
7.6	Remedy Program Participants, Status of Guaranteed Hours 3 Months and 15 Months After Training	91
7.7	Remedy Current Workers, Work Status of Program Participants and Controls at 6-Month, 12-Month, and 18-Month Follow-up	93
7.8	Remedy Current Workers, Work Status of Program Participants and Matched Controls at 6-Month, 12-Month, and 18-Month Follow-up	95
7.9	Relationship Between Prior Service and 18-Month Turnover, Program Participants and Matched Controls	96
7.10	18-Month Follow-up, Program Participants and Matched Controls	96
7.11	18-Month Follow-up, Program Participants and Matched Controls: Hours of Service During Demonstration Period	97
7.12	Remedy New Workers, Work Status of Program Participants and Controls at 6-Month, 12-Month, and 18-Month Follow-up	98
7.13	Remedy New Workers, Hours of Service During Demonstration Period	99
8.1	Attitudes of Home Attendants, Long Life and Independent Living	107
8.2	Continuity of Care Among Program Participants and Controls at One-Year Follow-up	114

8.3	Reasons for Changing Clients, Comparison of Program Participants and Controls at One-Year Follow-up	115
8.4	Work Status of Program Participants and Controls at One-Year Follow-up	115
8.5	Continuity of Care, Comparison of Program Participants and Controls Whose Cases Were Still "Open"	116
8.6	Work Status of Program Participants and Controls Whose Cases Were Open at One-Year Follow-up	117
9.1	Attitudes of Home Aides, Syracuse and Milwaukee Quality Care	127
9.2	Proportion of Quality Care Aides Who Agreed to Participate	130
9.3	Program Status: Syracuse and Milwaukee	131
9.4	Quality Care Milwaukee: 12-Month Follow-up, Work Status of Program Participants and Controls Including Program Dropouts	137
9.5	Quality Care Milwaukee: 18-Month Follow-up, Work Status of Program Participants and Controls Including Program Dropouts	138
9.6	Quality Care Syracuse: 12-Month Follow-up, Work Status of Program Participants and Controls Including Program Dropouts	139
9.7	Quality Care Syracuse: 18-Month Follow-up, Work Status of Program Participants and Controls Including Program Dropouts	139
9.8	Quality Care Syracuse: 12-Month Follow-up, Work Status of Program Participants and Controls Excluding 2-Week Dropouts	139
9.9	Quality Care Syracuse: 18-Month Follow-up, Work Status of Program Participants and Controls Excluding 2-Week Dropouts	140
9.10	Most and Least Important Program Aspects: Remaining Staff Aides	141
9.11	Other Attitudes toward the Program: Remaining Staff Aides	141
9.12	Syracuse: Differences in Job Satisfaction Among Staff Aides Comparing Baseline and 12-Month Follow-up	143
11.1	Proportion of Workers Contacted Who Agreed to Participate	167
11.2	Training Program Dropouts	169

11.3	Number and Percent Dropouts from the Full-time Work Requirement	170
11.4	Turnover Analysis—One-Year Follow-up, All Demonstration Sites	172
11.5	Turnover Analysis—One-Year Follow-up, Aggregate Data—All Demonstration Sites	173
11.6	Turnover Analysis—18-Month Follow-up, Two Demonstration Sites	174
11.7	Turnover Analysis—18-Month Follow-up, Aggregate Data—Two Demonstration Sites	175
11.8	Long Life and Independent Living, Continuity of Care Among Program Participants and Controls at One-Year Follow-up	176
11.9	Reasons for Changing Clients: Comparison of Program Participants and Controls at One-Year Follow-up	176
11.10	18-Month Follow-up, Remedy Program Participants and Matched Controls: Hours of Service During Demonstration Period	178
11.11	Remedy New Workers: Training Graduates Only, Turnover Analysis—One-Year Follow-up	179
11.12	Remedy New Workers: Training Graduates Only, Turnover Analysis—18-Month Follow-up	180
11.13	Remedy New Workers: Average Weekly Hours of Service During Demonstration Period	181
A.1	Characteristics of Agencies Participating in the Job Satisfaction Survey	212
A.2	Single-Item Measures	213
A.3	Multiple-Item Measures	214

Acknowledgments

The research, the work life demonstrations, and the writing of this book were funded by the Ford Foundation. We are especially grateful to Prudence Brown, Gordon Berlin, and Jan Jaffe of the Ford Foundation for their encouragement and support throughout the process. The project would not have been possible without the contributions of William Grinker, founder of Grinker, Walker and Associates, who shaped the demonstrations and nurtured them in their formative stages.

Nor could the study have proceeded without the cooperation of the organizations that participated in the demonstrations. For their patience, understanding, substantial data collection efforts, and above all their enthusiastic support for the goals of the project, we are indebted to the staff of the implementing agencies and their corporate or government sponsors. In particular, we wish to thank Emmett McDonough, Kaye Stinger, Lucille Moore, Lorraine Bergendorf-Clark, and Larraine Castellanos of Remedy Home and Health Care, Inc.; Fahari Jeffers of the United Domestic Workers; David Scheinman, Gerardo Canet, Theodore Kohan, Nancy Evale, and Vickie Sprinkman of Quality Care, Inc.; Carol Raphael of the New York City Human Resources Administration; Rosie Baker of Long Life Home Care Services, Inc.; and Allen Rosen of Home Care Services for Independent Living, Inc.

Judith Friedlaender and Tony Proscio—consultant and staff member, respectively, of Grinker, Walker and Associates—provided helpful advice on research design and data collection. Phyllis Quan provided invaluable assistance in implementing the San Diego demonstration. Kevin Smith (consultant), James Lynch (research assistant), and Ellen Hertzmark (consultant) assisted the research team at the Harvard School of Public Health in data analysis and interpretation. Joseph Stillman of Pickman Consulting Group read numerous drafts of the manuscript, provided many insightful comments on the project's findings and conclusions, and contributed the title *Who Cares for Them?*. He and Joanna Gould-Stuart also contributed key parts of Chapter 3. Lexa Hughes gave tirelessly of her efforts in preparing the manuscript and its numerous revisions.

Finally, we are grateful to the more than 1,200 home aides who responded to the lengthy survey administered as part of the project and to the 175 workers who participated in the work life demonstrations.

Part I

The Labor Market, the Work Force, and Industry Conditions

1

Providing Home Aide Services: The Challenge

INTRODUCTION

Large and growing numbers of the frail elderly and disabled depend on paid workers to assist them in daily life. This book focuses on the paid workers who serve as home aides, the paraprofessionals at the bottom of the service hierarchy that includes physicians, nurses, social workers, and physical and other therapists. In the United States more than a quarter of a million workers—mostly women, often minority—are employed as home aides, sometimes called homemakers, home health aides, home attendants, or the like.[1] The services they provide include personal care, such as bathing and toileting, and assistance with other activities of daily living, such as shopping, cooking, and eating. The positions they occupy are low skill, low wage, and low status, yet they constitute the foundation of the burgeoning home health industry, for without such basic care, many of the elderly and disabled would have to remain in hospitals or enter nursing homes. This book describes the home care workers, their problems on the job, and a variety of measures designed to improve the quality of their work life. An underlying assumption—supported by data presented in subsequent chapters—is that work life improvements will lead to improvements in the quality of service—in particular, continuity of care. The book has three specific objectives:

1. To identify critical factors affecting the working conditions and job satisfaction of the home aide work force
2. To assess the feasibility and evaluate the impact of changes designed to improve work life for these workers
3. To draw broader implications for managers and policy makers both in the home care sector and outside

The data and the recommendations presented are based largely on a three-year research and demonstration project funded by the Ford Foundation in the spring of 1985. That project mounted work life demonstrations in four cities (San Diego, Milwaukee, Syracuse, and New York), surveyed home aides in five cities,[2] and supported related evaluation and research efforts. The demonstration programs involved Remedy Home and Health Care, Inc., a major contractor under the California In-Home Supportive Services program; Quality Care, Inc. (now Kimberly Quality Care), one of the largest for-profit home care companies in the United States; and the New York City home attendant program, the largest Medicaid-financed home care program in the United States.

The book is divided into four parts. Part I presents a general discussion of the labor market, the work force, and the industry conditions that affect home care employment. Chapter 1 discusses the growing demand for home care and the work life issues that concern the industry. Chapter 2 describes general labor market trends that affect the home aide. Chapter 3 draws on in-home observations of the workers and their clients to describe the job of the home aide and the actual practice of home care. Chapter 4 uses survey data to describe the work attitudes of the home aide work force and to develop a causal model of job satisfaction and turnover. Chapter 5 focuses on financial conditions in the home care industry and their impact on work life issues.

Part II contains detailed case studies of the work life programs at each demonstration site. Each case study describes the participating agencies, their work force, specific work life changes implemented, and the effects of those changes, as well as organizational and environmental factors that affected program outcomes.

Part III draws on the case studies to present an overview of the work life programs and their implications. Chapter 10 discusses factors affecting adoption and implementation, while Chapter 11 discusses worker participation, turnover, and continuity of care.

Finally, Part IV summarizes the book's major findings (Chapter 12), then discusses management strategies and policy options (Chapter 13) for ensuring a sufficient and reliable home care work force. The rest of this chapter discusses the growth of the U.S. home care industry, the problems of the homemade work force, and the managerial concerns that underlie efforts to reduce turnover and improve service.

THE GROWING DEMAND FOR HOME CARE

Three major trends that have fostered the large-scale growth of home care services and a resulting increase in the number of home aides will continue to do so in the foreseeable future. These are (1) growth in the numbers of the elderly and, especially, the "old old," (2) growing limitations on the family's ability to provide informal care to family members, and (3) rapidly escalating health care costs, leading to a search for less costly alternatives to institutional care. In addition, the emergence of acquired immunodeficiency syndrome (AIDS) and the need to provide chronic care to those disabled by its effects are likely to be other factors fueling the future growth of home care, at least in communities with a high prevalence of the disease.

Growth in Numbers of the Elderly

The most significant factor affecting the growth of home care and therefore the demand for home aides has been and will continue to be the growth in the numbers of elderly, particularly the "old old"—those aged 85 and over. The number of Americans aged 65 and over grew from 17 million in 1960 to nearly 29 million in 1985 and was projected to increase by a third—from 29 million to 39 million—between 1985 and 2010. During the same period, the number of old old nearly doubled, and their number was projected to more than double again between 1985 and 2010—from about 2.7 million to nearly 6 million (GAO, September 1986; Suzman & Riley, 1985). Because chronic illness and the need for assistance with activities of daily living increase with age, the burden on the long-term care system has been growing and will continue to do so.

Overall estimates of the need for assistance vary widely, depending on underlying assumptions about population growth, rates of morbidity and mortality, and levels of individual functioning. Findings from the 1982 National Long-Term Care Survey showed that about 4.6 million or 19 percent of individuals aged 65 and older living in the community were in need of help with some activities of daily living (GAO, September 1986). Assuming no change in disability rates, Manton (1987) has estimated that by the year 2020 over 9 million elderly will require more than 242 million hours of assistance per week.

Decreasing Availability of Informal Family Care

Currently, the disabled elderly who live outside of a nursing home receive 80 percent of their care informally from relatives (GAO, September 1986). However, growing limits on the family's ability to provide care may increase reliance on so-called formal care givers—that is, paid providers of home health and homemaker/chore services—in the decades to come. As summarized by the Government Accounting Office (GAO, September 1986), factors limiting families' capacity to provide informal care are:

1. Increased life expectancy, delayed marriage, and declining fertility—all resulting in an increased ratio of elderly parents to children available to care for them
2. Differences in mortality by sex at all ages, leading to growing numbers of widowed elderly women without spouses to care for them
3. Aging of the population, increasing the probability that very old chronically ill parents

will have children who are themselves retired and may have low income or health problems limiting their ability to provide help

4. Increased participation of women in the labor force, resulting in the decreased availability or willingness of women to be the main providers of care for ill or dependent family members

While thus far the United States has relied heavily on nursing homes to care for those chronically ill who are without family or friends to care for them, the sheer numbers of the elderly, the relatively high costs of nursing home care, and limits on nursing home beds imposed by regulatory agencies in many states have forced an increase in the use of home care as an alternative. Nowhere is the reliance on home care as a substitute for nursing home care more extreme than in New York City, where the Medicaid program now has more elderly clients receiving home care than residing in long-term care facilities.

Escalating Health Care Costs

Health care expenditures for both acute and long-term care rose rapidly in the 1970s as a result of overall inflation but also as a result of the aging of the population, the development and diffusion of new technology and drugs, the concomitant increase in hospital service intensity, and the failure of cost control measures such as certificate of need regulations and physician peer review organizations to stem the growth in services. Medicare and Medicaid expenditures for the elderly grew faster than expenditures for those under 65 years, creating enormous pressure for cost control.

Although the 1980s brought serious debate among experts and policy makers about the cost-savings potential of home care, it was widely touted in the 1970s as a cost-effective alternative to institutional care—both hospital and nursing home care. Medicare's relatively generous funding of home health care was attributable in part to this belief, and the rapid growth of the home care industry was, in turn, largely attributable to Medicare funding.

In the 1980s, cost control has fueled demand for home care by means of Medicare's prospective payment system (PPS), put in place to control skyrocketing hospital costs. PPS encourages hospitals to discharge patients earlier than before by paying a fixed amount per diagnosis regardless of the length of hospital stay. According to the GAO, the new prospective payment system placed an "increased demand on home care, nursing home, and other support services that provide care for the homebound. For example, in fiscal year 1984 the percentage of times hospitals discharged Medicare patients to skilled nursing homes, intermediate care facilities, and home health agencies was 2.5 to 3 times as high for PPS hospitals as for non-PPS hospitals"[3] (GAO, September 1986:60).

AIDS

Exacerbating the health care cost problem in recent years and in cities with large high-risk populations has been the emergence of AIDS, a complex constellation of diseases that was first reported in the United States in the early 1980s. The nearly 8,000 AIDS cases reported in the United States in 1984 has grown roughly ten-fold by 1988 to more than 76,000, and over 42,000 individuals have already died. Moreover, while AIDS is still concentrated among male homosexuals and intravenous drug users, its spread to heterosexuals and, in particular, to women who are drug users or partners of drug users and to their offspring has caused widespread alarm. In New York City, one out of every sixty-one babies born in December 1987 tested positive for the AIDS antibody, "indicating that their mothers were infected and that many of the babies were carriers of the deadly virus" (Gross, 1988). AIDS has engendered substantial interest in home care both as a more humane alternative to hospital care for those suffering the chronic effects of the syndrome and as a less expensive alternative to the hospital setting (although its relevance to an addicted population that often does not have a stable home setting is uncertain).

NUMBERS OF PROVIDERS AND WORKERS

The trends described above contributed to a rapid expansion of home care providers in the 1970s and 1980s. The number of agencies certified to deliver services to Medicare beneficiaries increased from about 2,000 in the early 1970s to approximately 6,000 in 1986 (Abt Associates, 1984; HCFA, 1987b). In addition, numerous "unlicensed" agencies, which were not certified to deliver Medicare or Medicaid services directly, arranged to provide them indirectly by subcontracting with certified agencies (Ginzberg, Balinsky, & Ostow, 1984). Many of these unlicensed agencies were proprietary agencies, but many proprietary agencies also obtained Medicare certification.

Once a negligible part of the home care industry, the for-profit sector proliferated between 1972 and 1986: although there were only 43 Medicare-certified proprietary agencies in 1972 (Abt Associates, 1984), there were 1,900 by 1986, and they accounted for more than 30 percent of all agencies. In addition to serving Medicare beneficiaries, these for-profit companies sought out privately insured and self-paying segments of the market. Voluntary hospitals also entered the home care market in greater numbers, and the proportion of hospital-affiliated home health agencies increased from 10 percent to more than 20 percent between 1972 and 1986. Concomitantly, the market share of visiting nurse associations (VNAs) fell from about 25 percent in 1972 to 8 percent in 1986, and there were actually fewer VNAs operating in 1986 than in 1972. Especially in rural areas, county health departments were still an important source of service provision, and, overall, local governments comprised about 20 percent of Medicare service providers in 1986.

Estimates of the numbers of aides employed in the home care industry are far less precise. The National Association for Home Care estimated that there were 300,000 to 500,000 homemaker/home health aides in 1986, but this number was "soft" because it was based on industry "impressions" rather than on systematic research. The U.S. Bureau of the Census (1985) counted 350,000

"Health Aides, except Nursing" in 1985—a ten-fold increase from 1960. However, this number included some aides in institutional settings.[4] The Bureau of Labor Statistics (BLS) provided a 1986 estimate of 213,000 homemaker/home health and nursing aides in private households (U.S. Bureau of Labor Statistics, April 1988). However, this figure did not include home aides funded by state or local governments to work as "individual providers" (IPs) in "unorganized" settings for individual clients. A telephone survey of states with individual provider programs indicated that approximately 145,000 workers served as individual providers in 1986.

Thus a conservative estimate of the home aide work force, based on the BLS survey data adjusted for the numbers of individual providers paid by state and local governments, would be about 350,000 in 1986. Whatever the precise numbers, the BLS projected that by the year 2000, the number of home health aide jobs would increase by 80 percent, primarily because of the growing elderly population and the continuing trend to provide medical care outside the hospital setting (Silvestri & Lukasiewicz, 1987).

THE PROBLEM: WORK LIFE ISSUES FOR THE HOME AIDE WORK FORCE

As noted at the outset of this chapter, home aides are the least skilled workers in the home care service hierarchy.[5] The positions they occupy are low wage and low status. The work force is almost entirely female, and the services performed are typically regarded as "women's work." The typical home aide is poorly paid, is rarely salaried, lacks basic benefits such as health insurance or paid vacation or sick leave, receives minimal training and organizational support, and enjoys few opportunities for advancement. As discussed in Chapter 3, the home aide's job does provide opportunities for personal fulfillment. However, the objective conditions of employment are relatively poor. Managers, workers, and union representatives have identified five major work life issues for home aides.

1. Wage Levels and Wage Parity. Hourly wage rates for home aides lag behind most unskilled, nonsupervisory positions available (see Chapters 4 and 5). Survey data collected for this book and described in greater detail in Chapter 4 indicate that in 1986 the median wage of home aides was $4.30 per hour—comparable to the 1985 wage of workers in eating and drinking places (U.S. Bureau of Labor Statistics, March 1985).[6] Even if she worked full-time year-round, the average aide would earn less than $10,000 per year. Indeed, the home aides described in Chapter 4 reported an average personal income of about $8,000, and three-quarters earned less than $10,000 per year. As they were heads of household with one or two dependents, their income was barely at poverty level, defined as $8,738 for a family of three in 1986 (U.S. Bureau of the Census, 1987).

   Low wages were a particularly rankling issue for the home aide work force because of the disparity between home-based and institution-based workers. Although home aides carried out many of the same tasks as nursing aides in hospitals, they received at best three-quarters of their hospital counterparts' pay (Commonwealth of Massachusetts, Division of Employment Security, July 1986). Industry wage surveys of hospital employees in the five areas where demonstration programs were located found that wages of part-time nursing aides varied from a low of $5.56 per hour in upstate New York to a high of $7.00 per hour in southern California. Thus the nursing aides earned 30 to 60 percent more per hour than home aides in the same geographical area.[7] Disparities between home aides and those employed in long-term care facilities were generally smaller but existed nonetheless.

2. Part-time, Episodic Work. Most home care agencies prefer flexible part-time workers whose schedules can be readily adapted to changing client caseloads. Many agencies act as "temporary help" agencies, contracting with individual aides from a roster of those available. Aides are rarely assured a minimum number of hours per week and rarely salaried. If a client being cared for enters a hospital or dies, there is no guarantee that the home aide will be assigned to a new case without a disruption in pay. As a result, home aides often cannot be sure of full-time year-round work. Half the home aides surveyed for this book worked thirty or fewer hours per week, while more than 60 percent wished to work more than thirty hours. About one-fifth of the respondents worked at an additional job as well. In contrast, only about a quarter of nursing aides in hospitals and personal care facilities worked part-time in 1986 (U.S. Bureau of Labor Statistics, April 1988).
3. Benefits. As part-time workers, home aides are generally ineligible for benefits such as health insurance, paid vacation, or sick leave. Home care agencies rarely offer health insurance coverage to their aides. Only 19 percent of respondents to the home aide survey had health insurance coverage through their home care employer. About 8 percent had to rely on Medicaid, and about 20 percent had no health insurance at all. More detailed information on employment conditions presented in the case studies of this book shows that few employers offered vacation or sick leave—benefits highly prized by the work force.
4. Training and Support. Training requirements for home aides vary across states and by funding source. Relatively few agencies adhere to the sixty-hour training requirement for homemaker/home health aides put forward by the National Home Caring Council, a voluntary accrediting body, as the minimum industry standard. The lack of uniform standards and sophisticated training has become an issue because many of the most difficult chronic cases involving developmental disabilities, mental health, geriatric problems, and even terminal care are referred to home aides for personal care and emotional support (Mootz, 1986).

   The inadequacy of training is compounded by the lack of organizational support systems to help workers cope with difficult clients, feelings of isolation, or personal problems affecting their job performance and satisfaction. The typical home aide spends minimal time at the agency, has limited contact with coworkers, nurses, service coordinators, and schedulers, and receives little organizational recognition of her contributions to her clients' welfare (Canalis, 1987). As discussed in Chapter 4, perceived inadequacy of training increases the home aides' feelings of isolation in their work, and this sense of isolation or loneliness has a positive and direct effect on their intent to leave the job.
5. Opportunities for Advancement. Job titles, like training requirements, vary across states and by funding source as well. Home health aides, homemakers, personal care

workers, and home attendants, to name just a few, perform similar work but receive different pay, depending on their funding source. These largely artificial distinctions create the illusion of career ladders that, in fact, do not exist (Surpin, 1988; Surpin & Grumm, 1987). The industry as a whole does not provide systematic rewards to home aides for experience, good performance, acquisition of increased skills, or service in more difficult cases.

Given these employment conditions, it is not surprising that home care is an unattractive employment option for many entry-level workers. The job can be advertised, as one recent newspaper article pointed out, as offering "low pay; poor benefits; sometimes quirky clients" (*Record,* 1987). Poor wages and benefits, compounded by the physical and emotional strain of the work, the isolation from other workers, the lack of organizational support, and the absence of opportunities for advancement, have contributed to high turnover and difficulties in recruiting new workers. Amid signs that both quality and worker availability are inadequate to meet the current demand for service and even less adequate for the future (National Institute on Aging, 1987), worker recruitment and retention have become a major concern in the industry (*Caring,* 1988).

These, then, are the issues the work life programs sought to address. The picture was not entirely bleak, for while the conditions of employment in the home care industry were often inferior to those in other parts of the economy, there were indications that many employers were interested in finding ways to make things better (Canalis, 1987). Managerial interest in work life improvements stemmed partly from the self-interested belief that better working conditions would alleviate recruitment and retention problems, leading to higher volume and increased revenues, and partly from altruistic concern both for the status and satisfaction of the workers and for the availability and quality of care provided the client.

MANAGEMENT CONCERNS

Review of the home care literature and interviews with labor and management reveal five concerns motivating employers to address quality of work life issues: (1) worker recruitment, (2) worker turnover, (3) productivity, (4) quality of service, and (5) in some circumstances, union pressures.

Worker Recruitment

In recent years, increasing demand for home care and decreasing unemployment rates have created home aide shortages in many suburban areas and in high employment states. Recruitment is most difficult in states with the lowest unemployment rates, such as Massachusetts and New Jersey, where low wage employers face the greatest competition from employers offering more attractive employment opportunities (*Boston Globe,* 1987; *Record,* 1987). In Massachusetts, the state Rate Setting Commission estimated a 20 percent gap between hours of service authorized for the homebound elderly and hours actually provided by the state's home care corporations in 1986 (*Boston Globe,* 1987). A statewide provider task force concluded in March 1987 that "worker availability [had] become *the* critical resource issue for the years ahead—and for the present" and recommended a variety of actions to make the home aide's job more attractive, including improved compensation, better supervision and support, changes in job scheduling, and enhanced job status (Task Force, 1987:5). The key to the success of these recommendations, the task force noted, was a "regulatory environment that [would] allow and encourage innovative wage, benefit and recruitment policies" (Task Force, 1987:5).

A New York State provider task force cited similar problems and reached the same conclusions a few months later. Noting that the shortage of paraprofessional workers was of "crisis proportions" in New York, the task force made a series of recommendations, first of which was that Medicaid reimbursement rates be raised "swiftly" so that agencies could raise paraprofessional wages and benefits (Home Care Association of New York State, 1987). Without increased third-party payment, providers argued, they could not attract an adequate supply of workers. Shortages of entry-level workers, in turn, threatened access to care and diminished service volume and profits.

Worker Turnover

Human service agencies experience particularly high turnover rates (Montgomery, 1981). Reliable data on turnover rates among home aides are difficult to find because there have been few systematic studies and because agencies tend to compute turnover in different ways. The industrywide rate for home aides is thought to be about 60 percent (Surpin, November 1987). Twenty-two nonprofit home care agencies in Massachusetts reported an average turnover rate of 29 percent in 1985, with a range of 5 percent to 67 percent (Massachusetts Council for Homemaker-Home Health Aide Services, 1985). Montgomery's (1981) study of turnover among direct service providers employed by forty-two health and human service organizations in a mid-sized metropolitan area found a one-year turnover rate of 33.3 percent among in-home service workers, compared to 19.4 percent for hospital workers. (The study sample included nurses as well as aides.) As the case studies in Chapters 7, 8, and 9 report, one-year turnover rates at the demonstration sites ranged from 27 percent in a group of long-term New York City home attendants to 81 percent in a cohort of newly hired homemakers in San Diego.

Because home aides receive little formal training from their employers and because many home care employers function essentially as temporary help agencies, high turnover is not necessarily as disruptive to the home care industry as it would be to an industry heavily reliant on permanent full-time labor. Nevertheless, even for agencies accustomed to relying on temporary part-time workers, turnover can cause burdensome recruitment and orientation costs, decreased productivity, and decreased client satisfaction.

Productivity

Increased productivity has not traditionally been a major concern of home care managers. However, as third-party payers tighten their payments for home visits, agencies face the challenge of providing quality care at a lower cost per visit (Bonstein & Mueller, 1985). One response is to require aides who work as full-time staff to increase their number of visits—that is, to increase their productivity. A second response, noted in Chapter 2, is to place increased reliance on part-time "nonbenefited" workers. Now, even these workers are being asked to increase their productivity by accomplishing their tasks in a shorter time and by visiting more clients per day (Liebman, 1986). Worker stress associated with efforts to improve productivity is increasingly perceived by home care managers as a work life issue. To reduce the disruptive effects of stress, managers are considering improved scheduling practices, travel pay, and a variety of support services.

Quality of Service

Studies of the quality of care delivered by health organizations have rarely considered the possible impact of care givers' satisfaction on clients or the potential for management to influence quality by providing working conditions conducive to staff satisfaction (Weisman & Nathanson, 1985). Yet home care managers generally believe that well-trained, satisfied home aides will provide better care than minimally trained aides dissatisfied with their working conditions. Worker reliability, a criticial dimension of quality to dependent clients with chronic needs, is perceived to be especially sensitive to quality of work life issues and job satisfaction. Thus a recent article in the industry magazine, *Caring,* advised managers to "listen to the needs" of home aides and "improv[e] their work situation" to promote quality and excellence in care (Canalis, 1987:89).

Home care managers are also paying increased attention to home aides' skills in providing social support, counseling, problem identification, and crisis intervention—dimensions of quality that home care training programs by and large ignored in the past (Kaye, 1986). In particular, heightened public and professional awareness of the mental and emotional problems of elderly patients suffering from Alzheimer's disease and other debilitating conditions has sparked agency interest in efforts to improve the interpersonal and coping skills of aides who serve these difficult clients.

Union Pressures

Scattered across multiple work sites, home care workers are far more difficult to unionize than health care workers in institutional settings. The vast majority of home aides do not belong to unions, and the prospects for large-scale unionization of the industry appear dim. Nevertheless, the perceived threat of unionization hangs over many agency managers, leading to concern over employment conditions. Furthermore, in some large cities, unions have successfully organized aides who work for agencies that contract with state and local governments to provide publicly financed services. Freedom of information laws affecting government contracts, plus centralized program funding and administration, apparently facilitate unionization of workers in contract agencies. Unions in Boston, New York City, San Diego, and San Francisco, for example, have successfully gained paid holidays, vacation leave, sick time, and health insurance benefits for home aides employed by contract agencies serving publicly funded clients. In those areas where government funds can be garnered to finance increased program costs, managers have found it advantageous to join unions in lobbying public officials for funds to support work life improvements.

WORK LIFE PROGRAMS

Given evidence of both serious work life problems and employers' interest in addressing them, a basic premise of the demonstration programs was that the infusion of outside resources could tip the balance toward a more satisfactory employment situation for aides by establishing the feasibility and effectiveness of selected changes without financial risk to participating agencies. The measures designed and adopted as part of the demonstrations fall into the category of "quality of work life" (QWL) or, simply, work life programs. QWL is a broad concept—almost a "movement"—elaborated by a group of psychologists, sociologists, industrial relations experts, and others in the 1970s (Davis & Cherns, 1975). It includes such salient features of the job as the adequacy and fairness of compensation, health and safety conditions, employment or income security, opportunities to use and develop skills and knowledge, advancement opportunities, the social climate of the workplace, the availability of rules and procedures to safeguard workers' rights, and the opportunity to perform socially useful work (Walton, 1975). Job satisfaction has often served as the chief indicator of QWL, on the assumption that "the individual's own experience of satisfaction or dissatisfaction defines the quality of his [or her] own working life" (Seashore, 1975:106).

Organizations in the United States and other industrialized countries have adopted a variety of work life programs intended to improve job satisfaction as well as worker attendance, productivity, and length of service—all behaviors thought to be affected by satisfaction. Among these programs are structural and supervisory changes designed to enhance worker control and autonomy, worker training programs to develop new skills and expertise, job enrichment programs designed to utilize more fully workers' skills, changes in compensation and promotion schemes, and consciousness-raising and support groups for workers and sometimes their families (Walton, 1975).

Specifically, the work life programs described in this book included improvements in training, pay, benefits, opportunities for advancement, hours of work, support, and status:

- In San Diego, both entry-level and experienced workers received extended training in basic home care skills and a guaranteed thirty-five hour week. They also participated in a project-sponsored employee support and development group and received uniforms and badges as a sign of their special status.
- In New York City, experienced workers received specialized training in serving specifically defined difficult cases (e.g., Alzheimer's disease, organic brain syndrome, senile dementia) and a $.30 per hour wage increment. They also received ongoing professional support and status enhancements, including special titles, badges, and program publicity.
- In Syracuse and Milwaukee, experienced workers were promoted to full-time "staff aide" positions with a $.50 per hour wage increment, enriched fringe benefits, and staff status.

In each case, the immediate aim of the program was to increase worker satisfaction, decrease turnover, and thereby improve reliability and continuity of care. The effects of the programs, reported in Chapters 7, 8, 9, and 11, were evaluated using randomly selected demonstration and control groups within each site. Because the long-term objective of the programs was to demonstrate the feasibility of establishing and maintaining work life improvements for the home aide work force, factors affecting adoption and implementation were carefully documented for each site and are also discussed in the case studies and in Chapter 10.

Experience outside the home care industry indicates that work life programs have diffused far more widely in the "primary labor market," offering relatively stable, high paying employment, than in the "secondary labor market," characterized by marginal, low wage jobs. Furthermore, within the primary sector, organizations that have adopted the most far-reaching changes have generally been those where quality of work life, as measured by a variety of indicators, was already high. The result, ironically, has been that "the quality of working life in the best organizations [has become] even better and that in poor organizations [has become] relatively worse" (Davis & Cherns, 1975:8).

This book provides ample documentation of the ways in which the home aide's job epitomizes employment in the marginal secondary labor market. Furthermore, it provides financial data suggesting that the home care industry and its major employers of unskilled workers, although rapidly growing, are in a precarious financial position. At the same time, it provides a wealth of evidence that effective work life programs for the home aide work force can be implemented—programs that will reduce worker turnover and improve continuity of care. The challenge for the industry and for others in society concerned about the quality of work life and the quality of care is to overcome the political and financial barriers impeding change.

NOTES

1. Home aides work under many titles, including homemaker, home health aide, home attendant, personal care attendant, chore worker, etc. In theory, certified home health aides are distinguishable from the others by virtue of the training they receive and the more medically related tasks they are permitted to perform. In practice, the various titles have little functional distinction, so for the sake of brevity, we use the terms home aide, aide, or home care worker throughout this book.

2. Subsequent references to "the home aide survey" refer to this five-city survey described in Chapters 2 and 4 and in the Methodological Appendix.

3. Ironically, just as pressure for cost control in the institutional sector was creating increased demand for home care visits, not only by nurses but by nursing assistants and home health aides, the federal government began to institute cost control measures in federally funded home care programs as well. Medicare-funded home care was the first target, as the Health Care Financing Administration (HCFA) tightened enforcement of the program's regulations limiting utilization and controlling the rate of increase in unit costs (GAO, September 1986). Subsequently, HCFA issued proposed regulations that would significantly reduce federal funding for household or chore services provided as an adjunct to personal care under Medicaid (*Federal Register,* 1988). Both initiatives highlighted the problems of achieving consistency in federal policy.

4. The Census Bureau (1985) also counted 1.2 million "nursing aides, attendants, and orderlies," mostly working in institutional settings.

5. The following discussion of work life issues and management concerns has been adapted from P. Feldman and A. Sapienza, "Strategic Management of Quality of Work-life in the Home Care Industry," in A.S. Sethi and R.S. Schuler, eds., *Human Resource Management in the Health Care Sector* (Westport, Conn.: Greenwood Press, 1989).

6. Aggravating the problem of low wages is the problem of uncompensated travel time. Many, if not most, agencies do not pay workers for time spent traveling between clients. Thus the hourly wage is even lower than it appears.

7. Industry experts disagreed over the equivalency of home-based versus institution-based jobs for aides and, therefore, over the equitability of wage differences. Some argued that aides in hospitals and nursing homes worked harder than home aides because they performed tasks for a larger number of patients in any given time period, and therefore they deserved the higher wages they received. Others argued that home aides, while they served fewer individuals, bore greater responsibility for their patients' welfare and deserved at least equivalent wages for providing a full range of services in unsupervised and often difficult settings.

2

The Home Care Labor Market

Labor markets in the United States are segmented by occupation, race, and gender. Moreover, "the labor market segments in which women are concentrated tend to be disadvantaged in terms of skill, status, security, and earnings" (OECD, 1985:38). The lower ranks of the home care industry, occupied by the home aide work force, clearly constitute a "disadvantaged segment." This chapter first describes the general labor market trends that have affected home care, then presents more detailed data on the characteristics and working conditions of the home aide work force.

LABOR MARKET TRENDS AFFECTING THE HOME CARE INDUSTRY

The U.S. home care industry has been affected by three major structural changes that have occurred in the labor markets of the industrialized nations since World War II. First, there has been a rapid increase in the participation of women in the labor force. Second, overall employment in the service sector has overtaken that in agriculture and manufacturing. Third, and related to the preceding, the demand for part-time workers has outpaced that for full-time workers. Each of these changes will be discussed in more detail below.

Participation of Women

Between 1950 and 1980, the number of "economically active" men in the Western industrialized countries of the world grew by 25 percent, while the number of "economically active" women grew almost three times as much—by 74 percent (Paukert, 1984:10). Although women started from a much smaller base than men, their absolute increase in labor force participation has been much higher.

Many studies have examined the reasons for the growth of women's participation and have concluded that there are two principal factors. First, the "social climate of industrialized countries has changed very considerably . . . [and an] increasing proportion of women now feel they want the independence gained by paid employment" (Paukert, 1984:45). Second and of relevance to the home care worker, a "considerable proportion of women work because—like men—they have no option: it is an economic necessity" (Paukert, 1984:41). Those women who must work out of necessity are primarily single heads-of-household.

Although they are participating in increasing numbers, women are not participating equally with men in the desirable segments of labor markets. Instead:

> It is the less desirable and the marginal jobs in most sectors that tend to be held by women. . . . The rise in women's employment opportunities—to the extent that it materialized—has had relatively little impact on the long-established employment pattern characterised by a high concentration of women in a relatively small number of occupations, mainly of lower skill, lower status, and commanding lower wages (Paukert, 1984:10).

Economists and others have observed that the labor market in the United States consists of two sectors: a primary sector, offering jobs with high wages, good working conditions, employment stability, job security, and opportunities for advancement; and a secondary sector, made up of marginal jobs distinguished by low wages, poor working conditions, little chance of advancement, great instability, and little employment security (Piore, 1975). Many of the poor and many women are confined to the secondary labor market. As the following sections reveal, women's participation in the labor force has been primarily in the service sector—in human services, in part-time jobs, and often in inferior jobs.

Service Sector Employment

Before the Industrial Revolution, labor was concentrated in the agricultural sector of the nation's economy. From the Industrial Revolution through the late 1950s and early 1960s, labor was concentrated in manufacturing. But the employment pattern has shifted over the last few decades to the service sector, including the public sector, until in 1985 U.S. employment was divided into agriculture, 3 percent; manufacturing, 28 percent; and services, 69 percent. This same shift is mirrored in all industrial nations (OECD, 1985).

The service sector is expected to remain the major employment category for two reasons. First, productivity increases more rapidly in manufacturing than in services because machinery is continually substituted for labor. Very little substitution can occur in services. Thus, labor shifts from manufacturing to services naturally. Second, "as a country gets richer, it can be expected to spend more on services, particularly services such as health and education, and demand for these services increases" (Paukert, 1984:47). In the United States, for example, the proportion of the gross national product (GNP) spent on health rose from 5.3 percent in 1960 to about 11 percent in 1987.

The service sector is the primary employer of women. In 1980, of women who worked in the United States, less than 2 percent worked in agriculture, and less than 18 percent worked in manufacturing, but more than 80 percent worked in services (OECD, 1985).

The public sector invariably provides much of the employment in health, education, and social welfare services (termed "human services" and including home care). And the public sector also provides much of the employment of women.

> [In the United States] in 1980 nearly 30 percent of the 40 million women in the labour force worked in human services, compared with only 10 percent of the 53 million men in the work force. Comparing patterns of job growth for women and men between 1940 and 1980, the social welfare industry created jobs for one out of every three women entering the labour force but only for one out of every seven men (Paukert, 1984:49).

As the service sector has grown, so too has the demand for part-time employment. In the United States, as in most industrialized countries, the service sector accounts for the largest share of part-time employment. Thus, most of the women who work in services are working part-time, despite the "economic necessity" of their working.

Part-time Employment

A recent study of women's employment concluded that the growth of the service sector led to the growth of part-time employment because "many service sector activities benefit from the use of part-time workers" (OECD, 1985:15). As noted earlier, productivity increases faster in manufacturing than in services, primarily because of the substitution of machinery for labor (e.g., robots in factories). In manufacturing, then, a decline in demand for a product can be matched by a decline in factory production. Factories can be run at less than full capacity. Within certain limits, an increase in demand can be matched by running these factories at higher and higher percentages of full capacity.

In contrast, services tend to be labor-intensive and characterized by the high fixed cost of this labor. In many service businesses there is very little machinery to slow down or speed up, so when changes in demand occur, the matching of labor to demand can be difficult. Most hospitals employ the same number of nurses in December as they employ in June, despite the fact that admissions in December are lower than in June.

One alternative to keeping a high fixed-cost structure in services is to employ part-time staff, thus shifting some of the fixed (full-time staff) cost to variable (part-time staff) cost. Fast-food restaurants handle the peak hours of mealtimes by employing part-time workers. Rather than hire, for example, five full-time workers who will be overworked for twenty hours a week and underworked for the other twenty hours, the restaurants will hire seven twenty-hour workers for mealtimes and two twenty-hour workers for the remainder. The difference in worked hours will be twenty hours. But the savings in wages will be even greater, because part-time workers earn less and are usually not entitled to such benefits as paid holidays, sick leave, vacations, and health insurance. In brief, the ''greater flexibility and low cost of part-time work have been . . . factors of interest to employers, particularly in times of fluctuating business'' (Paukert, 1984:50).

The service sector in the United States accounts for more than 80 percent of part-time work, and women account for 70 percent of all part-time employment. For some women part-time employment may be advantageous because it allows them to continue bearing the larger share of household responsibilities. For others, however, part-time employment is one of the disadvantages they experience as a result of being confined to jobs in the secondary labor market:

> Part-time work is for some . . . a form of underemployment . . . [that is], marginal jobs and inequitable pay. Marginal jobs refer to those in the secondary labour market, with low wages and benefits and high labour turnover. Inequitable pay refers to earnings that are not commensurable with a person's qualifications. There are many indications that women suffer disproportionately from these forms of underemployment. . . .
>
> Also, part-time workers may experience a depreciation of any skills they do have, since on-the-job training is rarely offered to them. Advancement opportunities are often minimal; furthermore, the exclusion of part-time workers from pension schemes . . . means that there will be no retirement income on the basis of employment related pension schemes. Part-time workers frequently have less job security since they are often the first to be laid off (OECD, 1985:17).

Labor Market Segregation

The preponderance of women in part-time, service sector jobs is part of the phenomenon of gender segregation, a persistent feature of labor markets in the United States and many other industrialized countries:

> For reasons connected with the general perception of the roles of men and women within society, men are often chosen to do supervisory jobs, while women are chosen for [care of children and sick persons], cleaning, or repetitive work. . . . [The] industries with the highest proportion of women are also those paying the lowest wages for a given level of skill. . . .
>
> [In addition, because] the demand for part-time work tends to be concentrated in the relatively low-status jobs in the service sector, part-time work may be an important factor tending to increase segregation by gender (OECD, 1985:52-53).

Labor markets are gender-segregated both horizontally and vertically. That is, women (or men) dominate certain occupations (horizontal segregation); and women (or men) dominate certain skill levels within the same occupation (vertical segregation). Labor market analysts have observed that most women are found in jobs with certain presumed gender-linked characteristics, such as an extension of housework or child care. Not surprisingly, the industries in which these characteristics are found "tend to be less profitable and have less market power" (Stevenson, 1973:250).

The predominance of women in such occupations (horizontal segregation) has given rise to the "crowding hypothesis" as one of the reasons for women's low wages. If women are "crowded into a limited number of occupations, and virtually denied access to all others," then the supply of labor for these occupations is artificially expanded—with the result that women's pay is depressed (Stevenson, 1975:247).

In the health care industry, most of the occupations are gender-segregated (the usual criterion is that one gender accounts for 70 percent or more of those employed). Those occupations in which women predominate can, as expected from the above findings, be characterized as "caring, consoling, counseling, nursing and nurturing" occupations (Butter et al., 1985:10). In this sector, women are "severely underrepresented in the six highest income occupations" and earn less in virtually every occupation than their male counterparts, as shown in Table 2.1 (Butter et al., 1985:13). Furthermore, horizontal and vertical segregation in the health care industry is also associated with racial segregation: "Black women are highly concentrated in nonhospital services and in the convalescent home industry" and are almost four times more likely than white women in this sector to have earnings below the poverty level (Woody & Malson, 1984). This labor market segregation of women and minorities has deep economic, social, and historical roots.

The Roots of Segregation by Gender and Race

Societies stereotype women and men as suited for different work roles: men for supervising, for high-skilled jobs, for physically demanding labor; women for work that is an extension of home work and child care.

The economic advantages of gender-segregated labor markets have been well documented:

> The segregation of men's and women's jobs provides a category of lower paid workers which reduces the firm's wage bill. . . . Men's and women's jobs also tend to be structured differently. Men's jobs are structured in such a way as to encourage productivity (thereby discouraging turnover) and by offering training and experience they become characterised by relatively long promotion ladders. Women's jobs tend to be structured in such a way as to minimize the cost of turnover, although providing fewer advancement possibilities, even with rising seniority and experience (OECD, 1985:86).

Table 2.1
Income Differentials Between Males and Females, Selected Health Occupations

Occupation	1983 Median Incomes Males	Females	Percent of Males' Earnings Paid to Females	Percent of Females in Occupation
Optometry*	$44,194	$18,480	41.7%	5.7%
Veterinary Medicine (1980)	38,808	21,622	55.7	12.3
Medicine (1979)	67,450	39,820	59.0	12.0
Physician Assist.	20,789	12,993	62.5	36.4
Dentistry*	32,646	20,987	64.3	3.8
Physical Therap.	31,327	21,128	67.4	71.5
Health Admin.	31,216	22,638	72.4	51.0
Medical Soc. Work.	20,688	16,020	77.4	66.4
Respiratory Therap.	20,011	15,586	77.9	56.4
Aide, Attendant, Orderly	12,018	9,664	80.4	87.9
Dietician	18,228	15,036	82.5	92.7
Radiologic Tech.	19,860	16,485	83.0	72.9
Health Aides (non-nurs.)	12,730	10,775	84.6	84.5
Pharmacist	27,494	23,613	85.9	19.0
Clinical Lab Tech.	19,288	16,733	86.7	75.6
Dental Assist.	12,260	10,749	87.7	98.0
Occupational Therap.	20,948	18,393	87.8	93.2
Speech Therap.	20,840	19,152	91.9	89.4
Medical Librarian	20,912	19,322	92.4	83.0
Psychologist	21,715	21,052	96.9	47.0
Registered Nurse	20,962	20,901	99.7	96.0
Health Rec. Spec.	13,844	13,955	101.0	91.1
Practical Nurse	14,205	14,527	102.0	96.7

From I. Butter, et al., "Sex and Status." Copyright 1985 by the American Public Health Association. Reprinted with permission.

Sources:
U.S. Department of Labor, Bureau of Labor Statistics, Unpublished Tabulations from the Current Population Survey, 1983 Annual Averages.
Medical Economics, 1980, February: 98-110.
Telephone interview with the American Veterinary Medicine Association, November 1984.
* The main source of data, the BLS earnings series, excludes self-employed workers, therefore excluding the majority of workers in Medicine, Osteopathy, Dentistry, Chiropractic, Podiatry, Optometry, and Veterinary Medicine. We therefore explored other sources but succeeded in only two cases: Medicine and Veterinary Medicine. Annual averages from the BLS were added to the Table for Optometry and Dentistry though these data are probably biased because of exclusion of the self-employed. For Podiatry, Chiropractic, and Osteopathic Medicine we were not able to obtain any data.

Apart from economic incentives such as those described above, whence do work-related gender stereotypes arise? Psychological research on gender belief systems—including ''stereotypes of women and men, attitudes towards appropriate roles and behaviors of women and men'' (Deaux & Kite, 1987:97)—suggests that early socialization experiences lay the foundation. Such experiences include family upbringing, classroom education, and public media exposure.

These early experiences are apparently shared by many cultures, as illustrated by cross-cultural similarities in perceptions of men as "stronger and more active, characterized by high needs for achievement, dominance, autonomy, and aggression. Women, in contrast [are] viewed as weaker and less active, more concerned with affiliation, nurturance, and deference" (Deaux & Kite, 1987:99).

Emerging from these perceptions of gender are perceptions of role, including roles in society and work that women and men should occupy. "Thus, if one assumes that women are skilled in some domains and men in others, one may look to a member of one group and not the other when attempting to get a particular task accomplished" (Deaux & Kite, 1987:106). If society assumes that women are skilled in at-home work and child care, then the current segregation of labor markets is almost inevitable. If society values perceived strength, dominance, and aggression more highly in accomplishing tasks, then paying differentially by gender is a logical concomitant.

Black women, in particular, have been the victims of such stereotyping. In reviewing racial patterns of occupations during the industrialization of the United States, Glenn and Tolbert note: "[Women] of color were confined to the lowest rungs of female-typed occupations. Outside of agriculture, women of color were limited to the least desirable women's jobs and were paid less than white women. They were overwhelmingly concentrated in private household work or other service employment, typically the most technologically backward sector" (1987:319).

After World War II, and particularly with civil rights and equal employment legislation, women of color moved into previously unoccupied jobs, but they remain "nonetheless ghettoized within [them]" (Glenn & Tolbert, 1987:320). As pointed out earlier, jobs are vertically segregated by skill and pay levels as well as horizontally by gender, and women of color are disproportionately found in the lowest tiers. Woody and Malson observe: "In the case of black women . . . skills and education have improved substantially over past decades. Current median years completed in school by black women are nearly equal to white men and women and exceed that of black males. Wages and salaries paid black women, however, although improving, still lag considerably behind other groups" (1984:11).

Also, women of color "as low-skilled or marginal workers, tend to be recruited more often in [secondary or low value] industries" (Woody & Malson, 1984:13). Table 2.2 illustrates the characteristics of primary and secondary industries. Home care clearly falls into the latter category.

CHARACTERISTICS OF THE HOME AIDE WORK FORCE

Where does home care fit in this picture? It is a service sector occupation, clearly segregated by gender and by race. Workers are predominantly female—consistent with jobs that are deemed to involve gender-related charac-

Table 2.2
Typology of Industry Characteristics

Influential Factors	Industry Characteristics	
	A. Primary/High Wage	B. Secondary/Low Wage
1. Growth in average hourly wage	High average growth	Low average growth
2. Demand for labor	High	Mixed (some low, some high)
3. Productivity	High	Low or mixed
4. Profit trends	High profit margins	Low profit margins
5. Concentration v. Competition	Few, large firms dominate markets	Many small firms, high competition
6. Capital investment	High rates of capital investment per worker	Low capital investment per worker
7. Product demand	Low elasticity, low substitutability; little foreign competition	High elasticity of product demand
8. Public visibility	High visibility	Low visibility
9. Unionization	High rates of unionization, national collective bargaining contracts	Low unionization, local, fragmented collective bargaining

From B. Woody & M. Malson, "In Crisis: Low Income Black Employed Women in the U.S. Workplace." Wellesley College Center for Research on Women, Wellesley, MA. 1984, Working Paper No. 131, p.14. Reprinted with permission.

Source: Bluestone, B. 1971. The Characteristics of Marginal Industries. In Problems in Political Economy, D.M. Gordon (Ed.). Lexington, Mass.: D.C. Heath Company.

teristics such as caring for the infirm and homemaking. Workers are also disproportionately black and minority—consistent with jobs that are deemed to be of low skill and low status compared with other health care jobs. Such jobs are also low paying.

Survey data collected from 1,284 home aides in five cities document key characteristics of the workers and their jobs (see Table 2.3).[1] The mean hourly pay of the survey respondents was $4.61; the median was $4.31; and three-quarters reported wages of $4.85 per hour or less. Furthermore, the median personal income in this sample was only $7,000.

As is typical of jobs in the secondary labor market, the home aides' job is often part-time, and more than half the survey respondents worked fewer than thirty-five hours per week. Because of low pay and their role as single heads-of-

Table 2.3
Characteristics of Survey Respondents

		(Missing responses)
Median age in years	45	
Median years education	12	
Percent not high school grads.	39	
Percent Female	98	
Percent Black	49	
Percent Hispanic	7	
Percent Married	42	
Mean number of children under 6 years	.6	(798)
Mean number of children between 7-21 years	1.5	(528)
Percent workers who care for an aged parent	18	
Percent primary wage earner	65	
Median hourly pay ($)	4.31	(387)
Median personal income ($)	7,000	
Median household income ($)	13,000	(403)
Percent family income under $10,000	45	
Percent health insurance through agency or union	19	
Percent no health insurance	22	
Median years on the job	3	(335)
Percent with more than 1 job	18	
Percent workers who usually work fewer than 35 hrs/week	54	
Percent workers who usually work 35 hrs/week or more	46	
Percent workers who usually work more than 40 hrs/week	25	
Percent workers who have a car	49	

N = 1284

household (65 percent of survey respondents were their family's primary wage earner), home care workers often take on additional jobs (some working three or more). Nearly a fifth of the survey respondents held more than one job to supplement their earnings, and the percentage was nearer 30 percent when New York City workers, who are more likely than most to serve clients with long hours, were excluded. This burden made it highly unlikely that many workers would be able to continue their education beyond high school to better their earning potential. (Nearly 40 percent of the sample respondents had not finished high school, while another 40 percent had completed their education at the twelfth grade.)

Also typical of workers in the secondary labor market, many of the home aides lack basic health insurance benefits as part of their employment package. Only 19 percent of those in the sample received health insurance through their company or union, and 22 percent lacked health insurance altogether. Because the respondents were generally the primary wage earners in the family, the consequences of lack of health insurance affected other family members as well.

Finally, it should be noted that half the workers were reliant on public transportation. This reliance of necessity limited the number of clients they could serve in one day; it also added unpaid time to their workweek if they worked for agencies that did not pay for travel time. (Of the seventeen agencies surveyed, more than half did not pay workers for time spent traveling between clients.) Furthermore, if unexpected changes were made in their work assignments, workers might have a reduced workday because they could not easily travel to another location at short notice.

SUMMARY AND IMPLICATIONS

More women are in the work force today than ever before. Yet despite the postwar decades of increasing labor force participation, the majority of women are found in "women's work," especially in human services. In these horizontally segregated occupations, many women work part-time because labor-intensive service industries frequently match demand fluctuations by using flexible (i.e., less than full-time) employment.

Labor markets are segregated by skill level within occupation (vertical segregation) as well. For women, this often means not only that they occupy "women's" jobs but also that they occupy the lower skill, status, and wage levels of these jobs. And black and other minority women are at the lowest levels within this vertical structure. Despite civil rights and equal employment legislation, the structural barriers to mobility in horizontally and vertically segregated jobs remain formidable.

The home aides' job is the archetype of "women's work," and most workers who hold the job are disadvantaged in many respects. As a 1985 study of New York City home care workers noted:

> The most common salary is less than $5,000 a year. . . . Not surprisingly, severe economic hardship was also found: 80 percent of the workers are unable to afford adequate housing, 35 percent are frequently unable to afford enough food for their families, while an additional 50 percent reported they sometimes lack money for food. Many workers struggle with the persistent threat of homelessness and hunger (Donovan, 1987b:31).

Commenting on statistics like these, one New York City provider observed that home aides were "subsidizing the cost of home care" (Surpin & Grumm, 1987).

Two fragile populations—the frail elderly and disabled, on the one hand, and their poorly paid care givers, on the other—are caught in the middle of this dilemma. Both populations are vulnerable by virtue of their household situation (they tend to live alone or are single parents) and their income (low). The relationship of the client and the home aide is graphically described in the next chapter. If the two groups are forced to a confrontation in the battle to control health care costs, the outcome can only be Pyrrhic.

NOTE

1. For discussion of the development and administration of the home aide survey see the Methodological Appendix.

3

The Job of the Home Aide

The home aide (almost always a woman, paid at wages that are effectively at or near the level of public assistance, with few or no fringe benefits) receives little or no training and is assigned to cases about which she is told little. Once in the home, she is left for the most part to decide for herself—or with the client or client's family, neighbors, or friends—what the needs of the client are and what she should do to address them. Unless she or the client is particularly demanding or difficult, or a crisis occurs, she generally receives little if any direct supervision beyond the control of schedule, time sheets, and paychecks. (One agency supervisor said: "I can only go by the book, because I don't know what she does. I'm sure she'll do what needs to be done.")[1]

The aide is isolated from her peers and rarely ever sees a supervisor on site.[2] She is usually alone with an old woman who is ill, possibly in pain, perhaps disoriented or abusive. Apart from her client, the aide's most frequent contact is with the client's family, which often treats her as a domestic servant. (Families are almost never defined as a formal part of the case but are often a central and difficult facet of the aide's work.) Often neither the client nor the family has been told what to expect, what the aide will or will not do.

The central fact of the aide's job is that she is on her own—essentially isolated from day-to-day instruction, supervision, and support. (As one home aide put it, "I try to deal with Gloria by myself; nobody knows what we're going through—only God and the home attendant know.") If the client is well cared for, it is because she has been lucky enough to be assigned an aide who is experienced, naturally observant and responsive, and deeply committed despite what for many would be very difficult working conditions. (One agency supervisor said, "This job requires that [aides] function a lot off of instinct.") If the aide is satisfied, it is because she feels personally responsible for her clients and obtains gratification from helping them.

The following brief description of a day in the life of a home aide is a composite drawn from observations of several workers and their clients. Although the names and some of the details of the cases have been disguised, the quotations are verbatim. In the final sections of the chapter the description of the worker's day is used in conjunction with data drawn from a set of forty-eight three-hour visits to clients' homes in New York City (Stillman & Gould-Stuart, 1988) and with home aide survey data to generalize about both the difficulties and rewards of the job.

A DAY IN THE LIFE OF A HOME AIDE

7:30 A.M.

The buzz of the alarm coincided with the sound of a glass being dropped. Mrs. Bowen shut off the alarm. She dressed and went to the kitchen, where her daughter and grandchildren, who lived with her, were finishing breakfast.

The telephone rang. It was Mrs. Bowen's supervisor, explaining that the third client she was scheduled to see that day had to be canceled—he had been hospitalized two days before with a fever.

Mrs. Bowen's third client would have been Mr. G, a young man in his late twenties with muscular dystrophy. He lived alone in an apartment complex for the disabled and needed shopping and cooking assistance twice a week. He had become very depressed over the last few months because of the rapid advance of his disease. Institutionalization was a definite possibility. Mrs. Bowen wrote a mental note to herself to call the hospital that afternoon and talk to, or at least to leave a message for, Mr. G.

8:35 A.M.

Mrs. Bowen arrived at the subway after a short walk from her apartment. As usual, the cars were crowded, and she stood the seven stops to her station. In another crowd she waited for the bus and, at 9:07, got off a few blocks from the home of her first client that day, Mrs. Emma P.

Mrs. P had retired last year, after thirty-two years in the dietary department of a major teaching hospital. A warm, friendly woman, she was now seriously ill with congestive heart failure but determined to stay in her own home as long as possible. She had been hospitalized the week before, and this day was the first time Mrs. Bowen would see her since she had been discharged.

Mrs. Bowen walked quickly down the street where Mrs. P lived on the first floor of a two-family house. The neighborhood had once been better kept. Now, weeds and cars sprouted in the front yards, several houses had been burned and were boarded up, fences sagged, and litter was strewn on the sidewalks. Mrs. Bowen was glad it was spring and the mornings were light—she would not walk alone in the dark through these streets. Even so, she held her pocketbook tightly under her arm and kept a wary eye on the surroundings.

9:12 A.M.

Mrs. Bowen arrived at Mrs. P's house. The screen door to Mrs. P's apartment was empty of screens and hung crookedly. Mrs. Bowen rang the bell and was greeted by the overnight worker, who stayed with Mrs. P when Mrs. P's daughter was not available. In fact, Mrs. Bowen had stayed overnight herself a few times, when it had been impossible to find anybody else.

Mrs. Bowen apologized for being a few minutes late—the subway had been slower than usual, causing her to miss the bus that would have dropped her off in Mrs. P's neighborhood on time. The overnight worker left, and Mrs. Bowen greeted Mrs. P with a hug and asked how she had slept. Mrs. P was sitting in a hospital bed that took up most of the dining room. The overnight worker or her daughter slept in the small bedroom at the front of the house, across from the living room. Mrs. Bowen went into the kitchen and grimaced at the breakfast dishes left on the counter, table, and sink. The overnight worker had fed Mrs. P but, again, had not cleaned up. Mrs. Bowen said she would tidy the kitchen and then give Mrs. P her bath.

Although obviously feeling very weak, Mrs. P asked after Mrs. Bowen's daughter and grandchildren and Mrs. Bowen's son, who lived in another city. The two compared notes, laughingly, on grandchildren, while Mrs. Bowen worked in the kitchen and then went to the bathroom to draw a bath. Mrs. Bowen had to help Mrs. P out of bed and walk slowly, supporting her, to the bathroom. The promised wheelchair had not been delivered yet. The process of bathing took about half an hour because the bath lift was broken, and the procedure left Mrs. P tired and somewhat short of breath. After she got her back into bed, Mrs. Bowen tucked Mrs. P in and went back to the kitchen to clean it and get the lunch ready. She expected the visiting nurse to come that afternoon to check Mrs. P's condition.

"I feel as though I'm making a difference in someone's life," Mrs. Bowen explained as she washed the dishes. "I *like* to help older people. With me here, they can stay in their homes and not have to go to a nursing home. And I enjoy the feeling of doing some necessary job for people, to keep them independent."

Mrs. P's daughter had her own family as well as a job and did what she could in her mother's house. However, without Mrs. Bowen and the workers who stayed overnight, Mrs. P would have had to be put in a nursing home. Her disease was severe and, although she was cheerful with Mrs. Bowen, both women knew her remaining time was very short. This was the hard part of the job—losing a person you got to know almost as well as your own family. In fact,

Mrs. Bowen explained, she often felt as if she were taking care of her own mother, and she was sad to know this woman would die soon. "So many are suffering and in such pain—a little kindness goes a long way."

When Mrs. P. woke up, Mrs. Bowen made a pot of tea and sat beside the bed while they both drank it. Mrs. Bowen listened as Mrs. P recounted the stories of her job, including the story that Mrs. Bowen had heard many times before of how Mrs. P had struggled to get to work in the blizzard of 1978.

11:00 A.M.

Mrs. Bowen went through the house again, to make sure everything was in order for the neighbor who was coming to look after Mrs. P in the afternoon. Mrs. P asked Mrs. Bowen why she had to leave so soon, and Mrs. Bowen explained that some new regulations handed down by the county home care program meant that from now on she would have to do her usual three-hour job in two hours.

11:25 A.M.

The neighbor had arrived late, so Mrs. Bowen hurried back to the bus stop. After a change to another bus, she arrived at a high-rise apartment for the elderly in another part of the city.

12:10 P.M.

Mrs. Bowen greeted several home care workers from her own agency and other agencies in the foyer of the apartment building. During the elevator ride to the fourteenth floor, she talked with a supervisor from her agency, who was on her way to look in on another client. The supervisor asked Mrs. Bowen when she had last seen Helen T, Mrs. Bowen's supervisor, and she answered that it had been about three weeks earlier.

12:13 P.M.

Mrs. Bowen knocked on the door to number 14H, and a voice inside said, "Go away!" Mrs. Bowen knocked again and identified herself—there was some grumbling inside, but the door was opened by Miss B. Miss B began complaining immediately that she was hungry, that there was no food, and that Mrs. Bowen was late again.

Mrs. Bowen put her arm around Miss B's shoulders and gently led her to the couch. The tiny apartment was crammed with furniture, mementoes, pictures, knickknacks. The couch, overstuffed red velvet with fringe, looked out of place against the spare lines of the apartment. Mrs. Bowen said she would go immediately to the small market at the end of the block and pick up the items on Miss B's list. Then they would have lunch.

Miss B called after Mrs. Bowen to hurry because there was laundry to do as well. In the elevator going down, Mrs. Bowen said: "Sometimes clients expect more than what you are supposed to do, or don't think it's necessary to say 'thank you' for what you do." Apparently Miss B complained no matter how hard Mrs. Bowen tried to please her. In fact, Miss B had once called Mrs. Bowen's supervisor to say that Mrs. Bowen had kept some of the change from a shopping trip. The supervisor was used to hearing this complaint from Miss B about every home care worker that was assigned to her. In fact, Mrs. Bowen had now outlasted other workers. Why? Mrs. Bowen explained that Miss B had worked her way up from a secretary to vice president at a local bank. When she wasn't complaining, she talked about her experience. "[Miss B] has some very interesting things to talk about, and I can learn from her. This is another part of the job I like—dealing with older people, because they know so much!"

1:30 P.M.

After Mrs. Bowen put the food away, made lunch, and carefully counted out the change against the receipt, she cleaned up and then went into the bedroom to check the laundry. Miss B did not stop complaining, but Mrs. Bowen said later that this behavior was unusual and Miss B was probably feeling lonely. Mrs. Bowen sat with Miss B in the living room and played cards with her, listening patiently, until it was time to leave.

2:35 P.M.

Because her third client had been canceled, Mrs. Bowen decided to drop by her agency that afternoon and pick up her check. She had worked for this agency for nearly six years and earned the maximum hourly wage: $5.47. However, because she was not on salary, her weekly check reflected factors beyond her control such as whether clients had to be hospitalized suddenly (like Mr. G), leaving her without a scheduled replacement.

3:07 P.M.

Mrs. Bowen knocked on the door frame of her supervisor's office and chatted briefly with her about the cases. Mrs. Bowen said she was afraid Mrs. P was getting worse, and the supervisor agreed that Mrs. Bowen faced another loss with her death.

Mrs. Bowen picked up her pay—$111 for the prior week—and said quietly, "Low wages degrade and anger me!" She knew the agency had gone to the State House many times to lobby for their home care workers. However, reimbursement still did not take into account the real value of home care. On the bus back home, Mrs. Bowen said it was becoming harder and harder for her to justify the problems and emotional stress of her job with the pay and benefits that local agencies could offer. For younger women, she noted, competing job opportunities in the city's hotels were more attractive than home care. This fact made the available work force smaller than ever. How it would all end, she did not know.

THE PRACTICE OF HOME CARE

As the preceding story should make clear, the job of the home aide encompasses many tasks. Mrs. Bowen, our fictionalized worker, was coping with the severe depression of Mr. G; the physical frailty of Mrs. P, recently discharged from the hospital suffering heart failure and a prognosis of imminent death; the loneliness of Miss P, expressed as complaints about Mrs. Bowen's work; and the routine activities of shopping, cooking, cleaning, and helping with work around the house. For her clients, Mrs. Bowen functioned as ''social worker, confidante, nurse, and manager of the home environment'' (Parks, 1986:2).

The Clients

In general, clients observed during field visits to their homes could be divided into four broad categories based on the kinds of demands their condition placed upon the home aide:[3]

1. Bedridden clients
2. Alzheimer's, severe psychiatric, and senile dementia clients
3. Wheelchair-bound clients
4. Ambulatory, alert clients

These categories sometimes blurred because clients had multiple diagnoses, different functional abilities with the same diagnosis, and different stages of a given disease. Although neither clinical nor entirely distinct types, the four categories generally posed somewhat different problems for the home aide and required somewhat different skills and tasks.

First were the bedridden clients, suffering, for example, from strokes, advanced Alzheimer's disease, and Parkinson's disease. While sometimes able to speak, these clients were always totally dependent on their home aides (or, in the absence of the home aide, other care givers) for personal care. The home aides had to turn these clients every two hours to prevent bedsores; bathe, diaper, and feed them; and change their sheets and bedclothes while they were in bed. They could not leave the client's bedside for more than brief periods as they might be needed at any moment. Their principal duties away from the client included preparing meals (often pureed) and washing the client's sheets, towels, and bedclothes. Because the client was bedridden, most of the required cleaning chores were in the client's room (although the clients' families sometimes attempted, sometimes successfully, to get the aide to do more).

Second were clients who suffered from mild to severe forms of Alzheimer's disease and senile dementia as well as severe psychiatric disorders or severe mental retardation. Individuals in this group were not wheelchair-bound and were physically able to perform a range of functional activities. Generally, however, the clients' behavior and ability to function safely or responsibly were notably impaired, and the job of the home aide was to protect the client and perform a variety of personal care and household activities.

Third were wheelchair-bound individuals (sometimes using a walker or cane). These clients were generally mentally alert but needed varying degrees of assistance in feeding, bathing, dressing, and toileting; many had suffered from strokes.

Finally there were mentally alert and ambulatory clients, who could perform a range of functions independently. Constituting roughly half of the caseload, they were suffering from diseases such as diabetes, arthritis, and high blood pressure or from visual or hearing impairments. Some were very frail but could do some things for themselves, such as eating and toileting. Some could do more, including making their bed, going down for the mail, or preparing some food. But many needed assistance with shopping and household chores in addition to personal care, such as bathing or dressing.

Job Problems and Difficulties

The main job difficulties home aides encountered in attending to their clients were:

- Problems with clients' behavior
- Problems with the behavior of clients' family members
- Sexual harassment
- Difficult sleep-in conditions
- Boredom
- Job tasks for bedridden clients
- Problems with weekend or replacement aides
- Problems with inadequate information about the job or inadequate equipment or supplies
- Transportation problems
- Unsafe neighborhoods and buildings

Problems with Clients' Behavior. During the field visits carried out in New York City, problems resulting from the behavior of clients and their family members, taken together, were cited by home aides more often than any other problem area. This finding was not surprising because the field visits were made to a number of aides who were serving behaviorally difficult cases as part of the work life demonstration in that city.[4] Most distressing to the workers serving these cases were instances of abusive, bizarre, angry, stubborn, cursing, depressed, sad, forgetful, and fearful behavior on the part of Alzheimer's and severe psychiatric as well as nonpsychiatric cases. While such instances were perhaps more frequently mentioned by the New York City respondents, they were also mentioned by workers at all other sites. (Remember Mrs. Bowen's depressed muscular dystrophy client and the complaints and accusations the aide endured from Miss B.) For example, one aide reported that her client with Alzheimer's disease viciously cursed and tried to bite her when she bathed her. Other problems with Alzheimer's and psychiatric cases included clients walking out of their apartments without clothes, smoking and burning things, and throwing food.

One aide was continually ordered, over her objections, to go to the store to buy things the client already had but insisted she didn't. Then the aide was chastised by the client's daughter on her return from work for buying the items. Another aide with a particularly forgetful client found that when she arrived at her client's house in the morning, the client had already left to do errands, having forgotten the time. Sometimes she had to wait twenty minutes before the client returned from the store, usually empty-handed. This home aide worried that her client would become so disoriented outside that she would not find her way home.

Two aides reported that their clients did not allow them to go outside for a break, even when they worked twenty-four hours a day, five days a week. Others reported not receiving enough money to do necessary laundry, shopping, etc. (This problem was usually associated with the clients' suspicions abut the home aides' use of their money, as in the case of Miss B.)

Problems with Family Members' Behavior. Workers often complained that clients' family members were overly demanding and critical. Some aides indicated that family members ordered them about as domestic workers. In one case, a home aide complained that her client's daughter harassed her if she had to take time off from work. Other difficulties reported were family members' not giving a twenty-four-hour worker relief time for doing an errand, despite their own presence in the house. Family members' abuse of clients was also cited: in one case a client's sister and her friends wanted the client's apartment and so harassed the client and the sleep-in aide, entering the apartment at night and intimidating them.

Sexual Harassment. A related problem, reluctantly discussed by workers, was sexual harassment. A few home aides reported having been sexually approached by their male clients. Some home aides were annoyed or upset by elderly male clients who made sexual overtures, while other home aides were able to handle this behavior with equanimity. They were in a more threatening situation, however, when family members or neighbors with more physical strength harassed them because they were vulnerable to assaults in their isolated settings. In addition, if an aide reported an incident to her agency and the agency conveyed the allegation to the family, it was possible that the family would deny the incident and demand a new aide. The complaining worker might lose her job and might not easily find a case with a similar schedule or location.

Sleep-in Conditions. Some home aides complained about difficult sleep-in conditions. One slept in a bed in the living room but had no privacy because the client's daughter frequently walked through the room and turned on the light as the aide tried to sleep. Others had to sleep in their clients' rooms and suffer a lack of privacy. (Some were able to work out more suitable sleeping arrangements with the intervention of their supervisors.) Some home aides described how clients called them during the night or how they had to be vigilant of wandering clients at night, although they were paid only for their daytime working hours.[5] Thus, they found themselves up and about during the night after a full day's work and became exhausted. The only solution they found was to take a day off now and then, but respite from sleep-in cases was dependent on a sympathetic supervisor willing and able to find a temporary replacement worker.

Boredom. Another job difficulty, boredom, was acknowledged by many of the aides who served "long hours" cases (i.e., cases assigned thirty-five, forty, or more hours per week of care). Most appeared to have accepted boredom as part of the job and developed ways to overcome it. One worker explained that when she was really bored, she sometimes emptied her client's closet, cleaned it, and washed and ironed her summer dresses. Others cited reading, crocheting, and finding little projects around the house to conquer boredom during periods of inactivity.

Television watching was also a time-consuming activity in many homes, but mostly one that was shared with the clients, who used it to entertain themselves, since few other options were available. A few home aides took breaks at specific times during the day and watched television during these times for their own entertainment; others noted that occasional telephone conversations with family members helped them to remain indoors with their elderly clients for long hours.

Workers who complained most about being lonely or bored may have also been reflecting more generalized dissatisfaction with their jobs. For example, one home aide was bored and dissatisfied with her job, even though her client would have been considered a "plum" by most home aides and agency staff. Although totally blind, the 82-year-old client was ambulatory, dressed and bathed himself, made his own bed and breakfast, and had a cheerful disposition. However, his 25-year-old aide felt there was no room for mobility or challenge in her position. Her youth and career goals, in addition to an easy placement that left her with little to do during the day, made her unhappy with her job, even though she and her client seemed to like each other. (Remember that Mrs. Bowen had observed how younger women found competing opportunities in local hotels to be more attractive than home care.)

Job Tasks for Bedridden Clients. A small number of home aides reported that the most difficult part of their job was some aspect of their daily physical work: diapering, making the bed with the client in it, or lifting the client.

Weekend or Replacement Aides. An additional problem cited by some home aides was dealing with weekend, sleep-in, or replacement workers who they believed took poor care of their clients when they themselves were off-duty. A few home aides noted that weekend workers did not cook or clean for their clients but left everything for the aides to do during the week. One described how she routinely cooked on Fridays for the weekend, knowing that the weekend worker would not shop or prepare any food for her client. (Note that picking up after Mrs. P's overnight worker was a chore that Mrs. Bowen routinely faced.)

Home aides reported their clients' expressions of anxiety about changes in personnel: clients sometimes did not eat when a replacement or weekend person was there; sometimes they refused to be bathed by someone they did not know well; sometimes they showed signs of depression when their regular aide was away.

Problems with Information, Equipment, and Supplies. A substantial proportion of workers (25 to 30 percent) responding to the home aide survey reported a constellation of problems having to do with inadequate information about clients, inadequate instructions for clients' care, inadequate instructions about where and when to report for work, and lack of necessary supplies and/or equipment. (Mrs. Bowen, for example, lacked a wheelchair and bath lift for Mrs. P.)

Transportation Problems. Public transportation was often the only mode of travel for the home aide. Most of the workers could not afford their own car. (Note that Mrs. Bowen faced at least ninety minutes of travel on public transportation to see only two clients.) Aides at some of the New York City home attendant agencies, who worked only four hours per day, had to spend $4.00 per day on carfare—an amount equivalent to about 25 percent of their take-home pay. Long travel distances and two-fare transportation costs to the clients' homes were given as reasons by a few home aides for accepting sleep-in positions. The home aide survey found that about 40 percent of workers experienced occasional transportation problems, while a smaller proportion frequently experienced such problems.

Unsafe Neighborhoods and Buildings. Finally, another job difficulty cited was the danger of walking in clients' neighborhoods and apartment buildings. This problem was endemic in New York City, particularly in areas where workers felt most vulnerable to assaults from crack users. However, dangerous conditions were cited by workers in all cities included in the survey. (One Boston worker observed during the project period had been mugged the prior week while traveling to a client.) One home aide hoped that wearing her uniform (following her agency's rules) would ward off attackers, while another used the opposite strategy, dressing in plain clothes to appear as a neighborhood resident. In one Brooklyn agency, nurses making home visits in certain areas were routinely escorted by male staff members, but home aides received no such protection. A few reported that their husbands had to pick them up from work for safety reasons.

SOURCES OF JOB SATISFACTION AND MOTIVATION

Why did Mrs. Bowen and others like her stay in the home aide's job? The literature on job motivation suggests that there are three characteristics of "motivating" jobs: (1) the job allows the worker to feel personally responsible for meaningful portions of the work; (2) the job provides feedback to the worker; and (3) the job provides outcomes that are intrinsically meaningful and worthwhile to the individual worker (Hackman & Lawler, 1979).

Home care, in spite of the numerous problems described above, can be a motivating job. The upside of worker isolation is independence and a task situation in which she is personally responsible. In the home aide survey, respondents overwhelmingly expressed a sense of personal responsibility and involvement in their work. Approximately 80 percent of respondents at each site surveyed strongly agreed that they felt personally responsible for the work they did on the job and that they were personally involved with their work.

The home aides' commitment was often exemplified by their personal involvement in their cases outside of their working hours. One worker refused to take another case while her permanent client was hospitalized so that she could be free to visit her daily, without pay or reimbursement for travel. Another stayed late whenever her client's daughter could not get home from work at her usual time to take over the care of her parent, and the aide often prepared the daughter's dinner, knowing how harried she was. Other home aides similarly explained that they frequently did more than their jobs required. For example, they often gave medication to their clients and sometimes did some medical procedures (e.g., catheter irrigation), although they were not supposed to. If they did not, however, their clients would not have been able to get their medications by themselves and would have suffered serious health consequences.

Positive feedback to the worker was sometimes immediate, in the smile and laughs with a client, in the confiding of troubles, in the grasp of a hand as the worker left at the end of a visit. Even sporadic feedback, however, provided gratification to many workers. One home aide described her role as follows: "What I like most is giving her [the client] love and warmth and treating her like a human being. The love I give her keeps her going. Here, I'm helping someone and I know I'm appreciated. She reaches out and grabs my hand, kisses my jaw, and says, I love you, and then says nothing for the next six months. Those times when she can show her love are worth everything."

The personal relationship between the home aide and the client is an integral part of the aide's work and of the client's care. This is true even in an institutional setting, where to a greater or lesser extent the client is expected to adjust to institutional norms, and where no one worker deals exclusively with one patient. When the work takes place in the client's home, and the aide and client are either constantly alone or with others from the client's personal life, the relationship between the two is an even more salient aspect of the job.

In the home visits undertaken to complement the work life demonstrations (Stillman & Gould-Stuart, 1988), good relationships between aides and clients took many forms—familial, warm, friendly sparring, slightly formal—but the common feature was that the aide was aware of and responsive to the client's general condition, not only her immediate physical or mental symptoms but also her likes and dislikes, her dealings with family and others, her fears and other concerns, her daily habits and patterns of behavior. Finally, in caring for her clients, the home aide was demonstrably contributing to an intrinsically meaningful and worthwhile outcome: "Doing some necessary job for people . . . [so] they can stay in their homes and not have to go to a nursing home." The home aide survey found that the aides were overwhelmingly satisfied with the helping aspects of their job. Eighty to 90 percent of survey respondents at each site expressed satisfaction with "the chance to help people" and "the chance to accomplish something worthwhile."

The home aides described their generous acts with pride, noting that their commitment to their clients could not be given a dollar value, and all agreed that workers who worked only for the money would be poor home aides. Expressing the inherent worth of their work seemed to improve their morale and deflect their attention from the low pay, long hours, and low status of their job. The next chapter uses survey data collected as an adjunct to the demonstrations to explore the attitudes of the work force in greater detail and to develop a model of the determinants of job satisfaction and turnover.

NOTES

1. Pages 29 and 34-40 of this chapter are excerpted largely from Stillman, J. & Gould-Stuart, J. Quality of Work and Quality of Home Care. New York: Pickman Consulting Group, Inc. Prepared for the Ford Foundation.

2. In most states there are few if any supervisory requirements for agencies serving private pay clients. Indeed, many states do not even license agencies that serve only private pay clients. Publicly funded home care programs generally provide some sort of site visits to clients' homes. However, these visits may be made by county social workers, nurses, or others who are not direct supervisors of the home aide.

3. This typology and subsequent generalizations are based in part on forty-eight three-hour home visits conducted to observe and record the activities and interactions of home attendants and their clients from three New York City agencies, two of which were participants in the Ford demonstration (Stillman & Gould-Stuart, 1988).

4. See Chapter 8 of this book for a full description of the New York City demonstration.

5. In the New York City home attendant program, aides who worked twenty-four hours received hourly pay for their first twelve hours and one additional dollar for the second twelve hours, on the assumption that they were off-duty then. However, none of the twenty-four-hour home attendants in this study considered that they could be off-duty when their client was awake at night or might need them at any hour.

4

Understanding Job Satisfaction and Turnover

What are the critical factors affecting job satisfaction among home aides? To answer this question survey data collected from 1,284 aides in five cities were used to develop several models of job satisfaction and "intent to turnover" (i.e., intent tc leave the job). This chapter discusses the rationale for examining worker attitudes and presents the models developed to explain job satisfaction and turnover.[1]

THE RATIONALE FOR EXAMINING WORKER ATTITUDES

Job satisfaction has probably attracted more research than any other outcome in the field of organizational behavior (Staw, 1984). One count, taken in 1976, identified more than 3,000 studies that contained some documentation or examination of job satisfaction (Staw, 1984). Much of the early interest in job satisfaction arose from the belief that satisfaction affected productivity: the assumption was that a more satisfied, committed, or involved worker would be a more productive worker. However, unambiguous empirical evidence to support the link between attitudes and productivity was not forthcoming (Mitchell, 1979). "Research on job satisfaction per se probably peaked in the 1960s and then declined when the presumed link between satisfaction and productivity was called into question" (Staw, 1984:631).

Research on satisfaction began to show signs of resurgence in the 1980s for several reasons. First, researchers found evidence that linked attitudes to the specific behavioral outcomes of absenteeism and turnover, "once again providing an economic rationale for their study" (Staw, 1984:631). Second, concerns over the quality of work life led to renewed study of job satisfaction on the assumption that "the individual's own experience of satisfaction or dissatisfaction defines the quality of his [or her] own working life'' (Seashore, 1975:106). Third, growing interest in the relationships between work and mental health (Kahn, 1980) and between work and family life (Kabanoff, 1980) also fueled new interest in the study of job satisfaction.

The rationale for studying satisfaction among home aides is three-fold: (1) Job satisfaction is generally considered an important determinant of worker absenteeism and turnover. High absenteeism and turnover disrupt agency operations and continuity of service. Thus improved understanding of the determinants of worker satisfaction could facilitate agency management; increase worker reliability; and improve continuity of care, a critical dimension of service quality. (2) Job satisfaction may also be correlated with other less quantifiable dimensions of quality, such as the nature of communication between worker and client and the degree of rapport established during worker-client interactions (Weisman & Nathanson, 1985). (3) Finally, job satisfaction may be viewed as an intrinsically valuable outcome in itself. Home aides perform a socially important function in exchange for minimal remuneration. Job satisfaction may be among the most significant rewards for this difficult job, and managers may wish to improve job satisfaction, job commitment, and job involvement whether or not their impact on absenteeism or turnover can be quantified.

WORKER ATTITUDES TOWARD THE JOB

As might be expected, given the work life problems and the labor market statistics cited in Chapters 1 through 3, the survey respondents reported a good deal of dissatisfaction with pay, benefits, and opportunities for advancement (see Table 4.1). About half of the respondents were dissatisfied with pay, benefits, or both pay and benefits, and about a third were dissatisfied with opportunities for advancement. A fifth of the survey respondents were dissatisfied with the number of hours they worked each week, and 13 percent felt their training was inadequate. Across all sites, a consistent 15 to 18 percent of respondents reported feeling lonely on the job, and a similar proportion said they intended to look for a new job in the coming year.

On the other hand, the respondents overwhelmingly reported satisfaction with their supervisor, their company or agency, and with the helping aspects of the job. As discussed in Chapter 3, home aides' work does provide intrinsic gratification, and as can be seen from Table 4.1, more than two-thirds of the respondents reported intrinsic satisfaction with the job (i.e., with aspects such as doing ''worthwhile work,'' learning new things, and doing ''work suited to [their] abilities''). Furthermore, over 80 percent of the respondents ''slightly'' or ''strongly'' agreed with the statement ''all in all, I am satisfied with my job.''

These findings may understate the degree of dissatisfaction and overstate the degree of satisfaction among the home aide work force, insofar as survey respondents constitute a more stable and possibly more satisfied segment of the work force than nonrespondents.[2] Furthermore, the survey data may understate

Table 4.1
Attitudes of Survey Respondents, 17 Sites

	Satisfied* (Slightly or Very)	Dissatisfied* (Slightly or Very)
Pay	35%	51%**
Benefits	34%	52%
Pay/Benefits construct	24%	55%
Opportunity to advance	44%	34%
Hours Worked	69%	21%
Training Adequacy	81%	13%
Isolation	74%	16%
Opportunity to Help	93%	3%
Treatment by Supervisor	86%	7%
Treatment by Company	78%	11%
Intrinsic job satisfaction	68%	11%
Overall job satisfaction	84%	9%
Will look for a new job:		18%

N = 1284

* Workers responded on a 5-point scale including very satisfied, slightly satisfied, neither satisfied nor dissatisfied, slightly dissatisfied, very dissatisfied.

** Rows do not add to 100% because middle category "neither satisfied nor dissatisfied" is not reported.

the numbers of workers who intend to leave their jobs as home aides, insofar as dissatisfaction with pay and benefits is a predictor of intent to turnover.

EXPLAINING JOB SATISFACTION AND TURNOVER

Research on job satisfaction has provided a wealth of information on the correlates of job satisfaction, while research on turnover has attempted to specify further the relationship between job satisfaction and a worker's decision to leave the job.

Large-scale surveys as well as countless studies with more limited samples have examined the relationship between various working conditions, pay, supervision, promotion, and job features with satisfaction. As one might expect, data show that satisfaction covaries with level of pay, degree of promotional opportunities, the consideration of supervisors, recognition, pleasant working conditions, and the use of skills and abilities (Staw, 1984:631-32).

Models of turnover have posited that job satisfaction—or dissatisfaction—in turn "leads to thoughts of quitting, to evaluation of the utility of searching behavior, job search, evaluation of alternatives, comparison of alternatives versus the present job, intention to quit or stay, and finally to turnover or retention behavior" (Staw, 1984:642). This literature suggests that there is an inverse relationship between satisfaction and turnover (e.g., Mobley, 1982; Porter & Steers, 1973). Specific variables associated with increased job satisfaction or decreased turnover include personal factors (age, tenure, family responsibilities, similarity of job to vocational interest and educational level, and personality characteristics); work environment factors (attitudes toward job content and role); and organizational factors (pay, supervision, etc.).

The empirical studies have shown that satisfaction is generally correlated with turnover, but the magnitude of the relationship is generally not large (Price & Mueller, 1986; Staw, 1984).[3] Price and Mueller, for example, found that two of the determinants of turnover of hospital nurses were job satisfaction and commitment. The explained variance in individual turnover was only 12 percent. "The dominant pattern, however, [was] one of consistency between the findings and the model" (Price & Mueller, 1986:205).

A handful of studies has examined job satisfaction and/or turnover among home care workers. This research has identified several aspects that are satisfying about the home care job. When asked what they felt were the best aspects of the job, workers have responded: helping others and doing worthwhile work (Atkins et al., 1982); doing worthwhile work and having flexible hours and client relationships (Stelmach et al., 1981); and providing comfort for others (Gotay, 1983).

Least satisfying aspects have included low pay, no benefits, and odd hours (Atkins et al., 1982); poor work schedules, wages, and benefits (Stelmach et al., 1981); and job conditions (Tiagha, 1981).

Two studies attempted to identify aspects that were predictive of turnover. In a study of forty workers, Stelmach et al. (1981) found that past experience in home care and a caseload of patients with less intense needs contributed significantly to overall job satisfaction and low intent to leave the job. In the Atkins et al. (1982) survey of fifty-six home care workers, no single reason was found for turnover, although "attitudes toward disabled persons" and a personality dimension ("vigor") were found to be statistically significant predictors of turnover.

The Model

The model of home aide attitudes (Figure 4.1) described herein explored three domains: demographic factors, the work experience, and outcomes. It focused

Figure 4.1
Causal Model

Demographic Factors
Age
Race
Marital status
Education
Duration of job

The Work Experience
Supervisor supportiveness
Training adequacy
Task significance
Worker-client bond
Task variety
Information problems
Equipment problems
Personal responsibility
Task unpredictability
Loneliness
Satisfaction with pay and benefits
Perceived pay equity
Lock in

Outcomes
Intrinsic job satisfaction
Intent to leave

on two outcomes—intrinsic job satisfaction and intent to turnover—as defined below:

Intrinsic job satisfaction ("the chance to learn new things," "the chance to do work suited to my abilities," "the chance to take part in making decisions," "the chance to accomplish something worthwhile")

Intent to turnover ("I will probably look for a new job in the next year")

The model hypothesized that these outcomes were determined both by individual characteristics that workers brought to the job and by workers' perceptions about various aspects of the work itself. The work experience included supervisory support, task and role aspects, extrinsic rewards (pay and benefits), and intrinsic rewards (e.g., ability to do worthwhile work).

The specific elements of the causal model are illustrated in Figure 4.1.

Demographic factors and work experience factors and the items used to measure them were as follows:

Age (years)

Race (black, Hispanic, white)

Marital status (married or not married)

Education (years)

Duration of job (years with that agency)

Supervisor supportiveness ("My supervisor sets high standards for my performance; lets me know how I am doing in my job; is concerned about me as a person; is available when I need him/her")

Training adequacy ("I have enough training to do my job well")

Task significance ("My client's well-being depends on how well I do my work")

Worker-client bond ("I am often the only person my client can share his or her feelings with"; "I feel very close to my clients")

Task variety ("I get to do a number of different things on my job")

Information problems on the job ("information about clients," "instructions for clients' care," "changes in work assignments")

Equipment problems on the job ("lack of supplies or equipment," "broken equipment")

Personal responsibility ("I feel personally responsible for the work I do on my job")

Task unpredictability ("On my job, I often have to handle surprising or unpredictable situations")

Loneliness ("I feel lonely in this job")

Satisfaction with pay and benefits

Perceived pay equity ("All in all, my pay is fair"; "Considering my skills and effort, I make a fair wage")

Lock-in ("It would be very hard for me to find another job, even if I wanted to")

Results

Use of the path analysis method of regression[4] estimated the variables in the model, using survey data from the entire sample of home aides. Determinants that significantly affected intrinsic job satisfaction or intent to leave the job are listed in Table 4.2.

Figure 4.2 illustrates the significant variables that emerged from the path analysis. The direction of both the direct and indirect effects is shown by the arrow; a negative impact is indicated by a minus sign. Effects of about .15 are generally taken to be important. As shown in Figure 4.2, the determinants with a direct effect on intrinsic job satisfaction were task variety, supervisor supportiveness, and satisfaction with pay and benefits—with supervisor supportiveness appearing to be somewhat less important than the other two variables. The determinants with a direct effect on intent to leave were age, loneliness, and satisfaction with pay and benefits.

As has been found in other studies, age was one of the principal determinants of intent to leave the job—younger workers were more likely to express intent to leave than older workers. Age was also, in this study and others, highly correlated with years on the current job. Loneliness was also a determinant of intent to leave, and loneliness on the job was significantly influenced by

Table 4.2
Results of the Regression Analysis

Determinant	Direct Effects On Satis.	Direct Effects On Intent	Indirect Effects On Satis.	Indirect Effects On Intent
Age		-.18		
Race			-.15	
Supervisor supportiveness	.15		.28	
Training adequacy				-.25
Task variety	.21			
Loneliness		.14		
Satisfaction with pay and benefits	.22	-.14		

Figure 4.2
Causal Model: Satisfaction and Intent to Leave

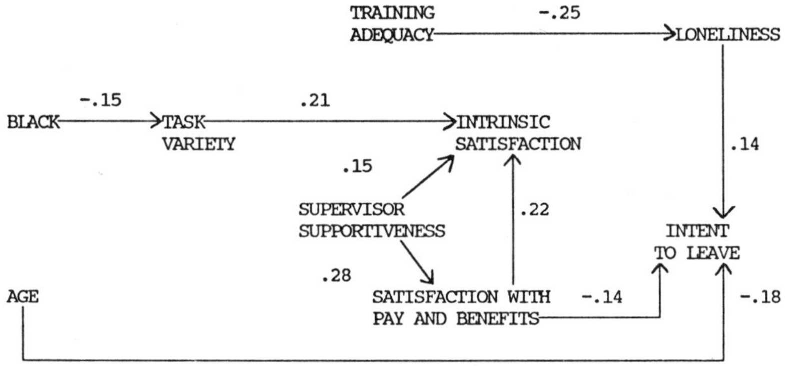

N = 836

perceived adequacy of training. Workers who felt their training was adequate were less likely to feel lonely; hence, they were less likely to consider leaving the home care job. One surprising finding was the lack of connection between supervisor supportiveness and loneliness. Contrary to expectation, higher levels of satisfaction with supervisor support did not evidently mitigate loneliness on the job.

Another determinant of home aides' intent to leave was their satisfaction with pay and benefits: workers who were satisfied with these extrinsic aspects of the job were less likely to consider leaving than those who were dissatisfied. The expectation was that intrinsic job satisfaction would also reduce intent to leave, but this relationship did not appear. The consistently high scores of intrinsic job satisfaction in the sample (mean = 4.09 out of 5.00) and the lack of variability of these scores (standard deviation = 0.93) may explain this finding.

Note that the supervisor was important in influencing workers' satisfaction with pay and benefits, as well as (to a lesser degree) their intrinsic job satisfaction. Observations in the field indicated that it was usually the supervisor who kept workers informed (to the extent they were informed) of third-party payment policies affecting wages and benefits and attempts by the agency and others to secure more generous payment. It was also the supervisor who provided the only real feedback from the agency about the importance of the work performed. Given the infrequency of contacts between supervisors and home aides, however, such feedback was generally quite minimal.

Task variety was also a determinant of workers' intrinsic job satisfaction. The ability to be involved in a number of different activities on the job was an important intrinsic motivator (this relationship was suggested by Hackman and Lawler, 1979). However, it should be noted that race had an impact on the perception of task variety. Black workers were less likely to feel that their job was varied; thus, their intrinsic job satisfaction was negatively affected.

Real or perceived discrimination might be one reason for black workers' perceptions of job monotony: to the extent that such workers were channeled into the home aide's job because of lack of other opportunities, they might have experienced greater boredom (see the discussion of boredom in Chapter 3) than white workers who took the job "voluntarily." In relationships not described in the path analysis in Figure 4.2, race was also found to influence negatively the worker-client bond (perhaps because of widely acknowledged preferences of white clients for white workers), equipment problems on the job, and perceived pay equity.

The original causal model (Figure 4.1) hypothesized that other items would also be important in explaining the outcomes of interest (i.e., intrinsic job satisfaction and intent to leave the job). Those attitudinal items that did not show up as significant explanatory variables included task significance, the worker-client bond, job problems, personal responsibility, task unpredictability, perceived pay equity, and lock-in (the perception by workers that they could not leave the job, even if they wanted to)—all variables that have appeared in one or another studies of satisfaction and turnover. Nevertheless, the model that emerged from the path analysis is generally consistent with other research in the field linking various personal characteristics and aspects of the job to intentions to stay or leave.

The survey data were also analyzed according to (1) agency corporate status (for-profit, not-for-profit) and (2) type of clients served by the agency (publicly reimbursed clients or a mix of publicly and privately reimbursed clients). The determinants of intrinsic job satisfaction and intent to leave, for workers in for-profit and not-for-profit agencies, were remarkably similar to the overall sample as well as to each other. This finding suggests that the corporate status of the agency was not a particularly salient feature of work life to the home aides. When agencies were categorized according to the type of clients they served (publicly reimbursed or a mixture of publicly and privately reimbursed clients), many of the determinants of intrinsic job satisfaction and intent to leave were also similar. However, there were some differences by type of client. Given the fact that the home aides spent virtually all of their work time with their clients and little if any time at the agency, it is not at all surprising that the mix of clients the worker served apparently exerted more influence on her attitudes about the job than the corporate status of the agency.

For publicly reimbursed clients, the model in Figure 4.3 was indicated. Determinants of intrinsic job satisfaction and intent to leave for these clients are listed in Table 4.3. For a mixture of publicly and privately reimbursed clients, the model in Figure 4.4 was indicated. Determinants of intrinsic job satisfaction and intent leave for these clients are listed in Table 4.4.

It is interesting that race,[5] task variety, task unpredictability, equipment problems, and worker-client bond appeared as significant explanatory variables only in the model of publicly reimbursed clients, while education, personal responsibility, and duration of job appeared only in the model of mixed public and

Figure 4.3
Causal Model: Satisfaction and Intent to Leave, Public Client Agencies

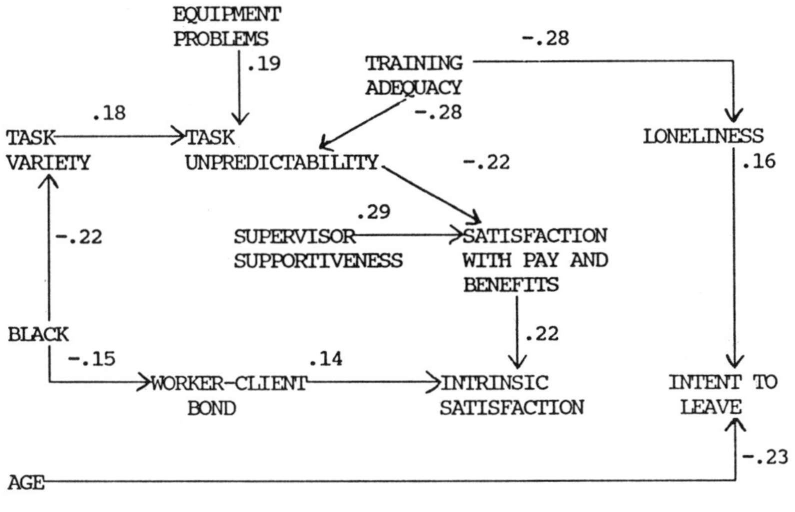

N = 348

Table 4.3
Regression Results—Public Client Agencies

Determinant	Direct Effects On Satis.	Direct Effects On Intent	Indirect Effects On Satis.	Indirect Effects On Intent
Age		-.23		
Race			-.22 (through variety)	
			-.15 (through worker-client bond)	
Supervisor supportiveness			.29	
Training adequacy				-.28
Worker-client bond	.14			
Task variety			.18	
Equipment problems			.19	
Task unpredictability			-.22	
Loneliness		.16		
Satisfaction with pay and benefits	.22			

private clients. In agencies serving only public clients, black workers were less satisfied than other workers with the amount of variety they had on the job, with the unpredictability of tasks, and with their relationships with clients. These perceptions, in turn, led to lower job satisfaction. It is possible that public clients have less influence than private pay clients over the selection of aides who serve them. This possibility could lead to greater conflict between clients and workers (particularly between white clients and black workers), making both race and worker-client bonds more salient issues in the public client agencies. It is also entirely plausible that public clients, who must meet a means test to receive service, have fewer supplies and equipment in the house; hence the salience of that item in the public client model.

Why education, duration of job, and personal responsibility appeared significant only in the mixed client model is less clear. Perhaps workers employed by the mixed client agencies (which employ a broader mix of workers as well) perceived a greater discrepancy between their education and their work than those employed by public agencies with their more homogeneous work force. Thus more educated workers were more likely to express intent to turnover. It is also possible that workers in agencies serving a mix of public and private clients

Figure 4.4
Causal Model: Satisfaction and Intent to Leave, Mixed Client Agencies

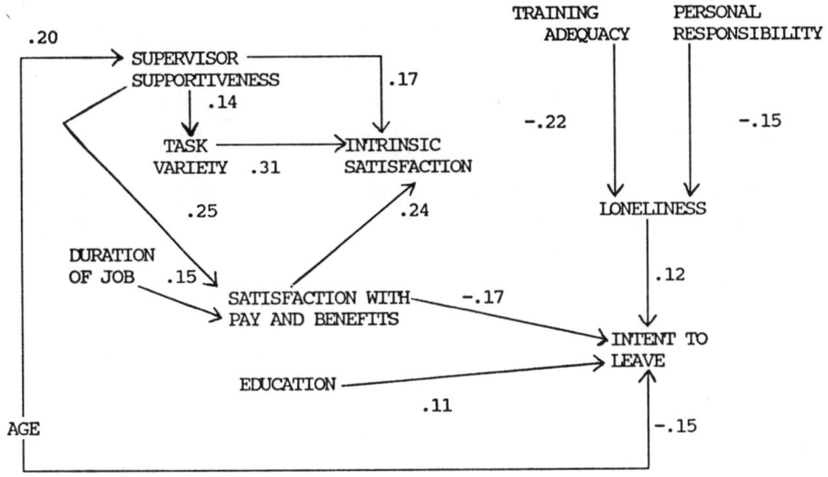

N = 487

Table 4.4
Regression Results—Mixed Client Agencies

Determinant	Direct Effects On Satis.	Direct Effects On Intent	Indirect Effects On Satis.	Indirect Effects On Intent
Age		-.15	.20	
Education		.11		
Duration of job				.15
Supervisor supportiveness	.17		.14 (through variety)	
			.25 (through pay satisfaction)	
Training adequacy				-.22
Task variety	.31			
Personal responsibility				-.15
Loneliness		.12		
Satisfaction with pay and benefits	.24	-.17		

were less bound by bureaucratic and agency rules, hence the greater importance of personal responsibility in determining attitudes toward the job. In agencies with greater possibilities for experiencing personal responsibility, it is entirely plausible, as the model indicates, that workers with a strong sense of responsibility would be less likely to leave the job. The fact that job duration was positively correlated with satisfaction in these agencies suggests, too, that because they were less bound by bureaucratic constraints, the mixed client agencies may have been in a better position to reward long-term workers with better pay and benefits.

SUMMARY AND IMPLICATIONS

In all of the models developed using the survey data, age and/or race were important personal characteristics contributing to job satisfaction and/or intent to leave the job. Training adequacy, task variety, and supervisor supportiveness—all factors to some extent subject to managerial prerogative—were also important determinants of worker attitudes, affecting perceptions of loneliness on the job, satisfaction with the work itself, and satisfaction with pay and benefits. Loneliness and satisfaction with pay and benefits were, in turn, the significant attitudinal determinants of intent to turnover.

Because the home aide work force is disproportionately black, the significance of race as a predictor of job satisfaction has particularly important (and potentially disturbing) managerial and social implications. At the least, this finding suggests that black workers experience particular difficulties on the job (especially related to worker-client relationships) that managers (especially those in agencies that serve principally public clients) have not effectively addressed. More disturbing, this finding suggests that some portion of the black work force may be confined—because of discrimination, lack of skills, lack of education, or lack of opportunity—in home aide jobs to which they are ill-suited. This situation cannot be good for either quality of work life or quality of care.

The importance of age as a predictor of turnover suggests that managers may want to focus their recruiting efforts on older workers, who because of temperament or lower employment aspirations, seem more inclined to stay with the job. This finding also suggests that younger workers may require special training, support, and/or supervision if their turnover is to be reduced. Given the general tendency of younger workers in all kinds of jobs to demonstrate higher turnover rates, however, there are probably limits to the effectiveness of age-focused activities.

Training adequacy, task variety, and supervisor supportiveness—all important determinants of worker loneliness, satisfaction, and/or turnover—are all to some extent subject to managerial discretion. Dictated largely by the needs of the client, task variety may be the most difficult area for managers or policy makers to address. Nevertheless, agencies may be able to make improvements in this area by using training to develop better mechanisms for coping with the boring aspects of the job and by using scheduling to vary workers' routines. As for training and support, the work life demonstrations, described in Chapters 6 through 9, indicate how successfully changes in these aspects of the job can reduce worker turnover.

Like task variety, loneliness is also largely dictated by the nature of the job itself, which often requires long hours in the company of no one but an uncommunicative or difficult client. Nevertheless, the inverse relationship found in the analysis between perceived training adequacy and loneliness suggests that agencies can mitigate workers' perceptions of isolation. And, again, the work life demonstrations addressed this issue with apparent success.

Finally, unlike monotony or loneliness, low pay and poor benefits are clearly not inherent to the home aide's job, although their prevalence in the industry have made them seem so. The significance of dissatisfaction with pay and benefits as a predictor of intent to leave the job suggests that improvements in this area ought to yield significant reductions in worker turnover, and the work life demonstrations provide sound evidence that this result is the case. Chapter 5 examines the financial condition of the home care industry and its current capacity to upgrade employment by providing better pay scales and improved working conditions.

NOTES

1. Details on development and administration of the job satisfaction questionnaire and on development of the models are presented in Methodological Appendix.
2. See the discussion of selection bias in Methodological Appendix.
3. Price and Mueller state that "with individuals as the focus, seldom does one find an unexplained variance of more than 20 percent and it is common to find studies explaining less than 10 percent" (1986:203).
4. See Methodological Appendix for an explanation of path analysis.
5. The proportion of black workers in the "publicly reimbursed" sample was 73 percent; in the "publicly and privately reimbursed" sample it was 26 percent.

5

Financial Conditions in the Home Care Industry

Is the home care delivery system adequate, from a financial perspective, to meet the current and future needs of elderly people wanting to live at home despite growing disabilities? The financial health of suppliers of custodial home care services is of particular concern because of the vagaries of health insurance coverage. Because of coverage limitations of insurers, home care services are classified as either acute/medically related (and, therefore, usually covered by insurance) or custodial/supportive (and, therefore, largely not covered by insurance). Unskilled (i.e., home aide) services are used for both segments, and often the same client requires both medical and custodial home care.

This chapter examines how publicly owned for-profit providers of unskilled home care services have performed financially in the early to mid-1980s. A basic premise is that financial health is a necessary prerequisite to a high quality delivery system. Publicly owned for-profit providers would be expected to pursue the most financially rewarding segments of the home care market. The majority of agencies providing unskilled care are proprietary; since 1980, many such agencies previously forced by state licensing requirements to be nonprofit have converted to for-profit status because of Medicare certification changes. Thus, the experience of the publicly held for-profit chains is likely to be representative of the majority of unskilled providers. If the publicly held group has been unsuccessful in achieving profitable performance, it is likely that other providers competing for the same customers with the same basic service are also experiencing financial difficulties. If the home care delivery system is financially unstable, the long-run outlook for high quality, accessible service is at best uncertain and, at worst, unlikely.

DEMAND CHARACTERISTICS OF THE INDUSTRY

As noted in the introduction to this book, aging of the population and the related increased requirements for personal assistance at home have fueled demand. Of the nearly 3 million people 85 and older in 1985, an estimated 30 to 45 percent needed some kind of personal assistance (GAO, September 1986; Scanlon & Feder, 1984). This age cohort will continue to outstrip general population growth well into the twenty-first century.

Currently 5 to 10 percent of those needing assistance in activities of daily living must rely entirely on paid care givers, and this percentage is likely to grow as younger women who formerly provided unpaid care join the work force and as the children of the elderly grow older. Unpaid care givers such as family and friends cannot meet all the needs of another 16 to 25 percent of people needing personal care assistance (Scanlon & Feder, 1984). Recent evidence published by the Government Accounting Office (GAO) suggested that about 45 percent of all Medicare users of home health care must purchase additional services beyond those that Medicare and unpaid care givers offer (GAO, December 1986). Most of the purchased care is for unskilled assistance; only 25 percent of the total 1982 disabled elderly population getting any home assistance received skilled (nursing) care (Liu et al., 1985).

SUPPLY CHARACTERISTICS OF THE INDUSTRY

On the supply side, two related trends emerged: Medicare became a major payer for unskilled services associated with acute care, which constituted nearly 30 percent of total Medicare-reimbursed home visits in 1983, and for-profits became the fastest growing group of providers during the early 1980s. In 1980, Medicare increased the number of for-profit agencies eligible for participation as skilled home care providers by eliminating the requirement of state licensure for Medicare certification. This change opened the door to many proprietary agencies previously barred from certification by state regulations. It also encouraged many nonprofit agencies to convert to for-profit status. Other 1980 Medicare changes encouraged service utilization by eliminating prior hospitalization and deductible requirements. In 1984, the Medicare prospective payment program for hospitals began, which contained strong incentives for hospitals to discharge elderly patients to acute home care. The number of Medicare-certified agencies grew from 2,924 in 1982 to 5,963 in 1986, and in the same period the proprietary share went from 17 to 30 percent of certified agencies. As a result of these changes, in a short time Medicare went from a relatively minor to a major financing source in the unskilled, albeit acute home care sector.

The payers for custodial care are largely Medicaid and self-paying patients. Self-paying patients play a major role in that Medicare does not pay for unskilled custodial services in the absence of acute skilled need, whereas Medicaid does not openly entitle home care in most states, with the notable exception of New York, where 80 percent of Medicaid home care dollars were spent in 1983 (GAO, September 1986). Most private insurance policies do not cover custodial levels of home care, and most privately insured individuals are under age 65, where home care demand is much lower.

Proprietary companies have traditionally supplied the custodial and acute home care market with unskilled workers: personal aides, home health aides, and homemakers. Workers are brokered by these proprietary agencies. Until they were permitted to become certified, a significant segment of the proprietaries' business was to provide unskilled hourly workers to nonprofit community, local public, and hospital-based certified agencies, under contract. Proprietaries also served the non-Medicare (i.e., Medicaid and private pay) market with both skilled and unskilled home health workers.

To many proprietary agencies, the Medicare changes signaled the opening of a lucrative market that they scrambled to enter. Between 1980 and 1985, the more aggressive agencies expanded geographically by acquiring established independent agencies in several states. The concept behind geographic expansion and multiagency chains was that economies of scale existed for activities such as obtaining and maintaining contracts with Medicare, Medicaid, and other state funding sources or recruiting and training workers. Also, some agencies perceived that greater geographic coverage promised new market opportunities such as health maintenance organizations (HMOs) requiring multistate provider networks.

Several of these multistate firms (Quality Care, Superior Care, Tender Loving Care, StaffBuilders, Professional Care, Continental Health Affiliates) grew large enough to go public. In addition, large public companies already in the industry with home health service subsidiaries (Upjohn, H&R Block, Olsten, Kelly) expanded their home care divisions, and both types sought Medicare certification for at least some of their agencies.

How profitable is the home care service market? What are its long-term prospects for growth and financial health? More important, is it likely to provide quality, cost-effective personal care assistance to a growing cohort of elderly people in need?

The findings presented below are not reassuring. The current financial environment is one of extreme constraint caused by the combined forces of public policy cost containment, frail elderly poverty, and overly rapid, poorly capitalized expansion of the fragmented delivery system for unskilled care. Opportunities for cross-subsidy of unskilled services by other home services and products appear inadequate and are diminishing under current competitive and cost-containment trends. These conditions limit the capacity of the home care industry to make sorely needed investments in quality of work life and quality of service.

OVERVIEW OF THE HOME CARE MARKET

The home health care market is predominantly a service one, as shown in Table 5.1, although the distribution of specialized and standard equipment, supplies, drugs, and solutions has grown to become a significant proportion of the medical (versus custodial) market, as well as the most profitable. Roughly $1 billion of medical market sales was for unskilled home services (part of primary services). These estimates, however, excluded custodial care. An estimate of the total sales of custodial services in 1985 is between $3 and $4 billion (FIND/SVP, 1987; Levit et al., 1985). Most of that service was delivered by unskilled homemakers and personal and home health aides. Somewhere between 30 to 40 percent of such care was paid for by patients themselves, with the remainder paid by Medicaid or other local public funding sources (Kavesh, 1986; Levit et al., 1985; Liu et al., 1985).

Although this chapter is devoted primarily to a discussion of the unskilled care providers' financial performance, the high technology and standard medical equipment segments are briefly summarized with regard to the nature of their businesses, key market trends, reimbursement, and profitability performance. These medically related product lines were increasingly undertaken by custodial home service providers as subsidiaries or joint ventures, presumably to generate profits to support the less profitable primary care services.

Table 5.1
Segments of Medical Home Care Market

Product/Service	1985 Sales $ millions	Projected Compound Growth Rate for Sales, through 1990
High technology products and services	1,218	17.3%
Standard medical equipment	901	12.1%
Primary services[a]	3,593	7.1%[b]
Total	5,712	

a) nurses, aides, therapists.

b) Relatively slow projected growth reflects payment constraints rather than demographic constraints.

Source: FIND/SVP. 1985. The Market for Home Health Products and Services. Health Industry Today, February: 46-51.

High Technology

The high technology segment is represented by the specialized providers of home infusion therapy (nutrition, hydration, antibiotics, chemotherapy, pain control), home renal dialysis, and respiratory and life support services. In 1984, infusion therapies were roughly $300 million in sales, as were respiratory services, whereas dialysis was around $200 million (Stephenson & Cron, 1986). Other technology-intensive services such as apnea monitors and bone growth stimulators also fell into this segment, at much lower 1984 revenues. Some of these high tech providers simply distributed drugs, solutions, and equipment of large manufacturers (i.e., New England Critical Care); others were vertically integrated with the product manufacturer (i.e., Baxter Travenol-Travacare and, now, Baxter-Travenol-Caremark). Highly specialized nursing services were critical to the distribution of some of the high technology products (i.e., antibiotics and chemotherapy). Vertical integration was increasingly common because it assured the manufacturer of access to a quality distribution network. Most sales were by hospital referral, so the distribution companies had to have very good product-service quality and local marketing capabilities.

Although many independent home health service agencies have entered or tried to enter this segment of the business, it has become one of the most competitive. Freestanding agencies must squeeze referrals out of hospitals, which are themselves pursuing the high technology home care business as a natural extension of acute inpatient care. Both must compete against national, vertically integrated high technology home health companies with significant marketing expertise and resources. Because high tech services are more likely to be provided to people under age 65 than the other home health segments, the opportunity to serve a privately insured, hence more lucrative, payer mix draws in a large number of sophisticated, well-financed providers. They in turn make tough competition for the predominantly primary service companies.

The high technology segment was relatively profitable in the early 1980s, as the technology to bring home acutely ill patients advanced significantly, and third-party coverage was expanded. In recent years, Caremark, which was predominantly a home infusion company, enjoyed operating margins of 14 to 15 percent on revenues of over $100 million. The alternate site division of Baxter Travenol, which included high technology home health and a number of other services and products, reported a 12 percent profit margin in 1986.

The prospects for this segment began to fade in the late 1980s, however, as Medicare, declaring many of the high technology products (oxygen, infusion therapies) to be commodities, began to crack down on allowable payment levels. Meanwhile, private third-party payers such as HMOs began negotiating for bids on a price basis. With nearly 1,000 hospitals entering this segment of the market, competition could erode profit margins as fast or faster than Medicare cost-containment policy.

Standard Medical Equipment

This segment is composed of thousands of specialized medical-surgical dealers and pharmacies, as well as a growing number of home health services agencies. They distribute durable (reusable) equipment such as beds and wheelchairs, as well as supplies such as ostomy, incontinence, and pressure sore products. A wide range of companies manufactures these products. Some manufacturers also engage in distribution, such as American Hospital Supply, which manufactured many of the products it distributed prior to its 1985 acquisition by Baxter Travenol. In addition, mass merchandising giants such as Sears, Roebuck & Co., Montgomery Ward, and J.C. Penney distribute standard equipment through mail-order catalogs and in-store home health centers.

Medicare, which pays for almost half of all home medical equipment purchases, has recently taken steps to reduce the generous profit margins earned in this business. It eliminated the rental option for equipment that is more economical to purchase and lowered allowable charge levels for most standard equipment and supplies. These moves had a significant impact on industry profit margins, which rapidly declined from an average 11.7 percent in 1982 to 6.2 percent in 1985 (Stephenson & Cron, 1986).

Thus neither high technology nor standard equipment segments of the home care market are expected to generate the generous cash flow of the past, at least for the near term. The industry leaders (Baxter Travenol, Abbott Labs, BOC Group-Glasrock, W.R. Grace & Co.-National Medical Care) are strong corporations, which are well prepared to enter the competitive battlefield, but they have for the most part avoided entering into the provision of unskilled services. Rather, providers of unskilled services, both for-profit and nonprofit, have sought joint ventures or tried to develop their own high tech and durable medical equipment (DME) services. Given the industry trends already described, these providers faced a very competitive, increasingly low-margin market with increasingly high entry costs for developing a referral network.

The Unskilled Service Segment

The largest segment of home care is service, and unskilled care, as mentioned earlier, is a significant share of both custodial and medical home care. Most unskilled-care clients in the custodial classification are disabled elderly people who have several chronic or permanent physical and mental impairments. The self-paying disabled people with the highest out-of-pocket expenditure tend to be senile and to need help with meals and medication. All self-paying disabled persons had greater prior use of hospitals and nursing homes than the general disabled population (Liu et al., 1985). Clients whose services are covered by state and local public funds are more likely to be low-income and to receive fewer hours of service[1] than the self-paying clients.

The larger regional and national service chains are more likely than the small, privately owned for-profit agency to serve directly the self-paying market, because of the high overhead costs associated with marketing and billing in a retail market. Most small local agencies seek a limited number of contracts with local public or Medicaid home care programs or sell services under contract to Medicare-certified acute home care agencies such as hospital-based or visiting nurse agencies. The contractor then deals with the headaches of obtaining client referrals and billing directly or to third parties.

As will be evident, the unskilled-care market segment, despite being served by a large number of for-profit companies, is not an attractive source of profits.

PERFORMANCE OF PUBLICLY HELD FOR-PROFIT HOME HEALTH SERVICE COMPANIES PROVIDING PRIMARY SERVICES

Ten of the twelve largest publicly held home care service companies reported specific information in their annual reports, audited financial statements, or prospectuses regarding the performance of their home care businesses. Contained in Table 5.2 is a list of the largest publicly held home health companies in all segments. The large service companies provided a mix of skilled and unskilled services. For instance, unskilled service accounted for over half the revenues of Quality Care and Upjohn. Five companies reported payer mix information. For the companies reporting payer mix, private paying clients were from 35 to 62 percent of all revenue sources; most of this care was unskilled, custodial service.

Institutional payers were from 5 to 30 percent of sources; for these, the home health agency supplied temporary nurses and aides to hospitals and nursing homes. Two companies reported contract sources for 14 to 19 percent of revenues. These were with state or local public agencies, usually for personal aide and homemaker services. Such contracts are often awarded to the lowest bidder or on a restricted cost basis that does not recognize profit.

Seven companies revealed detailed income statement information regarding the home health service business, and three others mentioned major strategic moves regarding the business, as shown in Table 5.3. Of the ten, only three indicated consistently positive profitability over a multiyear period. In one of those three, profit margins were dropping precipitously; in another, profits were improving as the company shifted from unskilled to high technology services; and in a third, the company was recently indicted for Medicaid fraud and forced to sell all of its operations. Summarized in Table 5.4 are the profitability data reported by the companies.

Adding to the financial constraint on providers' ability to serve the market was a large financial requirement for working capital experienced by most of the companies mentioned and caused by receivables commonly in the 50 to 150-day range. These financial data, although incomplete, are consistent, and indicated

Table 5.2
Home Health Care Services—Publicly Held For-Profit Companies and Subsidiaries

Parent Company	Operating Unit(s)	Approximate 1983/84 Revenues ($million)
1 Abbott Laboratories	Abbott HomeCare Division	50
* The BOC Group, Inc.	Glasrock Home Health Care, Inc.	150
1 C. R. Bard, Inc.	Bard Home Health Division	30
	Shield Healthcare Centers	25
* Baxter Travenol Laboratories, Inc.	Abbey Homecare, Inc.	125
	Travacare Division	80
1 Beverly Enterprises	Beverly Home Health Services	100
o H & R Block, Inc.	Medical Personnel Pool	61
* Caremark, Inc.	Caremark, Inc.	118
1 Colgate-Palmolive Company	Kendall McGaw Laboratories	20
o Continental Health Affiliates, Inc.	Continental Health Affiliates, Inc.	14
* W. R. Grace & Co.	National Medical Care, Inc.	25
o GrandMet USA, Inc.	Quality Care Inc.	125
* Healthdyne, Inc.	Healthdyne Health Care Services	50
* Hospital Corporation of America	Hospital Corporation of America	55
* MEDIQ Incorporated	MEDIQ Healthcare Resources	25
2 National Medical Enterprises, Inc.	Health Products and Services Group	195
* New England Critical Care, Inc.	New England Critical Care, Inc.	14
o The Olsten Corporation	The Olsten Corporation	28
3 Omnicare, Inc.	HPI Health Care Services, Inc.	20
o Pritchard Services Group of America, Inc.	Kimberly Services, Inc.	10
o Professional Care, Inc.	Professional Care, Inc.	35
o ServiceMaster Industries Inc.	ServiceMaster Industries Inc.	20
o Staff Builders,Inc.	Staff Builders, Inc.	60
o Superior Care, Inc.	Superior Care, Inc.	22
o Tender Loving Care Health Care Services, Inc.	Tender Loving Care Health Care Services, Inc.	15
* Union Carbide Corporation	Linde Home Care Medical Systems, Inc.	25
o The Upjohn Company	Upjohn HealthCare Services, Inc.	155
o Westworld Community Healthcare, Inc.	Westworld Community Healthcare, Inc.	20
	Group Total:	1,672
	Market Total:	2,445

o = mostly service, some unskilled
* = mostly hi-tech
1 = mostly DME, standard medical equipment and supplies
2 = mix, no one predominant segment apparent
3 = other, i.e., management services

Source: Medical and Healthcare Marketplace Guide, 1986. The International Biomedical Information Service, Inc. Miami.

Table 5.3
Profitability by Nonfinancial Evidence

Company	Source	Evidence
Olsten	1983 Annual Report	"Health care services not yet contributing to bottom line"
Kelly	1986 Annual Report	company has "realigned its health care division and eliminated all Medicare-certified agencies"
Upjohn	1984 and 1985 Annual Reports	company is "refocussing" business toward higher technology services, and away from (lower skill) home health services; 1985 home health service revenue growth: 3% over 1984 (after 2 years of double-digit growth)

that the primary home care service market does not offer reasonable financial stability to providers, not even to those most motivated to achieve strong financial performance, the publicly held chains.

Factors Contributing to Low Profitability

The lack of profits in the home care service market makes sense when who is paying the bill is considered. First are the self-payers. A GAO analysis of users of the Medicare acute home health benefit showed that nearly 64 percent were women, average age 77. Many of them exhausted their Medicare benefits and continued on a custodial private pay basis. Chronically ill home care clients were more likely to be female and a couple of years older than nonchronically ill clients (GAO, December 1986). Although the age cohort 65 to 69 had considerably more income in the 1980s than in previous generations, elderly people over age 75 often had limited economic resources. Single older persons, usually female, had significantly lower economic status than married older couples. In 1980, 52 percent of single persons aged 75 and older had income below $6,000, including annuitized nonhousing assets; 83 percent of this group had income less than $12,500. Regardless of marital status, 53 percent of the population over age 75 had cash and in-kind benefits that were only twice the poverty level or lower (Atkins, 1985). This fact did not leave a lot of discretionary income to pay for custodial home care services out-of-pocket, where the average reported 1982 payment of self-payers was $164 per month (Liu et al., 1986). Although some

Table 5.4
Evidence Regarding Profitability of Companies with Financial Statements or Prospectuses that Identify Home Health Sector Profitability

Company	1986 Home Care Revenues	Pretax Profit Margins As % Sales	Payer Mix		1985 Days In Receivables
Medical Personnel	$230 million	9% in 1984; 7% in 1985; 4% in 1986	1986: Medicare Instit. Private	 8% 30% 62%	n/a
Quality Care[a]	$160 million	Losses '79-81 2-5% Margin '82-84 Losses '85-86	1983: Medicare Instit. Contract	 31% 7% 19%	50 (1983)
TenderLovingCare	$30 million	Losses to 1% margins; 1983-85	n/a		
StaffBuilders	$48 million	Losses to 2% margins, 1983-84	n/a		94
SuperiorCare	$30 million	Losses, 1983-86	1985: Medicare Medicaid Contracts Private Pay Instit. Rentals	 14% 19% 14% 47% 5% 1%	76
Continental[b] Health Affiliates	$32 million	9%-16% 1982-84	1985: Medicare & Medicaid Private Pay, other	 62% 38%	154
Professional Care Inc.[c]	$56.2 million	loss, 1986, 3.5%-4.8% margins, 1982-85	1986: Private Pay Public & private insurers	 35% 65%	n/a

[a]Recently sold (1987) by Grandmet at a price below what was paid to acquire them in 1985.
[b]Reduced primary (skilled and unskilled) services from 83% to 46% of business. Also sold to a related company in 1982 at above market rates; age of receivables suggests that a large share of revenues reported may never be realized, and profits may be overstated.
[c]Company management indicted in August, 1986 for fraudulent billing and Medicaid compliance reporting in New York: 1987 - forced to sell off all New York assets.

broker agencies might have preferred to raise the average charge and simply provide fewer hours of care per client, this move would not necessarily have improved profitability. Many of the self-paying referrals came from nonprofit skilled agencies and hospitals, which were sensitive to the price patients had to pay out-of-pocket, especially when they had a choice. Home care is a competitive market in the sense that there are very low barriers to entry, hence usually a number of agencies competing for business (Dyckman et al., 1985). In addition, fewer hours per patient may require greater marketing and scheduling costs to obtain a sufficient volume of visits to cover overhead costs and maintain a work force.

Medicaid and local public contracting agencies did not improve the situation when they established cost-based hourly rates for personal care and home health aide services. State rate-setting agencies valued worker time at the minimum wage in many states (Liebman, 1986; Surpin & Grumm, 1987). In addition, many states have reduced the number of hours permitted per visit from four to two or three hours, and because travel is usually an excluded (nonreimbursable) expense, workers' effective hourly rates were lowered still further. Finally, states often capped the overhead allowable cost at levels that were based on averages, thus penalizing agencies that attempted to train workers, add fringe benefits, grow fast (high working capital interest charges), or broaden, through marketing efforts, their referral channels. Such cost-cutting measures by states simply shifted an even greater burden onto the worker (a longer day for the same total pay as before the shortened visit) and reduced the managerial flexibility of the agency that tried to improve its quality or its market position.

Nor did the acute medical home care market offer significant relief to those providers hoping that insurance coverage might improve their margins. In fact, Medicare has put many acute home care agencies in a precarious financial position. Medicare expenditures for home care grew phenomenally under the dual pressures of rapidly increasing demand and supply. In 1980, Medicare spent $640 million on home health benefits; in 1985, it spent $1.7 billion, an average annual growth rate of 33 percent. As with any fast-growing line item on a federal budget, home health services attracted much cost-cutting attention. In 1985 the Health Care Financing Agency published new cost limits that progressively lowered the ceilings on allowable costs per visit, reduced the ability of agencies to cross-subsidize among acute visit types (skilled nursing, physical therapy, and home health aide), and limited the number and frequency of home health aide visits. In addition, Medicare intermediaries were instructed to impose strict interpretations of medical necessity, such that claim denials increased 133 percent in 1986 over a preprospective payment period in 1983 (Perspectives, 1986). As a result of cost-containment efforts, many certified acute care agencies began looking for new revenue sources; a 1986 National Association for Home Care (NAHC) survey of 2,100 member agencies found that more than half were trying to reduce their dependence on Medicare (NAHC, 1986). The NAHC report suggested that the agencies would try to "raise revenues through the care of individuals who pay privately." This strategy, as has already been seen, was not likely to bolster the industry's financial condition.

IMPLICATIONS

The limited resources available to pay for custodial home care services make it an unattractive segment to enter as a home health provider or, more important, as an unskilled worker. Hourly wage rates lag behind most unskilled, nonsupervisory positions available, as shown in Table 5.5

If the industry is not able to attract and maintain a competent work force, quality and access will suffer. There are signs that both quality and worker availability are inadequate for today's needs and even less adequate for the future (National Institute on Aging, 1987). Financial woes of providers undermine efforts to improve the quality of care provided by the work force. The physical and emotional strain of the job is considerable and, coupled with the geographic difficulty of supervision, the managerial challenge to provide quality service is not easy to meet. Rapid turnover, poor reliability, low morale, and emotional and physical abuse of patient and worker are common problems in the industry. Furthermore, increasing demand for personal care service is likely to go unmet unless labor's wages and fringe benefits can be improved. In tight job markets, few workers are willing to contribute to society's commitment to the elderly at their own personal expense.

Home care, particularly that which maintains elderly and disabled people in their homes, is often viewed as the ideal solution to the need for quality and cost containment in the health delivery system. Keeping people out of nursing homes and hospitals by substituting home care is a goal of Medicare, Medicaid, and privately managed care plans nationwide. Home care benefits, however, appear

Table 5.5
Average Hourly Earnings, Nonsupervisory Workers in Selected Occupations: United States

	1983	1985	Average Weekly Hours
Homemaker/home aides	$3.20 - $7	$4.41	30[a]
	1983	1984	
Services - overall	$7.30	$7.53 - 7.60	
Retail - overall	5.74	5.87 - 5.90	
Selected occupations:			
Hotel worker		5.40 - 5.48	30.2
Laundry, cleaning		5.50 - 5.60	33.4 - 34
Beauty Shop		5.40 - 5.79	27.9 - 29
Nursing and personal care facilities		5.35 - 5.41	31.0 - 31.7
Department store		5.83 - 6.03	27.8 - 30.1
Grocery store		7.91 - 8.00	30.0 - 31.8
Eating and drinking places		4.31 - 4.34	25.7 - 27.2

[a] Ford Project Home Aide Survey (see Chapter 4 above).

Source: U.S. Bureau of Labor Statistics. 1985. Employment, Hours, and Earnings, 1909-1984. Bulletin 1312-12, Vol. 2: 698-784. Washington, D.C.: U.S. Government Printing Office.

to be overstated relative to their true costs. Third parties are refusing to pay the price for quality home care, and many elderly people, including the subgroup most at risk of needing home assistance, often cannot afford to pay enough to attract and maintain a quality work force.

Improvements in the quality of work life require the investment of resources in higher compensation, adequate benefits, better training and supervision, redesign of jobs to enhance worker satisfaction, development of opportunities for advancement, and the like. Industries and firms with poor working conditions and low profits or operating deficits are not likely to make such an investment.

In a normal market, the cure for low prices and lack of profits would be that many suppliers would leave the industry and that the remaining suppliers would bid up prices until attractive wages and profits could be earned. In the home care industry, however, prices are artificially constrained by third-party payers and also by the limited resources of the typical self-paying client. The experience of the work life demonstrations, described in detail in Part II, bears witness to the impact of these financial constraints on efforts to improve employment conditions. It also suggests that to fulfill the critical role society expects home care to play (from health care cost containment, to enabling women to remain in the work force, to bringing workers out of poverty), it will be necessary to devise better ways both to pay for home care and to provide the services.

NOTE

This chapter is taken from Kane, N. 1989. The Home Care Crisis of the Nineties. *The Gerontologist,* 29(1):24-31. Reprinted with permission from the Gerontological Society of America.

1. Except in New York City (see Chapter 8).

Part II

Case Studies of the Work Life Demonstrations

6

Introduction to the Case Studies

Part I discussed the employment conditions that contribute to dissatisfaction and turnover in the home aide work force, the concerns that create management interest in work life improvements, and the labor market trends and financial constraints that inhibit reform. The three chapters in Part II describe the demonstrations in detail, while Parts III and IV synthesize the project's findings and discuss their implications. This introduction to Part II reviews the assumptions underlying the project, briefly discusses the process governing site selection, and summarizes the main characteristics of each of the sites.

UNDERLYING ASSUMPTIONS

As noted in the introduction to this book, a basic premise of the project was that the infusion of outside resources could tip the balance toward a more satisfactory employment situation for aides by demonstrating the feasibility and effectiveness of selected work life improvements without financial risk to employers. While the conditions of employment for home aides are generally inferior to those of paraprofessionals in other health fields, many home care employers are seeking ways to narrow the gap. As noted in previous chapters, employers' desire for work life improvements stems partly from their self-interest in a more stable work force, partly from unionization or the threat of unionization, and partly from more altruistic concerns both for the status and satisfaction of the workers and for the quality of care provided the client. Working against these tendencies, however, are the basic economies of the industry. Narrow margins and vigorous competition make employers—both for-profit and nonprofit—highly risk-averse when it comes to experimenting with measures likely to increase the labor costs that constitute the bulk of their operating expenses.

The role of the Ford Foundation was to encourage such experimentation by underwriting for a trial period potentially costly but beneficial reforms. The working hypothesis was that efforts to restructure and upgrade the home aide's job would yield significant returns in worker satisfaction, worker retention, and continuity of care. These in turn would persuade the demonstration agencies to maintain the work life improvements at their own expense and encourage other agencies to adopt similar measures.

SITE SELECTION

Despite resources sufficient to fund only two to four demonstration agencies, depending on projected expenses at each site, the project sought national relevance and visibility. Given the growth and prominence of for-profit chains in the U.S. home care industry, participation of a large national chain was the first major objective of the site selection process. Given the significance of state and local governments in contracting for home care and their potential role in financing work life improvements, public sector involvement in at least one site was a second major objective. Third, given the role of unions in the workplace, union involvement in at least one site was also an important objective. Additional criteria were the local fiscal, political, and competitive environment for home care, local labor market conditions, the racial and ethnic mix of the home aide work force, worker/management dissatisfaction with existing employment conditions, agency size, managerial interest and commitment to the project, managerial capacity, and data accessibility.

Using these criteria, the project manager (Grinker, Walker and Associates) and the research team (from the Harvard School of Public Health) canvassed a variety of for-profit and nonprofit agencies in seven cities (Boston, New York, Philadelphia, Pittsburgh, Cleveland, San Francisco, and San Diego), seeking an appropriate mix of demonstration agencies. They also approached two of the largest national home care chains (Upjohn and Quality Care), as well as the New York City Human Resources Administration (HRA), which runs the largest Medicaid-funded home care program in the country. Remedy Home Care of San Diego, part of a regional chain providing contract services in California, was the first demonstration site selected. Subsequently, Quality Care, one of the five largest publicly held for-profit home care companies in the United States, agreed to participate, offering agencies in Syracuse and Milwaukee as demonstration sites. Finally, the New York City Human Resources Administration, whose Medical Assistance Program accounts for approximately three-quarters of all Medicaid home care expenditures nationwide, agreed to the participation of two of its contract agencies. From a list of agencies provided by HRA, the project manager and the research team selected two large agencies in Brooklyn, New

York (Long Life Home Care Services and Home Care Services for Independent Living).

MAIN CHARACTERISTICS OF THE DEMONSTRATION SITES

Table 6.1 indicates the diversity of the demonstration sites selected. Three of the sites (San Diego, Milwaukee, and Syracuse) involved for-profit agencies that

Table 6.1
Characteristics of Demonstration Sites

	Corporate Status	Client Base	Payment Source	Union Involvement
San Diego				
[Remedy Home & Health Care Services, Inc.]				
	For-profit regional chain	Public clients only	Low-bid county contract	Unionized
New York City				
[Long Life Home Care Services, Inc. Home Care Services for Independent Living, Inc.]				
	Non-profit independent agencies	Public clients only	Cost-based city (Medicaid) contract	Unionized
Milwaukee and Syracuse				
[Quality Care, Inc.]				
	For-profit national chain	Mixed public & private clients	Inst. contracts Cost-based county contracts Private pay	Non-Union

SUMMARY

For-profit	=	3 agencies
Non-profit	=	2 agencies
Union	=	3 agencies
Non-union	=	2 agencies
Public Clients Only	=	3 agencies
Mixed Clients	=	2 agencies
Public Funds Only	=	3 agencies
Mixed Funds	=	2 agencies

were part of larger home care companies; in contrast, the New York City demonstration involved two independent nonprofit organizations. Both the San Diego and the New York City demonstrations involved agencies that served publicly financed clients only and relied exclusively on public funds as their source of payment; in contrast, the Milwaukee and Syracuse agencies served a variety of public and private clients and drew on diverse revenue sources, including institutional and county contracts, Blue Cross, Medicare, Medicaid, and private paying clients. Finally, both the San Diego and New York City workers were unionized, while workers at the Milwaukee and Syracuse sites were not.

KEY ACTORS

Each of the demonstrations involved at least two sets of actors: (1) a corporate and/or public "sponsor," who authorized participation and entered into formal or informal agreement with the project management and research teams, and (2) the agencies actually responsible for implementing the interventions. Table 6.2 lists the actors at each site.

In *San Diego,* the county Department of Social Services (DSS) was the informal sponsor; Remedy Home and Health Care, Inc. was the formal sponsor; and the local Remedy office was the implementing agency. Because Remedy was the exclusive county contractor for In-Home Supportive Services, DSS consent to the project was key. DSS preferred, however, to keep its sponsorship informal; that way, the county could disclaim responsibility either for causing a possible failure or for institutionalizing a possible success. The homemakers' union, United Domestic Workers of America, endorsed the project, participated in its planning, and encouraged workers' cooperation. Remedy later subcontracted with two additional organizations—Allied Home Health Association and the University of California San Diego Medical Center—to provide the training and support components, respectively.

In *New York City,* the informal sponsor was the city Human Resources Administration (HRA), and the implementing agencies were Long Life Home Care Services and Home Care Services for Independent Living—both vendors for HRA's home attendant program. HRA, under growing public pressure to upgrade home attendant services, was very supportive of the undertaking, providing the names of appropriate agencies and encouraging participation. However, formal city participation would have required surmounting numerous bureaucratic and political hurdles. Thus HRA chose not to become a formal sponsor of the demonstration. Instead, the implementing agencies signed the formal letters of agreement authorizing the demonstration. Like Remedy in San Diego, Long Life and Independent were financed solely by public home care funds, and it is most unlikely that they would have agreed to participate without the consent of HRA. Although unionized (in fact their workers were represented

Table 6.2
Actors Involved in Adoption and Implementation

San Diego	
Informal Sponsor:	San Diego County Dept.of Social Services (DSS)
Formal Sponsor:	Remedy Home and Health Care, Inc.
Implementing Agency:	Local Remedy office
Subcontractors:	Allied Home Health Association; University of California, San Diego Medical Center
Union:	United Domestic Workers of America
New York City	
Informal Sponsor:	New York City Human Resources Administration (HRA)
Formal Sponsor:	(Not Applicable)
Implementing Agencies:	Long Life Home Care Services, Home Care Services for Independent Living
Unions:	Local 32B/J, Service Employees International; Local 1199 of the Drug, Hospital and Health Care Employees Union
Syracuse & Milwaukee	
Informal Sponsor:	(Not Applicable)
Formal Sponsor:	Quality Care, corporate
Implementing Agencies:	Q.C. Syracuse, Q.C. Milwaukee
Union:	(Not Applicable)

by two separate unions), the implementing agencies did not seek formal union approval, and the unions were not involved in planning the demonstration.

In *Syracuse* and *Milwaukee,* the formal sponsor of the demonstration was Quality Care corporate headquarters, and the implementing agencies were Quality Care Syracuse and Quality Care Milwaukee. As described in the Quality Care case study, corporate staff, responding to local office concerns about aide recruitment and retention, had begun to focus on work life issues before they ever heard of the Ford home care project. The project therefore struck a sympathetic chord. Neither the Syracuse nor the Milwaukee office was unionized or under immediate threat of unionization, so there was no union involvement.

CHARACTERISTICS OF THE WORK FORCE

At all the demonstration sites, program participants were drawn from the aide work force, consisting of homemakers, attendants, and home health aides. Table 6.3, based on data collected from the baseline survey, describes the pool of aides at each agency. At each site, the aide work force was almost entirely female, with a median age between 38 and 50. Between half and two-thirds of the aides at each site were single, and they reported a median of one to two dependents. Many of these women (ranging from 56 to 82 percent of survey respondents, depending on the agency) were the primary providers for their family.

The proportion of minority workers at the various sites ranged from more than 90 percent at the two Brooklyn agencies to 63 percent at Remedy San Diego, 29 percent at Quality Care Syracuse, and only 15 percent at Quality Care Milwaukee. Part of the range in race and ethnicity is undoubtedly attributable to differences in the local labor markets. For example, almost all the workers at Long Life and Independent Living were black (many of them Haitian, Jamaican, or individuals from other islands in the West Indies), and only 1 to 2 percent were Hispanic, reflecting the racial composition of the Brooklyn neighborhoods where the two agencies were located. In contrast, Remedy San Diego's work force was 20 percent black and 40 percent Hispanic, reflecting the high proportion of Mexican Americans and Mexican immigrants in the San Diego area. At the opposite extreme, only 15 percent of the Milwaukee Quality Care aides were minority group members—all black. The low proportion of minority workers in the Milwaukee agency is probably due in part to its suburban location, relatively inaccessible to inner-city residents reliant on public transportation.

Levels of education at the various agencies were generally low (a median of 11.0 to 12.0 years of school completed, compared to 12.5 for the U.S. female population aged 22 to 65) (U.S. Bureau of the Census, 1984). About half of the aides employed by Long Life and Independent Living had not completed high school. However, the Quality Care agencies had a higher proportion of high school graduates (68 percent in Syracuse and 73 percent in Milwaukee).

Although on average the workers at each agency had been in the labor force for ten or more years and in home care for three to seven years, their earnings were low. Depending on the agency, their median hourly pay ranged from $4.00 to $5.25, and 60 to 80 percent reported personal incomes under $10,000. Family income was also low, with one-third to two-thirds of the aides reporting family incomes of under $10,000 in 1985.

At Remedy and the two Quality Care agencies, the aide's job was essentially part-time (the average workweek ranged from twenty-five to thirty-one hours), and about a quarter of the work force held a second job. In contrast, Long Life and Independent Living provided—although they did not guarantee—full-time work to a high proportion of their aides (average reported workweek forty to forty-eight hours). As a result, fewer than 10 percent of their workers reported

Table 6.3
Characteristics of Home Attendants: Demonstration Agencies

	Independent Living	Long Life	Remedy	QC Syr.	QC Milw.
Percent Female	100	97	97	96	100
Percent Minority	92	93	63	29	15
Percent Black	90	91	20	29	15
Percent Hispanic	1	2	40	1	0
Median Age (yrs.)	42	44	47	38	50
Percent Single	61	66	54	62	53
Median Number Dependents	2	2	1	1	1
Percent with >1 Dependent	76	70	39	35	28
Percent Primary Provider	82	82	57	62	56
Median Years School Completed	11	12	12	12	12
Percent Education < 12th grade	53	48	43	32	27
Average years work experience	14	10	15	15	27
Median years in home care	5	4	7	4	3
Median yrs. in agency	4	3	3	1	3
Median Hrly. Pay	$4.45	$4.25	$4.07	$4.00	$5.25
Percent Personal Income <$10,000	59	72	63	81	69
Percent Family Income <$10,000	46	54	63	36	48
Average Workweek (hrs.)	48	40	27	31	25
Percent with another Job	9	8	23	29	26
N =	177	275	158	78	34

holding a second job. As can be seen from the Long Life/Independent Living case study, the high availability of full-time work at these agencies is attributable to the distinct character of the New York City home care program, which provides thirty-five or more hours of care each week to approximately 70 percent of the client caseload.

The case studies in the remainder of Part II describe in greater detail the demonstration agencies, their respective environments, the work life interventions adopted, factors affecting adoption and implementation, and the impact of the respective interventions.

7

Remedy Home and Health Care, Inc., San Diego

INTRODUCTION

Remedy Home and Health Care of San Diego is part of a regional for-profit chain that contracts with California counties to provide home care financed by the state's $500 million In-Home Supportive Services (IHSS) program. Winner of a competitively bid contract awarded by the county Board of Supervisors, Remedy was the exclusive San Diego IHSS contractor from December 1984 through February 1988. During the period of the project, the agency operated with an annual budget of $4.6 to $5.0 million, an office staff of approximately twenty, and a field staff of 700 to 750 aides—called homemakers. The homemakers provided housekeeping, chore services, and personal care to a caseload of approximately 2,000 elderly and disabled who could not have remained safely at home without assistance.

The San Diego contract covered the entire county, with a population of 2.2 million spread across an area of more than 4,000 square miles. In addition to Remedy, 5,000 to 6,000 individual providers (IPs)—minimum-wage workers hired and fired directly by their clients but paid by the county—also provided publicly financed in-home services to area residents.[1]

At the start of the project, Remedy's main San Diego office was located in an old two-story house near the center of the city and the South Bay area, home of many of its minority workers. The quarters were tight but manageable because after their initial hiring and training, homemakers were rarely required to report to the office. Time sheets and paychecks were generally collected or distributed by mail or at several more convenient locations throughout the county. In 1987 the agency moved to more modern and spacious quarters in an office complex outside the city center. In addition to its city office, Remedy also maintained an office in the northern part of the county, more accessible to workers in that area.

AGENCY AND CORPORATE MANAGEMENT

During the course of the demonstration, two women in succession held the job as director of Remedy San Diego. The first had come to the San Diego office in December 1984, after running a smaller Remedy office in Santa Barbara County. She left in September 1986 and was replaced by her office manager, who had started out as a homemaker. The primary responsibilities of the agency director were to oversee hiring and training, ensure smooth field operations, maintain union ties, and accommodate the various reporting requirements of the county Department of Social Services and Remedy corporate headquarters. The agency director worked under the area field director, a former member of the San Diego County Board of Supervisors and former head of Remedy's San Diego office (under a prior county contract), whose managerial and political experience was an asset in administering IHSS contracts. Strategic planning, budgeting, and most critical decision making were carried out at the corporate headquarters.

Remedy Home and Health Care, Inc., the parent corporation, had annual sales of approximately $17 million in 1984[2]—virtually all from IHSS contracts.[3] It shared new corporate headquarters in San Juan Capistrano, California, with Remedy Temporary Services, Inc., a $30 million per year operation—the largest independent temporary employment organization in California. Together, the two companies employed more than 5,000 employees at any one time and maintained a roster of an additional 10,000 temporary workers. Over the course of a year, they employed approximately 20,000 individuals. The two companies were founded in 1968 as a family business, and they are under common control.

The vice chairman of Remedy's board, son of the founder, was actively involved in running the business, especially the home and health care company. Because of Remedy's heavy involvement in the IHSS contract program, he spent a significant amount of his time speaking out on home care issues in Sacramento, negotiating with individual counties over home care contract issues and dealing with the leadership of the two unions (United Domestic Workers and Service Employees International) that have organized the contract workers in California.

THE UNION

Founded by a disciple of Cesar Chavez and modeled after the United Farm Workers Union, the United Domestic Workers of America (UDW) got its start in San Diego. It signed its first contract—with Remedy—in 1980. That contract provided a significant $.50 per hour wage increase (up from $3.10 per hour) for homemakers, plus benefits including paid vacation, sick leave, and subsidized health insurance for workers employed at least thirty hours per week. The formation of the union was marked by extraordinary consensus among the county, the UDW, and Remedy, all of which looked to better wages and benefits as a way of reducing high turnover among workers and allaying complaints about quality of service. At the time of the first contract signing, County Board of Supervisors Chairman Roger Hedgecock said of the negotiations, "We had, I think, a very large common ground and as a result I think this contract came together as well as it did" (*Los Angeles Times,* November 22, 1980).

Since then, relations among the county, the UDW, and the contractor have been marked occasionally by clashes over contract costs and wages. In 1982, for example, the Board of Supervisors became so concerned over the rising costs of homemaker services that it voted to cut the contract hours in half. By transferring 500,000 service hours from contract workers, who by then were paid $3.85 per hour, to individual providers, who were paid $3.35 per hour, the Supervisors hoped to cut about a quarter of a million dollars from the county budget (*San Diego Union,* July 28 & 30, 1982). Amid fierce union protest, acrimonious public debate, and close media attention, the Supervisors subsequently reversed their decision, claiming that new state funds had been found to fund the contract at its prior level of service. At the same time, however, the contract workers' starting wage was reduced to $3.75.

The dual mission of the union has been to unionize county contract agencies and to work for development of a statewide network of IHSS contracts. It has been relatively successful in the former, growing from 150 San Diego members in 1979 to some 4,500 members in eleven counties by 1986. Efforts to extend the contract system have been far less successful. Indeed, the trend seems to be the opposite. Like San Diego in 1982, other counties under pressure to maintain service volume while controlling burgeoning home care costs habitually look to the individual provider system as a cost-saving mechanism. In January 1987, for example, San Bernardino County canceled its contract with Remedy and reverted to individual providers to cut some $4 million from its projected $20 million IHSS budget.[4]

The IP system is a multiple threat to the union. It offers minimal wages and no benefits to the workers, while impeding efforts to organize or sustain union membership. Lacking a single responsible employer, the IPs are difficult to identify and contact. Furthermore, once the union finds and recruits them, it faces the formidable task of trying to negotiate contracts with each of the IP's individual "employers."[5] Reversions from contract to IP systems are also painful to the union, which loses face if it cannot prevent a local government from canceling a contract along with the employee wages and benefits that accompany it.

In their opposition to IP-only systems and their campaign for counties to adopt "mixed mode" systems allowing for contract agencies, the UDW and Remedy share a common interest. Remedy, like the union, looks to county contracts as a means to expand its organizational base and improve its financial position. And Remedy, like the union, loses both materially and symbolically when a county decides to abandon the contract mode. The role of the state and county governments as third-party payers facilitates cooperation between Remedy and the UDW. Rather than confronting each other in a zero-sum game over wages and benefits, the union and the contract agency can both improve their position by working together to persuade the state and the counties of the advantages of contracting out a portion of the IHSS program.[6]

EMPLOYMENT, LABOR MARKET CONDITIONS, AND WORK LIFE ISSUES

Under the terms of the Remedy-UDW contract in force during the period of the demonstration, Remedy homemakers earned from $3.75 to $5.28 per hour, depending on their experience and the level of impairment of the client they were serving. The workers responding to the baseline survey reported a mean wage of $4.16 per hour and a median of $4.07. The main benefits provided were vacation pay accrued at a rate equivalent to approximately forty hours of vacation pay for fifty forty-hour workweeks; sick pay accrued at the same rate; mileage reimbursement of $.26 per mile for travel between clients, or reimbursement of public transportation between clients; and voluntary health insurance with 75 percent employer participation for workers working thirty hours or more per week.

The Remedy pay rate was higher than the $3.66 to $3.72 the county paid its individual providers. However, Remedy workers earned 11 to 30 percent less than aides at the area's two major private nonprofit home care agencies[7] and even less relative to the average $7.00 per hour wage of part-time nursing aides in southern California hospitals (U.S. Bureau of Labor Statistics, Los Angeles-Long Beach, August 1985). Compared, too, to other occupations open to unskilled San Diego workers, the Remedy wage was low. For example, the area's Private Industry Council (PIC), established in conjunction with the Job Training Partnership Act (JTPA) to find jobs for disadvantaged people, set $5.00 per hour as the minimum starting wage it would consider. Thus the homemaker's job did not qualify for PIC-JTPA referrals. Most comparable to homemakers were janitors, porters, and cleaners in nonmanufacturing establishments, who earned a mean wage of $4.60 and a median of $4.00 per hour in 1987 (U.S. Bureau of Labor Statistics, 1987).[8]

The union's major complaints about working conditions focused on wages, training, and hours. With a starting wage of $3.75, Remedy homemakers made less in 1986 than they had before the Board of Supervisors' cost-cutting initiative in 1982. To save money, the county had also cut training hours; instead of the previously mandated fifty-hour training minimum, by 1985 workers needed only six hours of training to provide homemaking or chore services and an additional ten hours to provide services to a severely impaired client. Union representatives (and Remedy managers as well) were concerned that the reduced training requirement was insufficient to prepare homemakers to care for clients with increasing levels of impairment.

The union also complained about the issue of hours. The UDW-Remedy contract required Remedy to employ at least 50 percent of the homemaker work force for twenty-five hours or more, a condition it met. However, subsidized health insurance benefits were not available to homemakers unless they worked thirty or more hours per week. According to both the union and Remedy, workers had difficulty meeting the thirty-hour requirement because the county assigned the contractor proportionately more "short hours" cases, requiring only one to three hours of service in a given day, while it assigned to IPS the most severely impaired clients with the longest service hours. To meet the thirty-hour requirement, homemakers might have to serve four to six clients a day—an exhausting schedule. Serving so many cases imposed a heavy burden on workers, while scheduling workers to serve contiguous clients posed a difficult coordinating problem for Remedy's supervisors, particularly because the caseload was widely dispersed throughout the sprawling metropolitan area.

The baseline survey of Remedy workers corroborated the difficulty of reaching the thirty-hour threshold; on average, homemakers reported working twenty-seven and one-half hours per week, while they wished to work thirty-four hours per week. Fifty percent did not meet the thirty-hour threshold. The short workweek deprived them of benefits and also of needed income.

As Table 7.1 indicates, a majority of Remedy workers were dissatisfied with pay and benefits, while a substantial minority were also dissatisfied with opportunities for advancement and with hours worked. Between 50 and 60 percent expressed dissatisfaction with wages and benefits. Forty percent expressed dissatisfaction with their opportunity for advancement on the job, and about 20 percent expressed dissatisfaction with the number of hours they worked. On the other hand, more than 90 percent agreed with the statement "All in all, I am satisfied with my job," and only 13 percent indicated that they intended to look for a new job in the coming year.

In the view of both labor and management, turnover was a far more serious problem than the survey data might suggest, and worker dissatisfaction with pay, benefits, and hours was a major cause of the problem. Although only 13 percent of the homemakers responding to the baseline survey indicated they would look for a new job in the coming year, turnover rates were actually far higher—particularly among new workers. Data collected during the course of the demonstration revealed that a third of Remedy workers employed an average of nine months as of January 1986 left the agency within the following year, while 80 percent of a sample of new workers left within that period. Remedy's internal analyses indicated a 45 percent turnover rate overall, and Remedy supervisors cited high turnover as a persistent problem, interrupting service to clients and adding to managerial stress. Remedy's vice chairman was a strong advocate of enhanced training and higher wages to reduce turnover, improve service, and ease the managerial burden on his staff, and he was willing to work with the union in lobbying for a higher wage and training allowance from the county and the state.

Table 7.1
Attitudes of Remedy Homemakers

	Satisfied* (Slightly or Very)	Dissatisfied* (Slightly or Very)
Overall job satisfaction	93%	9%
Pay	31%	54%
Benefits	24%	60%
Opportunity for Advancement	37%	40%
Isolation	75%	12%
Hours Worked	65%	23%
Training Adequacy	78%	9%
Opportunity to Help People	93%	3%
Treatment by Supervisor	84%	8%
Treatment by Company	68%	12%
Will look for a new job in the next year:		13%

N = 158

* Workers responded on a 5 point scale including very satisfied, slightly satisfied, neither satisfied nor dissatisfied, slightly dissatisfied, very dissatisfied.

In the absence of improved working conditions and in the face of high turnover, Remedy's managers worried a good deal about aide recruitment. With an unemployment rate of 4.5 percent in 1986, the San Diego labor market was tight. Higher unemployment among inner-city blacks and Hispanics, plus a continuing influx of illegal aliens, provided a generally steady stream of homemakers within the immediate metropolitan area. However, homemaker jobs remained vacant in outlying northern and eastern areas of San Diego County, where minority workers were scarce and a budding electronics assembly industry offered full-time, high paying, entry-level work. In those areas, private home care agencies were paying \$7.00 to \$10.00 per hour to attract aides, and Remedy simply could not compete.

Remedy's managers also worried about worker accountability and the quality of care provided by homemakers earning little more than \$4.00 per hour. They argued that home care agencies offering higher wages and better benefits could exact greater effort and better performance from their workers. Unfortunately, the constraints of the IHSS program meant that public clients rarely benefited from the services of a well-paid and highly accountable work force.

COMPONENTS OF THE DEMONSTRATION

Given labor and management concerns over wages, hours, and training, Remedy proposed an ambitious program to upgrade the homemaker's job. In a letter to the project manager, Remedy proposed a demonstration program that would increase training hours ten-fold (from six to sixty hours), add responsibility for client needs assessment, develop a new wage structure built on the prior maximum attainable wage, double vacation and sick leave, significantly enhance the health insurance benefit, and address issues of supervision and worker isolation. While these measures seemed extravagant compared to existing employment conditions, Remedy management pointed out that in reality they would simply move a portion of the homemaker worker force closer to the norms established for paraprofessionals in other sectors of the health care system.

The demonstration program subsequently implemented was considerably more modest. Budget constraints required that the training and benefit package be trimmed. The county Department of Social Services, which administered the Remedy contract, was reluctant to involve homemakers in the client assessment process, which was the domain of more highly trained professionals, so the job enhancement idea was scrapped. Furthermore, the county vetoed the wage increment on the grounds that after the demonstration program ended, there would not likely be sufficient government funding to maintain the $5.00 plus per hour precedent.

The program components finally agreed upon were: (1) a *forty-hour training program* for selected new employees, included thirty hours of classroom and laboratory work plus ten hours of field training; (2) a *twenty-four-hour supplemental training program* for selected current workers; (3) *guaranteed full-time work* (thirty-five hours per week) for program participants; (4) *health insurance* for current worker participants subsidized at 90 percent; (5) a professionally developed *employee support and development group,* focusing on work-related and personal needs; and (6) measures to enhance worker *status,* including a special title and special uniforms and identity badges. Original plans called for training sixty randomly selected new workers in three groups, and fifty randomly selected current workers in two groups. In the end, for reasons discussed in the section on implementation, fifty-one homemakers participated in the program.

PROGRAM IMPLEMENTATION

Remedy and the UDW were enthusiastic about the project from the start. In addition to their substantive concerns about employment conditions for homemakers, they welcomed the attention of the Ford Foundation and Harvard

University, no doubt because they believed that participating in a successful demonstration would enhance their reputation and strengthen their hand in negotiating with the county—directly in the case of Remedy and indirectly in the case of the union.

In contrast to Remedy and the union, the county Department of Social Services (DSS) was ambivalent. On the one hand, the county would benefit from positive publicity associated with the demonstration. DSS had participated in other national demonstrations and prided itself on being responsive to outside initiatives and progressive in policy development. On the other hand, participating in the demonstration carried several apparent risks. Expanding the homemakers' role in the client assessment process, as envisioned in Remedy's initial proposal, would alter standard operating procedures and infringe on the responsibilities of county social workers. The wage increment, also envisioned in Remedy's initial proposal, could establish a costly and therefore dangerous precedent for future county contracts. Another consideration was that DSS might be subject to charges of favoritism if it worked closely with Remedy in implementing a demonstration and then subsequently awarded the company another IHSS contract. Furthermore, DSS, like other government contractors, preferred to dissociate itself from the union and thereby maintain the fiction that employment conditions were issues to be resolved by negotiations between labor and management, not by government involvement. Finally, once research started on the IHSS contract program, the researchers might want to expand their study to the IP program, a politically sensitive subject that the county wished to keep out of the limelight.

After objecting to specific program components and deliberating for some time about its appropriate role in the demonstration, DSS ultimately consented to the selection of San Diego as a project site but decided to avoid any formal involvement. Some seven months after submission of Remedy's initial proposal in July 1985, DSS gave informal approval for Remedy and Grinker, Walker and Associates—the project manager—to become the principal parties to the San Diego demonstration.

Two additional organizations became part of the demonstration. Allied Home Health Association, a local private nonprofit agency, was chosen to provide the training. The University of California San Diego (UCSD) Medical Center, the major hospital in San Diego, was chosen to develop and implement the support component. Once the county had decided on the terms of its involvement with the demonstration and Allied and UCSD Medical Center were on board, it took about two months to finalize the design of the training and support components, to circulate baseline questionnaires to workers, and to select program participants for a March 1986 start date.

Selecting Program Participants

Original plans called for a demonstration involving fifty current workers and sixty new workers, plus controls. All but twenty new workers would be trained at the start of the project; the final twenty would be trained several months later, after more new workers had been hired. Remedy and the UDW were sympathetic to the research agenda of the demonstration and willingly agreed to random selection of program participants. They thought it was important to upgrade a portion of the existing work force, hence the selection of current workers to constitute a sizable demonstration group. Because new workers typically demonstrated extremely high turnover rates, they were also an important focus of the demonstration. The assumption was that they, in particular, would respond positively to increased training, support, and the promise of a full-time job.

The project management and research teams selected the number of participants—fifty current workers and sixty new workers—as small enough to be affordable but large enough to make it possible to detect a program impact. These numbers were ultimately scaled down because difficulties in contacting potential program participants and high rates of refusal among those contacted made the recruitment process so time-consuming that it interfered with the operational responsibilities of Remedy's supervisors.

Table 7.2 indicates that the Remedy supervisors responsible for contacting the homemakers and inviting them to take part in the demonstration were able to reach only about 70 percent of current workers and 60 percent of new workers. The remaining 30 to 40 percent lacked telephones, didn't answer their telephones, and/or failed to return telephone messages left for them at work or at home. Compounding the problem of participant selection was the high refusal rate of those workers successfully contacted. As can be seen from Table 7.3, only a quarter of the current workers invited to participate accepted the offer, while nearly two-thirds of the new workers agreed to participate.

Among the one hundred current workers who declined to participate in the demonstration, 35 percent cited reasons related to the thirty-five-hour workweek. These reasons included conflict with another job, conflict with school, child care problems, and simply the desire to work fewer than thirty-five hours. The comparable percentage for new workers was 33 percent. The base-

Table 7.2
Proportion of Remedy Homemakers Successfully Contacted

	Current Worker	New Worker
Contact	134 (69%)	33 (58%)
No Contact	59 (31%)	24 (42%)
Total	193 (100%)	57 (100%)

Table 7.3
Proportion of Contacted Remedy Homemakers Who Agreed to Participate

	Current Worker	New Worker
Agreed	34 (25%)	21 (64%)
Refused	100 (75%)	12 (36%)
Total	134 (100%)	33 (100%)

line survey of Remedy homemakers had indicated that nearly two-thirds would work thirty-five hours or more per week if asked to do so by their employer, while 32 percent would not. The latter proportion is strikingly similar to the 35 percent of current workers and 33 percent of new workers who when contacted declined to participate in the program for reasons related to the thirty-five-hour per week commitment. Thirteen percent of current workers and 17 percent of new workers declined to participate on the grounds that they didn't need additional training. Other reasons cited were transportation problems, illness or death in the family, intent to leave the job soon, and a variety of "miscellaneous" reasons. Table 7.4 summarizes the information on workers' reasons for declining to participate in the demonstration.

Ultimately, the research team supplied the names of 193 randomly selected current workers to yield 34 current worker participants and 57 randomly selected new workers to yield 21 new worker participants.

Training

Four groups of new and current Remedy homemakers (21 new workers and 34 current workers) participated in the training programs during the months of March, April, and May 1986. All of Remedy's supervisors also attended at least one program so that they would be familiar with what their homemakers were learning and could provide field supervision as part of the training. Each of the current worker classes had 16 or 17 participants (not counting supervisors); each of the new worker classes had 10 or 11 participants (again, not counting supervisors). New workers were paid for training at the rate of $3.90 per hour, while current workers were paid at existing wage rates. Each worker also received a $5.00 per session stipend to cover travel time and expense. Training time, however, was in addition to client service so that during the training period, program participants in effect worked two extra hours per day.

Table 7.4
Remedy Homemakers' Reasons for Declining to Participate

	Current Workers	New Workers
Reasons related to hours:	35 (35%)	4 (33%)
conflict with other job	21 (21%)	2 (17%)
conflict with school	2 (2%)	1 (8%)
child care problems	5 (5%)	0
want to work <35 hrs.	7 (7%)	1 (8%)
Reasons related to training	13 (13%)	2 (17%)
Transportation problems	13 (13%)	1 (8%)
Illness or family death	0	3 (25%)
Intend to leave job soon	0	1 (8%)
Other: "not interested," "inconvenient," etc.	39 (39%)	1 (8%)
	100 (100%)	12 (100%)

Training for the new workers consisted of thirty-two hours of lecture, discussion, and hands-on laboratory work in the classroom, plus eight hours of field supervision. The curriculum was divided into seven parts, consisting of introductions to aging and caring, safety, care of the client's environment, personal care, nutrition, special procedures (e.g., observation of signs and symptoms), and emotional and social needs of clients and families. Training for the current workers consisted of twenty-four hours of lecture, discussion, and laboratory work, plus two hours of field supervision—all with an emphasis on personal care, special procedures, and the emotional and social needs of clients and families.

Allied's principal instructor was a registered nurse with long experience in community nursing and home care. For some of the classes she brought in other staff—for example, a social worker to lead the class on psycho-social needs of the elderly. None of the instructors was bilingual—a problem for several Spanish-speaking participants with limited English. After instructors and super-

Table 7.5
Remedy Homemakers: Completion of Training

	Current Workers	New Workers
Graduated	33 (97%)	14 (67%)
Dropped Out	1 (3%)	7 (33%)
Total	34 (100%)	21 (100%)

visors realized the extent of the language barrier, Remedy provided a bilingual supervisor to translate for the Spanish speakers.

During the course of training, program participants developed considerable rapport among themselves, with the instructor, and with their supervisors. Each group had a lively graduation ceremony, complete with photographs and homemade refreshments. Graduates also received bright red jackets—their own selection—which became a status symbol among other Remedy homemakers. Table 7.5 summarizes data on completion of training.

Support

The homemaker support component was designed to pick up where the training ended. A series of two-hour sessions focused on work-related and personal needs, self-esteem, group cohesion, and professional identity. The program heavily emphasized the development of workers' communications skills to improve their personal lives as well as their interactions with each other, with Remedy, and with their clients. Because of the emphasis on communication, the support program provided for both English- and Spanish-speaking groups. The program also provided a stipend of $15.00 per participant per session to cover time and travel costs.

The initial plan was to begin worker support sessions about a month after the end of the training module. However, staffing problems at UCSD led to lengthy delays in starting the support component (a three-month delay for English-speaking participants and nearly a twelve-month delay for some of the Spanish-speaking participants). In the end, at least in part because of the delays in start-up, only thirty to thirty-five homemakers—about two-thirds to three-quarters of the forty-seven current and new worker training graduates—participated in the support program.

Because of budgetary constraints, each support group was scheduled for only nine sessions, and there was no provision for formal follow-up by the professional staff. However, those participants who finally attended the support sessions were so enthusiastic that the groups combined and continued informally. With Remedy's encouragement, about thirty-five homemakers, five union representatives, and five Remedy supervisors met every three or four weeks through the end of 1987 to share problems, concerns, and plain "good times."

Guaranteed Hours

Of equal importance to training and support in the original conception of the San Diego demonstration was the guaranteed hours component. On the assumption that regular full-time work constituted a major improvement over the part-time, occasionally erratic schedules of many homemakers,[9] the demonstration provided that upon successful completion of training, program participants would be guaranteed thirty-five hours per week of employment. The aim was that within three months of completing training all program participants would be working at least thirty-five hours per week.

This part of the demonstration was not implemented as planned. Table 7.6 shows that three months after the last training group finished, 62 percent of the

Table 7.6
Remedy Program Participants, Status of Guaranteed Hours 3 Months and 15 Months After Training

	3 Mos.	15 Mos.
Total Training Graduates	47 (100%)	47 (100%)
Inactive	8 (17%)	21 (45%)
Active	39 (83%)	26 (55%)
Total Active Training Graduates	39 (100%)	26 (100%)
Working 35 hrs. or more	15 (38%)	16 (62%)
Working fewer than 35 hrs. (Average workweek=28 hrs.)	24 (62%)	10 (38%)
Total Active Training Graduates working fewer than 35 hrs.	24 (100%)	10 (100%)
Who want fewer than 35 hrs.	11 (46%)	5 (50%)
Who want 35 hrs. or more	13 (54%)	5 (50%)

active training graduates (i.e., those that were still on the job) were working fewer than thirty-five hours per week, while at the fifteen-month point, 38 percent were still not working thirty-five hours or more. Half of these workers indicated they did not want a thirty-five-hour workweek (despite the fact that this was an initial condition of program participation). The other half, however, claimed they did. Thus, throughout the demonstration, there remained a group of program participants who never experienced a regular thirty-five-hour week, although that had been an important initial objective of the project.

According to Remedy supervisors, difficulties in assigning thirty-five-hour schedules to program participants arose from several sources: (1) periodic county cutbacks designed to reduce contract costs and keep within the total county IHSS budget;[10] (2) inaccessibility of homemakers who lacked telephones; (3) inability or unwillingness of homemakers to take assignments when they interfered with child care or other personal arrangements; and (4) logistical problems in routing homemakers to contiguous clients. Toward the end of the demonstration, worker inaccessibility and transportation problems were apparently the main obstacles to assigning program participants full-time work.

PROGRAM COSTS

The Remedy demonstration cost approximately $725 per participant.[11] Of this cost, approximately 70 percent (about $500) represented direct costs associated with training and support—including instruction, materials, travel stipends, and hourly pay for the homemakers while attending training and support sessions. The remaining 30 percent of expenditures (about $225 per participant) went toward phasing in the guaranteed hours (7 percent), amenities for the workers (e.g., badges and uniforms—5 percent), and administration (including some training sessions for supervisors—18 percent). If this $725 were spread across a year (assuming the worker worked thirty-five hours per week for fifty weeks), it would have amounted to $.40 per hour—nearly 10 percent of the homemakers' average hourly wage of $4.16 or 6 percent of the $6.50 per hour paid by the county to Remedy.

PROGRAM EFFECTS

The main hypothesis of the Remedy demonstration was that it would reduce worker turnover—and consequently improve continuity of care to clients—by enhancing homemakers' skills, reducing their isolation, developing their professional identity, and offering them full-time work. As discussed above, neither the worker support component nor the guaranteed hours component was implemented as intended. Thus the program effects detected and described below are principally attributable to the special status accorded to the program participants and to their training and only secondarily to the other components of the demonstration.

To assess the effects of the demonstration on turnover, the turnover rates of program participants were compared to those of nonprogram participants at three points in time—three months, twelve months, and eighteen months after completion of their training. Table 7.7 presents turnover data for current workers and shows consistent differences between program participants and controls. At the six-month follow-up, only 12 percent of current worker program participants were inactive, compared to 28 percent of controls. At twelve months, 18 percent of participants were inactive, compared to 34 percent of controls, and at eighteen months, 26 percent of participants were inactive, compared to 46 percent of controls. Thus at each of the follow-up points, current worker program participants were 16 to 20 percent more likely to be working than nonprogram participants. Moreover, the difference between participants

Table 7.7
Remedy Current Workers, Work Status of Program Participants and Controls at 6-Month, 12-Month, and 18-Month Follow-up

6-Month

	Program Participants	Controls	Difference
Working	30 (88%)	324 (72%)	16%
Inactive	4 (12%)	126 (28%)	
Total	34 (100%)	450 (100%)	

[Chi square = 4.2 with 1 degree of freedom; p <.05.]

12-Month

	Program Participants	Controls	Difference
Working	28 (82%)	300 (66%)	16%
Inactive	6 (18%)	150 (34%)	
Total	34 (100%)	450 (100%)	

[Chi square = 3.3 with 1 degree of freedom; p <.10.)

18-Month

	Program Participants	Controls	Difference
Working	25 (74%)	245 (54%)	20%
Inactive	9 (26%)	205 (46%)	
Total	34 (100%)	450 (100%)	

[Chi square = 4.7 with 1 degree of freedom; p <.05.]

and controls was slightly stronger at the eighteen-month follow-up than earlier in the demonstration period. Thus the effects of the program on current workers appear to have been lasting.

Given the large number of homemakers who could not be reached or who declined to participate in the demonstration, it is possible that those who agreed to participate were a self-selected group whose turnover would have been low regardless of the demonstration. For example, at the start of the demonstration, program participants had already worked an average of 1,222 hours for Remedy in the past year (about twenty-four hours per week), while the "no contact/declined to participate" group had worked an average of 921 hours and the controls, 907 hours (about seventeen to eighteen hours per week). Given this evidence of self-selection among the current worker program participants, the decision was made to compare their turnover with the turnover of a matched group of randomly selected controls whose prior work experience was virtually identical.

As can be seen from Table 7.8, the differences between the thirty-four program participants and their thirty-four matched controls are somewhat smaller than the differences between participants and the entire control population of 450. Nevertheless, participants were still 11 to 18 percent more likely to be working at each of the follow-up points than those who did not participate in the demonstration.

To understand better the relationship between prior Remedy service and turnover, program participants and their matched controls were analyzed separately. Table 7.9 shows that for controls, prior service was a strong predictor of turnover. More than 80 percent of controls who at baseline had worked 1,413 hours or more (at least twenty-seven hours per week; N=14) were still on the job at the eighteen-month follow-up, compared to only 29 percent of those who were below the median 1,413 hours (N=5)—a difference of 53 percent. In contrast, 70 to 76 percent of program participants were still on the job at the eighteen-month point, regardless of their prior hours worked. Thus participation in the demonstration was clearly more important than prior service in affecting the turnover of the program participants.

The major impact of the demonstration appears to have been on workers with low prior service and workers with a moderate work attachment during the course of the program. Table 7.10 shows that participation in the demonstration had a strong impact on turnover for workers who had worked fewer than 1,413 hours in the prior year. Seventy-one percent of program participants in this group were still on the job at the eighteen-month follow-up compared to only 29 percent of controls, a 42 percent difference. One inference from these data is that the impact of the current worker program could have been increased by focusing on homemakers working fewer than twenty-five or thirty hours per week prior to the start of the program. The job commitment of such workers was arguably weaker than that of workers spending five or more hours per day on the

Table 7.8
Remedy Current Workers, Work Status of Program Participants and Matched Controls at 6-Month, 12-Month, and 18-Month Follow-up

6-Month

	Program Participants	Controls	Difference
Working	30 (88%)	26 (76%)	12%
Inactive	4 (12%)	8 (24%)	
Total	34 (100%)	34 (100%)	

[Chi square = 1.6 with 1 degree of freedom; p <.2.]

12-Month

	Program Participants	Controls	Difference
Working	28 (82%)	24 (71%)	11%
Inactive	6 (18%)	10 (29%)	
Total	34 (100%)	34(100%)	

[Chi square = 1.3 with 1 degree of freedom; p <.3)

18-Month

	Program Participants	Controls	Difference
Working	25 (74%)	19 (56%)	18%
Inactive	9 (26%)	15 (44%)	
Total	34 (100%)	34 (100%)	

[Chi square = 2.4 with 1 degree of freedom; p <.2.]

job, and the effect of training and support may have been to strengthen that commitment.

Analyzing the job experience of program participants and matched controls during the demonstration period further highlights the importance of hours spent on the job. The findings presented in Table 7.11 suggest that focusing training and support efforts on workers with a moderate work attachment (i.e., four to six hours per day) would likely yield the greatest benefits in terms of increased job commitment and reduced turnover. Table 7.11 shows a 33 percent difference in turnover at the eighteen-month follow-up point between program participants

Table 7.9
Relationship Between Prior Service and 18-Month Turnover. Program Participants and Matched Controls

	Program Participants		Matched Controls	
	High Prior Service*	Low Prior Service**	High Prior Service	Low Prior Service
Working	13 (76%)	12 (70%)	14 (82%)	5 (29%)
Inactive	4 (24%)	5 (30%)	3 (18%)	12 (71%)
	17 (100%)	17 (100%)	17 (100%)	17 (100%)
	[Chi Square=.2, not signif.]		[Chi Square=8.3, p<.01.]	

* High prior service = more than 1413 hours of prior service.
** Low prior service = 1412 or fewer hours of prior service.

Table 7.10
18-Month Follow-up, Program Participants and Matched Controls

	High Prior Service*			Low Prior Service**		
	Program Participants	Matched Controls	Diff.	Program Participants	Matched Controls	Diff.
Working	13 (76%)	14 (82%)	6%	12 (71%)	5 (29%)	42%
Inactive	4 (24%)	3 (18%)		5 (29%)	12 (71%)	
	17 (100%)	17 (100%)		17 (100%)	17 (100%)	
	[Chi Square=.2, not signif.]			[Chi Square=5.6, p<.02.]		

* High prior service = more than 1413 hours of prior service.
** Low prior service = 1412 or fewer hours of prior service.

and controls who fell into the "medium hours" category (twenty to twenty-nine hours per week or four to six hours per day). In contrast, among "high hours" workers, controls were actually more likely to be working than program participants, while among "low hours" workers, there was virtually no difference between participants and controls. A nearly full-time schedule (i.e., thirty hours or more per week) was apparently more important than training and support in influencing turnover. Furthermore, at the opposite end of the full-

Table 7.11
18-Month Follow-up, Program Participants and Matched Controls: Hours of Service During Demonstration Period

Medium Hours*

	Program Participants	Matched Controls	Difference
Working	14 (88%)	6 (55%)	33%
Inactive	2 (22%)	5 (45%)	
	16 (100%)	11 (100%)	

[Chi Square = 3.6; p <.1.]

High Hours**

	Program Participants	Matched Controls
Working	8 (80%)	8 (100%)
Inactive	2 (20%)	0
	10 (100%)	8 (100%)

[Chi Square = 1.8; p <.3.]

Low Hours***

	Program Participants	Matched Controls
Working	3 (38%)	5 (33%)
Inactive	5 (62%)	10 (67%)
	8 (100%)	15 (100%)

[Chi Square = 0.]

* Medium Hours = 20-29 hours per week on average.
** High hours = 30 hours per week or more on average.
*** Low hours = fewer than 20 hours per week on average.

time/part-time continuum, the training and support apparently did little to mitigate the effects of very part-time work.

Table 7.12 presents turnover data for new workers. The most striking thing about the table is the high turnover rate of both program participants and controls. In sharp contrast to current workers (Tables 7.7 and 7.8), more than half of both groups had already become inactive at the six-month follow-up point, and more than 80 percent were no longer working at the eighteen-month follow-up point. Nevertheless, a 20 percent difference between program participants and controls—comparable to the differences for current workers—held during the first year of follow-up, declining to a 3 percent difference by the end of eighteen months. Only 57 percent of program participants had become inactive at the six-month follow-up, compared to 78 percent of controls—a 21 percent difference.[12] Similarly, only 62 percent of participants were inactive at one year, compared to 81 percent of controls—a 19 percent

Table 7.12
Remedy New Workers, Work Status of Program Participants and Controls at 6-Month, 12-Month, and 18-Month Follow-up

6-Month

	Program Participants	Controls	Difference
Working	9 (43%)	8 (22%)	21%
Inactive	12 (57%)	29 (78%)	
Total	21 (100%)	37 (100%)	

[Chi square = 2.9 with 1 degree of freedom; p <.10.]

12-Month

	Program Participants	Controls	Difference
Working	8 (38%)	7 (19%)	19%
Inactive	13 (62%)	30 (81%)	
Total	21 (100%)	37(100%)	

[Chi square = 2.6 with 1 degree of freedom; p <.15.]

18-Month

	Program Participants	Controls	Difference
Working	3 (14%)	4 (11%)	3%
Inactive	18 (86%)	33 (89%)	
Total	21 (100%)	37 (100%)	

[Chi square = .2 with 1 degree of freedom; not significant.]

difference. At the end of eighteen months, however, the difference between the two groups was only 3 percent.

Despite the absence of statistical significance, it is reasonable to conclude that the demonstration's impact on new workers who participated in both the training and the support programs was real, at least for the first year of the demonstration, because it is similar to the effects observed for current workers in Tables 7.7 and 7.8 (see also discussion of effects in Chapter 11).

Turnover among new worker program participants during the six- and twelve-month follow-up periods consisted entirely of homemakers who dropped out of training (seven workers) and program graduates who left before the delayed start-up of their relevant English- or Spanish-speaking support group. It is

Table 7.13
Remedy New Workers, Hours of Service During Demonstration Period

	Program Participants	Controls
Working at 18 mos.	Mean = 34 hrs. Median = 40 hrs. N = 3	Mean = 25 hrs. Median = 31 hrs. N = 4
Inactive at 18 mos.	Mean = 15 hrs. Median = 16 hrs. N = 18	Mean = 14 hrs. Median = 11 hrs. N = 33

possible that the immediate availability of a support group for program graduates, unaccustomed as they were to the isolating aspects of the job, might have averted some of their turnover, although this statement is only speculation.

Nevertheless, it is clear from the high training dropout rate (33 percent) and the high eighteen-month turnover rate of the entire group, including participants in training and support, that other factors affected their willingness or ability to stay on the job during the first eighteen months or so. Short workweeks may well have been one of those factors, although in the absence of interview or questionnaire information about "leavers' " reasons for leaving, we can only speculate. New worker controls who eventually terminated averaged only fourteen hours per week on the job while they worked for Remedy, and their median workweek was eleven hours. New worker program participants (including training dropouts) who became inactive were not much higher; their average workweek was fifteen hours and their median, sixteen. In contrast, program participants who were still working at the eighteen-month follow-up worked on average thirty-four hours per week, while comparable controls worked on average twenty-five hours per week (see Table 7.13).

PROGRAM POSTSCRIPT

Remedy's San Diego agency director, her regional director, and Remedy corporate leadership did not perceive that the demonstration had an impact on turnover during the course of the project. The local director and her area director did perceive an impact on participants' self-esteem and job satisfaction. Their enthusiasm for both the training and support components mirrored that of the participants. Pending renewal of their county contract, they planned to subcontract with Allied to teach Remedy supervisors to carry out the training program—a less expensive option than paying Allied staff to serve as instructors. They also intended to continue the support program in the form it had taken since the end of UCSD's involvement. The plan was for each supervisor to organize regular informal meetings for the homemakers on her roster. Furthermore, based on the San Diego experience, the Remedy office in Tulare County—also a large contract operation—instituted a similar support program in 1987.

Remedy corporate leadership endorsed training and support efforts modeled after those of the demonstration but cautioned that these "softer" aspects of employment must never overshadow the importance of raising pay and benefits to meet the basic needs of the homemaker work force. The county had thwarted efforts to include a pay differential in the demonstration, but the county action simply heightened Remedy's concern over wages as an employment issue. As for the guarantee of full-time employment, the San Diego staff found it onerous to find at least thirty-five hours of work for every homemaker who wanted them, and corporate headquarters lost confidence in the feasibility of the thirty-five-hour guarantee early in the demonstration period.

Plans for continuing the expanded training and support went the way of guaranteed hours when Remedy lost the San Diego IHSS contract in 1988. National Homecare Systems of Chicago, a division of Wright Marketing, Inc., underbid Remedy by $1.1 million, in part by proposing to pay its homemakers a starting wage of $3.75 per hour instead of the $4.38 agreed upon by Remedy in negotiations with the union.[13] Despite angry worker protest, widespread media coverage, claims that the initial bidding process was unfair, and vacillation by the Board of Supervisors, the state Department of Social Services ruled that there were no improprieties in the initial bidding process. The state's ruling stipulated that National Homecare should be awarded the contract, unless the county wished to convert the whole contract program to an individual provider system—a prospect even more odious to the union than giving the contract to National Homecare. Meanwhile, the wage issue became less critical because the California legislature passed new minimum wage legislation requiring all employers to pay a wage of $4.25 per hour starting July 1988. In the end, after more than two months of delay, amid worries about the financial viability of the low bidder and unsuccessful efforts to get the state to back down, the Supervisors finally awarded the contract to National Homecare starting March 1988.

National Homecare hired Remedy's San Diego director and most of her office staff to run its San Diego operation, thus providing continuity of management. Furthermore, as described above, the director was an enthusiast when it came to training and support. National Homecare's first priority, however, was not job enrichment but delivering service and staying afloat while receiving from the county $7.48 per hour, a reimbursement rate $.73 per hour less than Remedy projected it would have needed to cover costs and earn a modest profit. In the end, the fate of the quality of work life improvements embodied in the demonstration was determined by the public financing system for in-home services and, in particular, by the requirement that the county provide an exclusive contract to the low bidder.[14]

NOTES

1. Statewide, approximately 20 percent of IHSS clients received services from contract agencies, mainly Remedy, while nearly 80 percent received services from

individual providers. One to 2 percent were served by aides employed directly as county workers (Zukas, Cone & Leon, 1984).

2. Financial statements after 1984 report consolidated revenues for Remedy Home and Health Care and Remedy Temporary Services.

3. During the period 1984-1988 Remedy Home and Health Care competitively bid and won twelve county IHSS contracts totaling over $66 million. At the time the Ford project started, Remedy held contracts with nine counties.

4. San Bernardino County later decided to return to a contract mode because it did not achieve the savings sought from the IP program. One consequence of shifting to a completely IP system had been that the volume of service hours per client increased, thus cancelling savings that might have been gained from the IPs' lower unit rate of reimbursement.

5. Under the individual provider mode of service, the counties authorize service hours, provide referral lists to clients who need help in finding a care giver, and issue the workers' paycheck. Two recent California court decisions have declared that IPs are county employees for the purposes of withholding, FICA, unemployment, and workmen's compensation (Attorney General, July 23, 1985; *Bonnette* v. *Calif.*, 1983; *IHSS* v. *Workers' Compensation Board,* 1984). However, the counties disclaim any other responsibility as employers. IP wages are typically lower than those of aides in contract agencies; there are no benefits; and the counties avoid training and supervisory responsibility, lest they be construed as employers subject to county civil service, liability, or union obligations.

6. According to Remedy, one of the principal advantages is cost control. Although unit reimbursement rates are higher for contracts than for IP services, overall costs of serving nonseverely impaired clients are lower for contracts. Contract services cost less because low paid IPs may inflate their hours to achieve adequate compensation, while there are strict volume controls on the contracts.

7. The San Diego Visiting Nurse Association (VNA) paid $4.12 to $4.95 per hour for noncertified homemakers and $5.66 to $6.84 per hour for certified aides in 1985. Since then, the VNA has disbanded its homemaker program. Aides at Allied, the area's other major nonprofit provider of homemaker services, reported average hourly wages of $4.61 in 1986.

8. The data on janitors, porters, and cleaners are for 1987; if Remedy 1986 survey data are updated by $.20 per hour to reflect a cost of living pay increase, the mean becomes $4.36 and the median, $4.27.

9. A third of Remedy homemakers responding to the baseline survey worked twenty-two hours or fewer each week, while half worked twenty-eight hours or fewer.

10. Periodic cutbacks were a customary "management tool" of the county. If projections indicated that the budget might be overspent, DSS would instruct social workers to cut the contractor's hours and shift more hours to individual providers. Toward the end of the fiscal year, if the budget allowed, the contractor's hours would be restored to the full 715,000-hour allotment.

11. This figure results from dividing total costs by the number of workers initially enrolled in each program.

12. This difference was not statistically significant. The significance level attained depends on the size of the sample used. If a sample is very large, even a very slight relationship will generally be statistically significant. In contrast, if a sample is small, even a good-size relationship may fail to "pass" a significance test. If the numbers in the cells of

a two-by-two table are doubled and the proportions are kept the same, the chi-square figure will also double—that is, chi-square varies directly with the number of cases (Blalock, 1972).

13. Remedy had agreed to a starting wage of $4.25 in year 1 of the contract and $4.50 in year 2, or a composite starting wage of $4.38.

14. Remedy and the United Domestic Workers continued to lobby in Sacramento for changes to the state law that requires IHSS contracts to go to the low bidder. Under legislation proposed by the union, counties would have the flexibility to consider factors such as client satisfaction, continuity and quality of service to clients, and employee relations, in addition to "pure cost" in awarding contracts through the competitive bidding process.

8

Independent Living and Long Life Home Care Services, New York

INTRODUCTION

Home Care Services for Independent Living (Independent Living) and Long Life Home Care Services (Long Life) are two of some sixty independent, private nonprofit agencies that contract with New York City to provide Medicaid-financed home attendant services to the frail elderly and disabled. Long Life is the larger of the two, with an annual budget of $10.5 million in 1986 and approximately 1,500 aides serving a caseload of 800 clients. Independent Living, with an annual budget of $9.9 million in 1986, employs approximately 1,000 aides to serve a caseload of approximately 600.[1] Both agencies are located in Brooklyn, where nearly 13,000 or 40 percent of New York City's home care clients are concentrated, and both serve a mix of elderly Jewish, black, and some Hispanic clients.

Located in the Bedford-Stuyvesant section of Brooklyn, Long Life occupies spacious offices in Restoration Plaza, an ambitious and tasteful factory renovation that is the cornerstone of redevelopment efforts in the area. Long Life is the offspring of an enterprising former day care center director, who with the support of local church groups and politicians won a $2.5 million city contract when New York City "vendorized" its home care program in 1980.

Located in the Flatbush section of Brooklyn, Independent Living occupies somewhat rundown offices in five adjoining store fronts. Although the premises are neither modern nor streamlined, the agency stays because the offices are architecturally accessible for the disabled, visible from the street, and well situated for recruiting new home attendants from the many new immigrants who live in the area. Like Long Life, Independent Living has been in operation since June 1980. It is an offshoot of the Brooklyn Center for Independence of the

Disabled, part of a nationwide movement of consumer-controlled self-help programs and independent living centers for the disabled.

THE HOME ATTENDANT'S JOB

Home attendant is an entry-level job requiring little training. Job applicants must be 18 years old, undergo a physical examination and drug screening (paid for by the vendor agency), and pass a two-day "rapid assessment" and certification examination that requires minimal competence in homemaking, personal care, and English language skills. If they fail the examination—as about 40 percent do—they must complete an additional three days of training.[2] Beyond the initial two to five days, each year home attendants are supposed to receive an additional six hours of in-service training, provided by the agency that employs them.

According to their formal job description, the home attendants are responsible for assisting with "feeding, ambulation, bathing, toileting, personal grooming, dressing, money management, general cleaning, marketing, laundry, ironing, meal preparation, and errands—as required to maintain the client in his/her own home." In actuality, this job description captures only a part of their varied, often trying, responsibilities. Approximately 70 percent of the home attendants' clients are so debilitated that they require thirty-five hours or more of care each week, and between 15 to 20 percent require twenty-four-hour live-in assistance (Human Resources Administration, May 1984). About two-thirds of the home attendants work thirty-five hours per week or more, usually for one client, and some work as many as five, six or seven twenty-four-hour days, providing live-in services. In this respect, the New York City home care program differs from public programs in many other states, where hours of care per recipient are fewer and aides serve proportionately more "short hours" cases.[3]

Most of the home attendants in New York City are unionized. Workers at Long Life belong to Local 32B/J of the Service Employees International Union, and workers at Independent Living belong to Local 1199 of the Drug, Hospital and Health Care Employees Union. Regardless of their union affiliation, all home attendants earned a starting wage of $3.95 per hour in 1985, or $4.25 per hour if they had been at the same agency for a year. Weekend work paid no more than weekday work, and live-in assignments paid for twelve rather than twenty-four hours per day. In addition to Social Security, unemployment insurance, and disability coverage, home attendants also received up to ten days of sick leave and up to ten days of annual leave, based on the number of hours they worked; paid training; and modest health insurance benefits.

Pay and, particularly, benefits were distinctly better than they had been prior to "vendorization," when the home attendants had worked as individual providers and were not unionized. Nevertheless, compensation was inferior to that in other parts of the health care sector. For example, part-time nursing aides in New York City hospitals earned an average hourly wage of $7.50 in 1985—$3 per hour more than home attendants—while hospital cleaners, food service helpers, and laundry workers made between $7 and $8 per hour (U.S. Bureau of Labor Statistics, August, 1985d). The disparity was particularly rankling to home care providers and workers because, they claimed, their clients increasingly comprised the acutely ill discharged early from hospital and the extremely debilitated unable to find space in a nursing home.

THE UNIONS

Ostensibly, wages, benefits, and other working conditions in the home attendant program are the product of negotiations between the contract agencies and the unions that represent the workers—Local 1199 of the Drug, Hospital and Health Care Employees Union; Locals 32B/J and 144 of the Service Employees International Union; and District Council 1707 of the American Federation of State, County and Municipal Employees. The city and the state, however, determine the final outcome of negotiations by establishing the reimbursement rate to agencies. Traditionally, the guidelines for wage increases have been established by the city's negotiations with its own unions, and final contracts between the home attendant agencies and their unions have typically awaited the city's wage settlement.

According to the unions, negotiations with the home attendant agencies are a "charade." "By setting up agencies that deal with the unions, the city does not have to deal with it. They [the agencies] sit down and negotiate it. But they are really bound hand and foot by what the city wants to give" (Moreno, September 28, 1987:33).

City officials assert that the wage and benefit package is an issue that must be settled between the unions and the contract agencies. They acknowledge that the agencies are constrained by what the city will pay for service; at the same time, they are clearly influenced by what happens at the bargaining table. "The unions have a collective power to make their demands known. If the unions are strong enough to be able to demand and get a bargaining agreement that is more than what we will reimburse, what [are we] going to do?" (Moreno, September 28, 1987:33).

The paucity of the home attendants' wage and benefit package has been attributed in part to the availability of a large inner-city immigrant work force, in many cases consisting of illegal aliens, willing to work under substandard conditions. A 1985 study conducted under the auspices of Local 1199 found that 96 percent of home attendants were black or Hispanic and about half were foreign-born, mostly from the West Indies (Donovan, 1986). "This is a job that is good for new immigrants," according to William Pernisek, president of the Home Care Council. "Americans, let's face it, won't work for these wages or in these jobs" (Moreno, September 28, 1987:33). Despite the inadequacy of pay and the disparity with other health care jobs, until the government started to enforce the Immigration Reform and Control Act of 1986, the contract agencies reported little difficulty in recruiting workers, except for weekend or live-in assignments. Apparently even foreign newcomers were reluctant to work without weekend pay differentials or for twenty-four hours at a stretch while being paid for only twelve.

Difficulties in mobilizing the home care work force have also been cited as a factor working against significant improvements in employment conditions. Major upgrading of wages and benefits for New York City hospital workers came only after lengthy and bitter strikes in the late 1950s and early 1960s. Union officials observed that efforts to organize home attendants for similar protests were hampered by the lack of a common work place (Moreno, September 28, 1987). Furthermore, during the early 1980s Local 1199, the major union representing the home attendants, was hampered by internal political divisions and was in severe disarray (Prial, 1987; Raskin, 1986).

WORKER ATTITUDES

Not surprisingly, a sizable number of workers at both Long Life and Independent Living expressed dissatisfaction with their pay and benefits when polled in 1986. Approximately 40 percent of home attendants surveyed at Long Life and 50 to 60 percent of those surveyed at Independent Living reported that they were "slightly" or "very" dissatisfied with pay and fringe benefits. Table 8.1 presents comparative data on the job satisfaction of workers at the two agencies.

Besides pay and benefits, other sources of dissatisfaction were the weekly work schedule, lack of opportunity for advancement, inadequate training, and loneliness on the job. At least 15 percent of workers in each agency expressed dissatisfaction with the number of hours they worked, their opportunities for advancement, and the adequacy of their training, while about one-fifth agreed with the statement "I feel lonely in this job." About one-fifth also indicated that they intended to look for a new job in the coming year.

On the other hand, 80 percent or more at both agencies expressed satisfaction with their supervision, with the way they were "treated" by the agency, and with the opportunity to help people. Furthermore, despite dissatisfaction with pay and benefits, overall job satisfaction was high. More than 80 percent of workers at both agencies agreed with the statement "All in all, I am satisfied with my job."

THE WORK LIFE DEMONSTRATION AT LONG LIFE AND INDEPENDENT LIVING

The project management and research team approached the New York City Human Resources Administration (HRA) to participate in the home care demonstration in the summer of 1985. By that time, New York's moratorium on the building of nursing home beds had been in effect for ten years, and the city was increasingly reliant on its home care program to meet the service needs of its growing elderly population. The city's home care program had doubled in size

Table 8.1
Attitudes of Home Attendants, Long Life and Independent Living

	Satisfied* (Slightly or Very)		Dissatisfied* (Slightly or Very)	
	Ind.	L.L.	Ind.	L.L.
Overall job satisfaction	83%	83%	10%	12%
Pay	27%	45%	60%	39%
Benefits	31%	44%	54%	38%
Opportunity for Advancement	55%	58%	21%	29%
Hours Worked	63%	75%	30%	17%
Isolation	69%	72%	24%	19%
Training Adequacy	78%	77%	17%	15%
Opportunity to Help People	80%	90%	5%	5%
Treatment by Supervisor	87%	88%	6%	6%
Treatment by Company	89%	83%	5%	10%
Will look for a new job in the next year:			14%	22%

* Workers responded on a 5 point scale including very satisfied, slightly satisfied, neither satisfied nor dissatisfied, slightly dissatisfied, very dissatisfied.

since 1981, and more Medicaid recipients were receiving home care than were residing in nursing homes (Cronin, 1987).

During this period of rapid growth, the home attendant program had been relatively free of scandal—only six agencies had their contracts terminated, none of them for fraud, client abuse, or serious misuse of funds. Nevertheless, officials in HRA were increasingly concerned that the low levels of payment provided the workers might be insufficient to sustain either continued program growth or the maintenance of quality standards. They perceived that the fundamental problem of the basic wage and benefit package could not be addressed through the vehicle of a demonstration program. They did look to the demonstration, however, as a way of testing the feasibility of a specialized training and compensation program leading both to improved service and to the creation of a career ladder for home attendants.

The home attendant agencies were already railing at the problems they faced as a result of systemic pressures on hospitals to discharge elderly patients "sicker and quicker" and on the city's Medical Assistance Program to keep elderly patients out of nursing homes. In the view of the agencies, more acutely ill and severely impaired patients were ending up as their charges, whether or not home care was appropriate. The home attendant had become the default solution of the city's long-term care system, but the attendants were poorly equipped to address the problems they faced.

On the one hand, home attendants were authorized to provide personal care but forbidden to provide health care. Legally, they could not change clients' dressings; administer medications, injections, or intravenous feedings; take care of ostomies or tracheotomies; or perform a host of other tasks related to their clients' medical needs but reserved by state law and regulation to certified home health aides. On the other hand, in part for reasons of cost control, relatively few clients were authorized by HRA social workers to receive the services of certified aides. In theory and according to regulation, the clients themselves or their friends or family members were responsible for carrying out these tasks; in practice, home attendants found themselves performing many of these services lest their clients suffer inattention. Meanwhile the agencies, prohibited by law from providing health care and lacking insurance protection for health care malpractice, were unable to acknowledge formally the expanded role of the home attendant, let alone offer appropriate training, compensation, or protection. As a result, they and their clients were at risk, as various forms of makeshift medical care were rendered by untrained and underpaid workers.

Short of becoming certified home health agencies—a status coveted by some of the home attendant agencies—a number of directors hoped to create a new senior, more experienced category of home care worker, between the home attendant and the home health aide. This new worker would be trained and paid commensurate with her heightened responsibilities. Acknowledging the growing acuity of the client caseload and providing selected workers with additional skills and compensation for dealing with these more difficult cases would, it was argued, upgrade both the job and quality of care provided by the home attendant.

Sympathetic to this proposal, HRA sought the approval of the state Department of Health (DOH), responsible for licensing and certifying aides, and the state Department of Social Services, responsible for Medicaid. DOH was responsive but cautioned that some of the practices envisioned for the new category of home attendant would be viewed as the practice of nursing by the state Education Department and would therefore be problematic. DSS, it seemed, was already engaged in the process of trying to define a new level of care ("Level 3") comparable to what was being proposed, and it suggested that the demonstration proposal be put aside. A demonstration effort at that point might conflict with rather than reinforce the DSS initiative, and, in any case, once the new level of care was instituted statewide, a demonstration would be redundant.[4]

Returning to the demonstration drawing board, the project management and research team, in conjunction with the agency directors and HRA, came up with a new but similar proposal that was approved by the state. In addition to clients with difficult and more intensive medical needs, there are also many clients in the home care system who have more intensive social and psychological needs than the average client. Many victims of Alzheimer's disease, stroke, senile dementia, or other mental impairment, for example, exhibit "problem behaviors" that challenge the endurance of the home attendants assigned to serve them and constitute a troublesome and expensive management problem for the agencies, who often have a hard time finding reliable aides to care for them on a long-term basis. Frequent requests by such clients to change home attendants and by home attendants to change clients consume the time and patience of the coordinators responsible for matching clients and home attendants. Home attendants serving these clients often experience burnout and ask to be reassigned to a less demanding case. Some leave the agency altogether. In effect, the psychologically neediest and most dependent clients often experience the most frequent and serious disruptions in care. The new proposal called for creating a specially trained and appropriately compensated corps of attendants to serve this population. The purpose of the demonstration was to reduce worker reassignments and turnover, to improve continuity of care, and to demonstrate the feasibility of training home attendants for more responsible positions as caretakers for individuals whose psychological and/or behavioral problems compounded their other problems of dependency.

The components of the demonstration were the following: (1) a thirty-five-hour home attendant *training program* providing elementary familiarity with the underlying causes and manifestations of "difficult" behaviors related to diagnoses such as Alzheimer's disease, senile dementia, and organic brain syndrome, as well as with methods of stress management and problem solving; (2) measures to enhance worker *status,* including a special uniform and certificate indicating the worker's specialized skills; (3) a *wage increment* of $.30 per hour for home attendants serving clients meeting the criteria for behaviorally difficult cases; and (4) periodic *follow-up and support* sessions for program participants.

PROGRAM IMPLEMENTATION

Start-up

By early summer of 1986, nearly a year after the project manager and research team had approached HRA, the demonstration proposal had finally cleared the bureaucratic hurdles in its path, and the program was ready to begin. That summer, Independent Living and Long Life provided the research team with lists of potential program participants, all of whom were serving behaviorally "difficult" clients—defined for the purposes of the project as those with diagnoses of organic brain syndrome, Alzheimer's disease, or senile dementia or with a record of being served by 10 or more different attendants in the prior twelve months (or 4 or more attendants in the prior six months). From those lists of approximately 300 workers, the research team randomly selected the names of home attendants to be contacted by their supervisors and offered the opportunity to participate in the demonstration. Ultimately 150 contacts were required to meet the program target of 100 participants—50 from each agency. The overall acceptance rate—that is, the rate at which home attendants agreed to participate—was two-thirds, 60 percent at Long Life and 75 percent at Independent Living. The remaining 142 home attendants (57 at Long Life and 85 at Independent Living) were designated as the control group. Although the controls were serving difficult clients (at least at the outset of the project), they received no special training or compensation.

Training

Between September 1986 and January 1987, six groups (three from each agency) of 16-17 program participants each met on three consecutive Saturdays for a full day of class. They then returned for four monthly half-day sessions, generally held during the week. On the whole, workers preferred to attend class during the week, so as not to interfere with weekend plans. In contrast, agency management strongly preferred the Saturday schedule, to minimize the need to find replacement workers to care for clients when program participants were attending class.

Altogether there were thirty-five hours of class time devoted to subjects such as stress management, aging, stroke, Alzheimer's disease and confusional states, developmental disabilities, mental illness, alcoholism, troublesome client behaviors, family dynamics, and death and dying. These class hours were supplemented by a series of "call-back" sessions scheduled to provide ongoing support at monthly intervals for several months after the end of the formal training program.[5]

The curriculum established clear informational goals but most strongly emphasized creative problem solving, practical ways to alleviate stress and avoid burnout, and the development of better communication skills. The class format was informal, encouraging individual participation and group support. Lecture was kept to a minimum, and most of the teaching relied on discussion of actual case materials, role playing, video, films, and other audiovisual aids. The instructor—a registered nurse/social worker/psychotherapist with considerable experience in training paraprofessionals—quickly established rapport with the workers and attendance was virtually perfect.

In keeping with the commitment to build home attendants' status and self-esteem, graduation exercises were elaborate. Program participants wore special jackets purchased by the project, adorned with badges featuring the agency logo and declaring: "I AM A S.H.A.R.P. HOME ATTENDANT"—SHARP standing for "Special Home Attendant Research Project." Both the head of the Medical Assistance Program and the head of the Office of Home Care Services within the Human Resources Administration attended the ceremonies and addressed the graduates, as did the instructor, the project manager, and the director of the research team. Diplomas were presented, food and drink were plentiful, photographs were taken, and the local press reported on the event (*Afro-American Times,* 1987). The spirits of the one hundred graduates gathered for the occasion were high.

The Wage Increment

After finishing training, attendants received a \$.30 per hour wage increment for the duration of the project, so long as they continued to serve a difficult client. The \$.30 per hour figure was chosen to be symmetrical with the \$.30 increment for 2,100 hours of service. Because of the demonstration status of the increment and to prevent commingling of Medicaid and demonstration funds, the workers received their increments in checks that were separate from their regular paychecks and often issued at different times. The separate paychecks were an administrative burden to the agencies and caused confusion among some of the home attendants, who didn't understand why they were getting separate checks and found it difficult to match their incremental pay with the check stubs from their regular pay. As a result, a few felt their agency was cheating them.

Assignment to Difficult Cases

During the course of the demonstration, some program participants also complained that their coordinators did not assign them to a new difficult case when their original client was hospitalized for an extended period or when the case was closed because the client entered a nursing home, moved out of the area, or died. Coordinators reported that they preferred to assign the SHARP workers to difficult cases because they were more competent and professional than home attendants who had not been through the training, but they didn't always have a difficult case available when a program participant's original case was closed.

Because workers are not on salary and are paid only when they serve a client, coordinators were afraid they would lose the home attendant to another agency if they didn't reassign her immediately. Rather than risk losing a skilled and reliable worker, the coordinator would assign her to a routine case. Furthermore, once the worker established a bond with her new client, the coordinator would keep her on that assignment in order not to disrupt the client's care. This practice meant that some program participants did not have the opportunity to utilize fully their newly acquired skills and that they were deprived of the wage differential.

Management Perspectives

Coordinators were generally pleased with the demonstration program. Their sentiments were similar to those expressed by one of the coordinators at Long Life: "My difficult cases are quieter now—the patients are calmed down. The attendants [i.e., the program participants] are more patient and understanding, and I have fewer changes to deal with now."

Aside from complaints about finding substitute workers while the program participants attended training or support sessions, the only other complaint expressed by the coordinators—usually in joking terms—was that it was harder to replace the specially trained workers during their vacations or illnesses. Because their clients had become accustomed to a higher standard of care, they often balked at the replacement workers assigned to them, thus creating more work for the coordinators.

Senior management were generally supportive of the project, but they never saw it as central to their mission or their agencies' performance. They had warned the participating home attendants at the outset that the program was only of a year's duration and that the incremental pay would cease unless HRA decided to pick up costs after the demonstration period lapsed. The agency directors might have lobbied HRA for a program extension, but they didn't. Toward the end of the demonstration, when lobbying would have been timely, they, along with the other home attendant agencies in the city, were busy negotiating with the unions (and testing the city waters) over a major across-the-board increase in wages and benefits (described at the end of this chapter). These negotiations took precedence over efforts to extend the demonstration.

PROGRAM COSTS

The cost of the demonstration was approximately $1,500 per program participant. Of this cost, 27 percent (approximately $400 per participant) went toward development and teaching of the training and support component; 60 percent (about $900 per participant) went toward training pay for the workers, salary differentials, and associated fringe benefits; and 13 percent (about $200 per participant) went toward administrative costs. If this $1,500 were spread across a year (assuming the worker worked forty hours per week for fifty weeks), it would have amounted to $.75 per hour—about 18 percent of the $4.25 hourly wage paid to workers with one year of service and about 16 percent of HRA's $4.75 hourly reimbursement to the agencies in 1986. If program costs had been cut to $1,200 per participant (e.g., by hiring a less expensive instructor for training and support and by reducing admnistrative costs to the 8 to 9 percent usually paid by the city), the increase in hourly worker costs, spread over a year, would have been $.60 per hour—about 14 percent of the $4.25 base hourly wage and 13 percent of the $4.75 reimbursement rate.

PROGRAM EFFECTS

As discussed above, the immediate purpose of the demonstration at Long Life and Independent Living was to reduce worker reassignments and turnover, thereby improving continuity of care to clients. The premise of the program was that the overall feasibility of developing a specially trained and compensated corps of home attendants would depend on such key factors as organizational and political support, available funding, and willing workers, and that these factors, in turn, would be heavily influenced by the demonstration's success in encouraging program participants to stick with their difficult clients. To assess the effects of the program on this outcome measure, the research team collected one-year follow-up data on one hundred program participants and 142 controls. The follow-up measurement point was October 1987, one year after the start of the demonstration training. At that point, the program at Long Life was drawing to a close in the sense that pay differentials were being terminated, while the program at Independent Living would run into the spring of 1988.

All program participants and controls were classified as to the client they were serving and their work status (working or inactive). The categories of analysis were:

1. *Same Client:* the attendant was servicing the same difficult client as at the start of the demonstration. Sixty-three program participants and 66 controls were still serving their original client at the point of follow-up.
2. *Different Client:* the attendant was serving a different client from the one she served at the start of the demonstration. She might be serving a different client because her original client was hospitalized or the case was closed or because she or the original client asked for a change. The subsequent client could be a difficult case according to the program definition or a routine case. Twenty-one program participants and 38 controls had changed clients during the follow-up period.
3. *Inactive:* the attendant quit, was fired, went on a leave of absence (e.g., for pregnancy or disability), or was not working for some other reason. Sixteen program participants and 38 controls fell into this category.

As can be seen from Table 8.2, one year after the start of the demonstration, program participants were significantly more likely to be working with their original difficult client than were the controls. Sixty-three percent of program participants, compared to only 46 percent of controls, were still with their original client—a 17 percent difference. Controls were significantly more likely to have changed clients (a 6 percent difference) or to be inactive (an 11 percent difference) than program participants. Thus a major objective of the program—to increase continuity of care among participants serving difficult clients—was achieved.

During the course of the demonstration 17 percent of the cases served by program participants and 14 percent of the cases served by controls involved either a client death or a case closing for other reasons. (The 3 percent difference is not statistically significant.) The death of a client or the closing of a case was an important factor contributing to the changing of clients by program participants,

Table 8.2
Continuity of Care Among Program Participants and Controls at One-Year Follow-up

	Participants	Controls
Same Client	63 (63%)	66 (46%)
Different Client	21 (21%)	38 (27%)
Inactive	16 (16%)	38 (27%)
Total	100 (100%)	142 (100%)

(Chi Square = 6.9, p <.05 with 2 degrees of freedom.)

but not by controls. As Table 8.3 shows, 62 percent of program participants who changed clients during the course of the demonstration did so because the client died or the case was closed. Only 38 percent changed cases because they or the client requested a change. (Half of these changes were requested by the home attendants and half by their clients.) In contrast, two-thirds of the controls changed cases because they or the client requested a change (a majority of these changes were requested by the home attendants), while only one-third changed because of a client death or case closing. One inference is that program participants were much more likely to change clients for reasons beyond their control, while controls were much more likely to change clients because of circumstances that could have been addressed had they benefited from the training, support, and wage differential for serving difficult clients.

Because program participants were specially trained and paid to serve difficult cases, the expectation was that those who changed clients would more likely be serving a difficult case at the one-year follow-up than controls who changed cases. Contrary to expectation, this did not turn out to be so.[6] One interpretation of this finding is that logistical problems encountered by coordinators in matching program participants to available cases—problems discussed in the section above on program implementation—account for the failure of the agencies to discriminate between program participants and controls in making reassignments to difficult cases.

The analysis also examined the effects of the demonstration on worker turnover. As in the case of continuity of care, the experience of program participants was significantly better than that of controls. However, the differences between them were not as great as for continuity of care. Table 8.4 indicates that 84

Table 8.3
Reasons for Changing Clients, Comparison of Program Participants and Controls at One-Year Follow-up

	Program Participants	Controls
Client died/hospitalized/ Case Closed	13 (61.9%)	13 (34.2%)
Change requested by Client or Home Attendant	8 (38.1%)*	25 (65.8%)**
	21 (100%)	38 (100%)

[Chi Square = 4.1, p <.05 with 1 degree of freedom.]

*Of these, 4 changes were requested by home attendants, and 4 by clients.

**Of these, 14 were requested by home attendants, and 11 by clients.

Table 8.4
Work Status of Program Participants and Controls at One-Year Follow-up

	Program Participants	Controls
Working	84 (84%)	104 (73%)
Inactive	16 (16%)	38 (27%)
Total	100 (100%)	142 (100%)

[Chi Square = 4.0 with one degree of freedom, p <.05.]

percent of program participants were working at the one-year follow-up, compared to only 73 percent of controls. Conversely, only 16 percent of program participants were inactive, compared to 27 percent of controls. This 11 percent difference is statistically significant but only about two-thirds the size of the 17 percent difference found in Table 8.2. This somewhat smaller impact on turnover than on continuity of care should not be surprising given the relatively long job tenure of both participants and controls at the outset of the demonstration. The baseline data show that these were well-seasoned workers: median job tenure for program participants and controls at both agencies was between three and four years. Thus the room for improvement with regard to reducing turnover was relatively small.

The "inactive" category was subsequently analyzed to determine to what extent client deaths, hospitalizations, or case closings were associated with home attendants' leaving the job. As noted in the discussion of program implementation above, workers who do not immediately receive an appropriate reassignment from agency coordinators are left without pay and may leave the agency for work elsewhere. This natural disruption in service is also an ideal time for a considerate worker to leave the agency for other reasons without inconveniencing the client or the coordinator. Client deaths or case closings were a contributing factor in about one-quarter to one-fifth of the cases in our sample. Twenty-five percent of program participants left the job immediately after a client death or case closing, compared to only 18 percent of controls; however, the 7 percent difference was not statistically significant. Approximately three-quarters to four-fifths of workers in both groups became inactive for other reasons, including leaving for maternity or disability reasons, quitting, or being fired. Because the reporting of these other reasons was unreliable and incomplete, it is not possible to provide an accurate breakdown.

Finally, the analysis examined the work status of two separate subgroups of the entire population of program participants and controls: (1) those whose original cases were still "open" at the one-year follow-up (i.e., the client had not died, experienced an extended hospitalization, entered a nursing home, or moved) and (2) those whose original cases were closed and who therefore experienced a major disruption in work status over which they had virtually no control. Table 8.5 shows that the effects of the demonstration on continuity of care among workers whose cases were still open at the one-year follow-up were

Table 8.5
Continuity of Care, Comparison of Program Participants and Controls Whose Cases Were Still "Open"

	Program Participants	Controls
Same Client	63 (76%)	66 (54%)
Different Client	8 (10%)	25 (21%)
Inactive	12 (14%)	31 (25%)
	83 (100%)	122 (100%)

[Chi Square = 10.16, p <.01 with 2 degrees of freedom.]

Table 8.6
Work Status of Program Participants and Controls Whose Cases Were Open at One-Year Follow-up

	Program Participants	Controls	Difference
Working	71 (86%)	91 (75%)	11%
Inactive	12 (14%)	31 (25%)	
Total	83 (100%)	122 (100%)	

[Chi Square = 3.5 with one degree of freedom; p<.10.]

even more pronounced than among the entire group of workers described in Table 8.2. Of program participants whose original difficult cases were still open, 76 percent were still with their original client at the one-year follow-up, compared to only 54 percent of controls—a 22 percent difference. Controls were significantly more likely to fall into the ''Different Client'' category (an 11 percent difference) and the inactive category (also an 11 percent difference) than were program participants.

The effect of the demonstration on turnover among these workers was weaker. As can be seen from Table 8.6, 86 percent of program participants whose cases were still open were still on the job at the one-year follow-up, compared to 75 percent of controls, an 11 percent difference (similar to the difference in Table 8.4). Conversely, 14 percent of program participants were inactive, compared to 25 percent of controls.

The same 11 percent difference held for the group of workers whose clients died or whose cases were closed, although the absolute percentages of working home attendants were lower. Seventy-six percent of program participants who experienced a major disruption in work because of a client death or case closing were on the job at the one-year follow-up, compared to only 65 percent of controls who experienced a similar disruption. Conversely, only 24 percent of program participants were inactive, compared to 35 percent of controls.

One inference from these data is that the potential for fully utilizing the skills of program participants and for reducing turnover among seasoned workers—whether or not specially trained—could be increased by providing transitional pay for home attendants who find themselves ''out of a job'' because their clients have died or experienced a major decline in health.

PROGRAM POSTSCRIPT

During the final months of the demonstration, the work life interventions implemented at Long Life and Independent Living were eclipsed by larger political events that would significantly upgrade home attendant employment citywide but leave the demonstration in limbo. Local 1199 had patched up its internal political divisions sufficiently to launch a major "crusade" on behalf of the home attendant work force (Crowe, 1988). The union's hospital and nursing home base was stable or shrinking, and the growing home care sector was a promising area for expansion. Enlisting the support of prominent religious leaders and politicians, the union precipitated a series of public hearings and rallies highlighting the problems of the home attendants and their critical role in providing services to the frail elderly and disabled. In the process, it forged an alliance with the other New York home care unions and with the vendor agencies (represented by the Home Care Council of New York City) to campaign for a "breakthrough" settlement for home attendants.

By the beginning of 1988, a variety of forces had converged to make such a breakthrough possible. Local hospitals were releasing elderly patients more quicky, waiting lists for nursing homes were growing, and the AIDS epidemic was creating a whole new category of individuals in need of home care. The result was an increase in the demand for home attendant services just as providers were beginning to feel the effects of the Immigration Reform and Control Act of 1986. Local philanthropic organizations and state policy groups began to study and report on the problems of New York's home care system, focusing in particular on work force issues (Community Service Society, 1987; Long Term Care Policy Coordinating Council, December 1986; United Hospital Fund, 1987). The media highlighted the "labor crisis" in home care, providing in-depth human interest coverage of home attendants and their clients, along with analysis of the issues involved and pungent quotes from workers, clients, agency directors, and public officials, all attesting to the need for dramatic improvements in employment conditions (Bernstein, September 27 and September 28, 1987; Iverem, 1988; Moreno, 1987; *New York Times,* March 14, 1988; Roberts, 1987; Sullivan, 1987; Wolff, 1987).

In a climate of growing political support, both reflected and reinforced by the media, the unions and the Home Care Council issued a joint position paper in January 1988 advocating significant increases in wages and benefits. Officials of the Human Resources Administration quickly expressed support for the position but deferred to the state for an increase in the Medicaid payment rate. Several months later, under heavy political pressure, the governor's office and the state Department of Social Services agreed that Medicaid would fund a package estimated to increase the cost of home attendant care in New York city by about $650 million over three years.[7]

The final agreement among the unions, the vendor agencies, the city, and the state increased attendant starting wages by 20 percent the first year, to $5.00 per hour (retroactive to December 1987); an additional 8 percent, to $5.40 in September 1988; and an additional 9 percent, to $5.90 per hour in the following July. (Prior wage increases had been in the 5 to 6 percent range.) With the $.30 per hour differential for one year's tenure at a given agency, most attendants would be earning $5.30 per hour as of July 1988. The agreement also provided for weekend differential pay of $.50 per hour, for a per diem increase of $6.25 for twenty-four-hour live-in attendants, for greatly expanded health insurance coverage, and for a joint union-management plan to administer these health benefits. The executive vice president of Local 1199 declared the settlement a ''major breakthrough for health care workers in their campaign for a living wage'' (Scott, 1988).

Preoccupied with these negotiations, neither Long Life nor Independent Living actively lobbied HRA to extend the life of the demonstration or to expand the program to additional workers. They were unwilling to expend their political capital on the SHARP home attendants, lest they jeopardize their chances for a positive response from HRA on the far larger and more significant pay and benefit issues pending. Thus the end of the demonstration period arrived without any decision on the part of HRA to extend the pay differential or to expand the program to additional workers or agencies. Because neither the HRA budget nor its contracts with the vendor agencies provided for a program extension in the current fiscal year, the SHARP home attendants stopped receiving their pay differential at the end of the demonstration period.

Before the 1988 wage and benefit agreement was approved by HRA and the state, the demonstration agencies had hesitated to confuse the issue or jeopardize the agreement by approaching HRA on behalf of the demonstration. Afterwards, the special training and the $.30 per hour wage differential seemed insignificant beside the 40 percent overall wage increase mandated by the agreement. Furthermore, during the course of the demonstration, the state Department of Social Services seemed nearer to implementing the new level of personal care (Level 3) envisioned at the outset of the project. The agency directors perceived that the advent of Level 3 would have more far-reaching implications for them than would the demonstration project, because it would affect more clients and therefore more workers. For that reason, too, they hestitated to push the concept of the program for the behaviorally difficult client.

In addition, although coordinators at both agencies expressed satisfaction with program graduates and their management of difficult cases, they never became ardent advocates of the program, perhaps because they feared that a corps of specially trained and paid home attendants might demand more attention or consideration than they were able to provide. The program also imposed on the coordinators a new set of responsibilities—that is, the need to find substitute workers for trainees, to systematically identify difficult cases, and to distinguish between routine and difficult cases in reassigning workers whose cases were closed—adding to their already heavy administrative burden. Thus the only strong advocates of maintaining the program were the program participants themselves, who lacked an organized voice for expressing their concerns once the demonstration ended and whose concerns about losing the differential were almost certainly mitigated on learning that they would receive a raise to $5.00 per hour in July, retroactive to December 1987.

In the end, without lobbying by the agencies or the workers, HRA was free to decide the future of the SHARP program based on ''the merits'' and on its own bureaucratic and fiscal priorities. The head of the Office of Home Care Services, the head of the Medical Assistance Administration, and her deputy for Program Planning and Evaluation all followed the demonstration with interest. They were eager to learn the results of the program and pleased to discover its effects on continuity of care and turnover. Reducing turnover, improving opportunities for workers, and upgrading care were high on their list of program priorities in 1987-1988, as they worried about possible worker shortages and found the home attendant program the focus of media and public attention. Using preliminary follow-up data from the evaluation, they proceeded to build the elements of the demonstration into the HRA budget for the fiscal year beginning 1 July 1988.

The budget request submitted to the mayor's Office of Management and Budget (OMB) for fiscal year 1988-1989 requested approximately $3 million to institute special training and a $.30 per hour wage differential for home attendants serving medically complex or behaviorally difficult clients. (The $3 million number was based on an estimated 7 percent of the caseload qualifying for the services of specially trained workers.) Medical complexity referred to the Level 3 program being developed by the state Department of Social Services, while behavioral difficulty encompassed the provisions of the demonstration project. Thus the budget request combined appropriations for both initiatives, on the grounds that they were similar in design and intent and that OMB would more likely approve the program for behaviorally difficult clients if it were billed as part of the new state regulations for Level 3 home attendants. OMB approved the budget request in July 1988. However, as of September 1988, plans for implementation had not been formulated.

Instead, the Office of Home Care Services was focusing its attention on two new demonstration programs, developed at the behest of David Dinkins, Manhattan Borough president and now mayor, whose support Local 1199 had earlier enlisted in the cause of the home attendant program. With a special budgetary appropriation obtained by Dinkins, HRA planned to implement a Field Support Demonstration program and a Worker Recognition program in some twenty home attendant agencies starting September 1988.

In the field support demonstration, participating agencies would designate a new corps of workers—Field Support Liaisons—who would be chosen from the existing home attendant work force to visit home attendants on the job, provide ongoing support, help identify and solve problems, and improve the linkages between home attendants in the field and administrative and professional staff in the agency. The stated goals of the demonstration were to: (1) reduce the isolation of home attendants in the field and thereby improve job satisfaction, (2) provide selected home attendants with an opportunity for job advancement, (3) reduce home attendant absenteeism and turnover, and (4) improve agency performance and the quality of service to clients. The idea for field support grew in part from the observations of the Ford project management and research teams that substantive support and supervision of home attendants were often lacking and in part from HRA's desire to beef up monitoring as well as support of the home attendant in the field.

In the Worker Recognition demonstration, participating agencies would receive a fixed sum of money, based on their client caseload, to fund programs they would design to reward deserving workers and improve home attendants' morale. With these demonstrations and their predecessor, HRA clearly showed its receptivity to programs aimed at upgrading the home attendant's job and improving service. Whether or not these programs could or would be institutionalized and incorporated into standard operating procedures was yet to be determined.

NOTES

1. Caseload figures are as of March 1986.

2. The city provides the training through contracts with several independent nonprofit contractors.

3. In California, for example, only 10 percent of the entire In-Home Supportive Services caseload received more than thirty-five hours of care per week in 1983. This 10 percent consisted principally of severely impaired individuals, who averaged about forty hours of care per week and who were generally served by individual providers rather than by workers employed at contract agencies (IHSS Survey, March 1983).

4. As of July 1988, regulations for the new Level 3 workers had been promulgated, but the administrative directive specifying allowable tasks and activities had not been finalized. The latter were enmeshed in political controversy stemming largely from the interests of the nursing community, on one hand, which sought to limit the scope of the Level 3 workers' responsibilities, and the disabled community, on the other, which sought to enlarge them. An early draft of the allowable tasks and activities did enlarge the responsibilities of the home attendant but not to the extent envisioned in the Ford proposal. For example, Level 3 attendants could clean ostomy or intravenous (IV) feeding equipment but not actually place an appliance or insert an IV.

5. Four monthly half-day sessions were held at one agency, and two were held at the other.

6. At the end of the one-year period, 57 percent of program participants and 71 percent of controls were serving a difficult case; this 14 percent difference was not statistically significant.

7. In fact, the cost of the settlement was uncertain, largely because of the difficulty in projecting the cost of the new health insurance benefits, and projections continued to change throughout the spring and summer of 1988.

9

Quality Care: Syracuse and Milwaukee

INTRODUCTION

Quality Care Syracuse and Quality Care Milwaukee—each established in 1978—are part of the large for-profit home health care chain now called Kimberly Quality Care. At the start of the project, both agencies were considered flagship offices by corporate headquarters because of their high volume, high growth, and superior management. In 1985 Quality Care Syracuse—including a main office and three rural satellites—provided about 6,000 hours of care each week to some 300 clients, generating weekly revenues of $45,000 to $50,000 and annual revenues of approximately $2.5 million. About half the agency's revenues came from contracts with nearby county departments of health and social services, about a quarter from private pay clients, and a quarter from other sources—including private hospitals and long-term care facilities, the local Visiting Nurse Association, and private insurers. Quality Care Milwaukee was technically two separate agencies sharing the same offices and the same manager. Its "noncertified" branch served private pay, privately insured, some institutional, and some county clients, generating weekly sales of $30,000 to $40,000 and yearly revenues of about $1.8 million in 1985. Nearly 60 percent of these revenues came from Wisconsin Blue Cross, which provided extremely generous home care benefits.[1] The smaller "certified" branch served Medicare and Medicaid clients and generated yearly revenues of approximately $380,000.

The main office of Syracuse Quality Care was located in an apartment complex just outside downtown Syracuse, convenient to bus routes and local highways. Its three satellites were in the small towns of Oswego, Auburn, and Geneva, New York. The main office occupied two connecting apartments in a building housing other offices, a Greek restaurant, and a garage, in addition to its noncommercial occupants. The Milwaukee office was located in a modern, sprawling office complex situated next to a quiet pond. It was well outside the city and not on major bus lines, thus relatively inaccessible to workers without their own means of transportation.

Both Syracuse and Milwaukee listed approximately 400 field workers—home health aides, homemakers, personal care attendants, and a smaller number of licensed practical nurses and registered nurses—on their master employee list, of whom a third to a half were actively serving clients. As with most home care agencies, much of their business took place over the telephone. However, a steady stream of job applicants and workers entered their offices to fill out forms, receive orientation or training, bring in time sheets, pick up paychecks, and the like.

AGENCY AND CORPORATE MANAGEMENT

The Local Agencies

The manager of the Syracuse office and its three satellites had been a nurse practitioner, then a nursing instructor for thirteen years, before joining Quality Care to start and operate the Oswego satellite. After successfully establishing the satellite, she took over all the Syracuse operations when her predecessor was promoted to a higher position in April 1985. The Milwaukee manager came to Quality Care from a career in laboratory sales and technical marketing. Starting in October 1985, she too replaced a predecessor who was promoted within the Quality Care corporate hierarchy.

Both managers concentrated their efforts on building service volume, maintaining healthy gross margins, and consolidating their agencies' reputation for providing quality service. Their bible was the ''Blue Book''—a summary of weekly billings by payer by site produced by corporate headquarters for all office managers. Sales volume was a target of close attention, and charts of weekly sales were prominently posted where the office staff could observe them.

The managers' concrete rewards—and those of their staff—were cash bonuses tied to volume and net profits. Under a corporate incentive plan established in 1986, every four months office managers and their staff could share a bonus of approximately 2 to 5 percent of net profits for that period, if the profits exceeded those of the prior year.[2] Bonuses, which could amount to more than $10,000 a year for managers and more than $1,000 a year for office staff, were a strong motivating force, and the key to qualifying for bonuses lay in efforts to maintain an adequate supply of aides through steady recruitment.

According to the managers, successful marketing—critical to building volume—was virtually inseparable from recruitment. If field staff supervisors could not find reliable aides ready to take contract assignment as they arose, efforts to fill quotas would be doomed to failure. Seeking steady growth, the managers put heavy emphasis on attracting new workers.

Corporate Headquarters

Growth was also a hallmark of the corporation as a whole. Quality Care grew out of a physicians' on-call organization—Health Delivery Systems—founded by physician-entrepreneur Dr. David Scheinman in 1969. Its first office opened in Hicksville, New York, in 1972, and brought in revenues of $300,000. Shortly thereafter the company expanded its home care business and became a publicly owned corporation, changing its name to Quality Care in 1978. By 1983 Quality Care had established 165 offices in forty-three states, the District of Columbia, and Canada and was one of the three largest home health care companies in the United States, with revenues of more than $100 million.[3]

Despite, or perhaps because of, rapid growth between 1978 and 1981, Quality Care experienced financial losses during that period (see Chapter 5). Between 1982 and 1984, however, it posted record earnings and revenues and improved its profit position. Nevertheless, it made just $3.5 million in profits in 1984, less than 3 percent of sales (*Business Week,* 1985).

Seeking a "well-heeled parent" who could finance additional expansion and cushion the company from cash flow problems, in 1985 Quality Care sold out to Grand Metropolitan PLC—a British conglomerate with vast interests in liquor, food, and retailing (*Business Week,* 1985; Cole, 1988). The founder of the company stayed on as chairman and chief executive officer until late 1986, when he stepped down to become a consultant.

GrandMet's ownership of Quality Care lasted about two and a half years. In the summer of 1987, GrandMet sold Quality Care to Life Time Industries, another British concern, for $100 million (about $25 million less than its 1985 acquisition price) (*Business Week,* 1985; Lohr, 1988). Life Time Industries had previously acquired Kimberly Home Care, and together Kimberly and Quality Care would constitute more than 70 percent of Life Time's business.

Under the terms of the Life Time buy-out, Kimberly and Quality Care merged, forming a $300 million company—the largest home care chain in the United States. The merged company moved to new headquarters in Boston and set about consolidating operations at the regional and local level. With consolidation down the line, corporate leadership expected significant economies of scale leading to increased profits and a brighter financial future than either company could have experienced independently.

WORKING CONDITIONS

Wages and benefits at Quality Care subsidiaries reflected local labor market conditions. Neither Quality Care Syracuse nor Quality Care Milwaukee was unionized, nor were its immediate competitors. The wage and benefit package of each agency closely resembled the packages of its nearest proprietary competitors. However, the major nonprofit home care organizations in each area offered a longer workweek and better benefits than the for-profits.

Hourly wages at Milwaukee Quality Care were about a dollar higher than in Syracuse, reflecting the Milwaukee area's generally higher pay levels. In 1986, starting wages for homemaker, personal care attendants, and certified home health aides ranged from $3.80 to $4.10 per hour at Quality Care Syracuse. Personal care attendants at Milwaukee Quality Care started at $4.50 per hour, while home health aides, who constituted most of the aide work force, were paid $5.25 per hour for part-time daily work, with a $.25 per hour differential for nights and weekends. The Syracuse aides responding to the baseline survey reported an average hourly wage of $4.13 and an average workweek of thirty-one hours, while the Milwaukee aides reported an average hourly wage of $5.28 and an average workweek of twenty-five hours. (Twenty-nine percent of the Syracuse respondents and 26 percent of the Milwaukee respondents also held another job in addition to their work at Quality Care.)

At each site, the home aides earned about the same hourly wage as aides in area nursing homes and personal care facilities (U.S. Bureau of Labor Statistics, March 1987), but about $1.50 less per hour than aides employed by local hospitals. For example, in upstate New York in August 1985, part-time hospital aides earned $5.55 per hour (compared to the average $4.13 wage reported at Quality Care) (U.S. Bureau of Labor Statistics, Buffalo-Niagara Falls, August 1985); while in Milwaukee, part-time hospital aides averaged $6.89 per hour (compared to the $5.28 average reported at Quality Care) (U.S. Bureau of Labor Statistics, Milwaukee, August 1985). Even part-time hospital food helpers earned more than the home aides ($5.21 per hour in upstate New York and $5.48 per hour in Milwaukee).

Quality Care Milwaukee offered virtually no benefits to its workers, while vacation pay was the only substantial benefit provided by Syracuse Quality Care. After a year of service, the Syracuse aides received vacation pay equivalent to the average number of hours per week worked during the prior year, up to a maximum of forty hours. Any vacation time taken during the course of a year, however, was unpaid, as was sick leave.

WORKER ATTITUDES AND JOB SATISFACTION

As can be seen from Table 9.1, dissatisfaction with benefits at both Quality Care Syracuse and Quality Care Milwaukee was high; 80 to 88 percent of aides at both agencies reported they were slightly or very dissatisfied with the benefits they received. Dissatisfaction with pay was less prevalent at the Milwaukee Quality Care office than at the Syracuse office, as might be expected given the higher hourly wage in Milwaukee. Nevertheless dissatisfaction with pay was substantial at both agencies. Nearly 50 percent of the Milwaukee aides surveyed and 62 percent of the Syracuse respondents expressed dissatisfaction with pay. Approximately 40 percent of the aides surveyed at each site also expressed dissatisfaction with opportunities for advancement, although nearly as many reported that they were satisfied with this aspect of the job. Syracuse Quality

Table 9.1
Attitudes of Home Aides, Syracuse and Milwaukee Quality Care

	Satisfied* (Slightly or Very)		Dissatisfied* (Slightly or Very)	
	Syracuse	Milwaukee	Syracuse	Milwaukee
Overall job satis.	88%	86%	2%	6%
Pay	27%	42%	62%	48%
Benefits	10%	9%	80%	88%
Opportunity for Advancement	29%	44%	41%	41%
Hours Worked	71%	79%	25%	18%
Isolation	82%	74%	6%	12%
Training Adequacy	81%	88%	13%	8%
Opportunity to Help	98%	100%	0	0
Treatment by Supervisor	79%	86%	10%	6%
Treatment by Company	67%	94%	17%	9%
Will look for a job in the next year:			20%	18%
N =	78	34		

* Workers responded on a 5 point scale including very satisfied, slightly satisfied, neither satisfied nor dissatisfied, slightly dissatisfied, very dissatisfied.

Care aides, who worked more hours on average than their Milwaukee counterparts, were more likely to be dissatisfied with the hours they worked than aides at their sister agency. However, more than 70 percent of the aides in both agencies reported satisfaction with hours worked.

Aides at both agencies generally expressed satisfaction with their supervisors and with their treatment by the company. Virtually all expressed satisfaction with the opportunity to help people in their work, and only 6 to 12 percent reported they felt lonely on the job. Overall job satisfaction was high (86 to 88 percent), and the job tenure of workers surveyed at Milwaukee Quality Care (an average of three years) was comparable to that of workers at Remedy, Long Life, and Independent Living. However, job tenure at Quality Care Syracuse (an average of two years) was somewhat lower.

THE WORK LIFE DEMONSTRATIONS AT QUALITY CARE

At the start of the project both agencies were in more or less continuous search of new home aides to fill service gaps created by turnover and to support their growing service volume. Predicted worker shortages—not just in Syracuse or Milwaukee, but in other offices throughout the country—had caught the attention of corporate leadership, which was beginning to focus on issues of aide recruitment and retention.

The major appeal of the demonstration to the chief executive officer and his corporate staff was the opportunity to use outside funds to experiment with new ways of attracting and keeping unskilled workers. Two demonstration proposals received serious consideration. One called for developing a transportation network to move home aides from inner-city areas where recruitment was relatively easy to suburban areas where public transportation was poor and agencies had difficulty deploying workers. This idea was ultimately rejected on the grounds that it would be too costly and difficult to design and sustain a system for transporting significant numbers of workers to widely scattered clients at two-hour or four-hour intervals on a regular basis. The second proposal called for developing a "staff aide" program intended to provide full-time work and associated benefits to a select group of aides at one or two Quality Care sites. This proposal received enthusiastic endorsement from Quality Care regional and local staff, who were already beginning to experiment with the idea in several locations but were hesitant to institute a major initiative because of the personnel costs involved.

Field and corporate staff cited seven compelling reasons for using staff aides at the local level: (1) to fulfill contractual requirements—that is, to guarantee service; (2) to fill difficult and/or short-term cases; (3) to provide backup for last minute employee cancellations; (4) to provide evidence of capacity to deliver service when marketing for contracts or traditional referrals; (5) to reduce the use of overtime pay; (6) to offer aides an opportunity for advancement; and (7) to market opportunities to new workers. In an idealized analogy, the staff aides were likened to a Green Beret strike force that could be dispatched expeditiously to trouble spots and areas of opportunity in order to increase business.

Persuaded that the potential benefits of a staff aide program were substantial, Quality Care and the management and research teams agreed to institute such a demonstration at two sites—Syracuse and Milwaukee.[4] The explicit objective of the demonstration, described in the letter of agreement signed at the start of the project, was

> to test the proposition that, by creating or expanding a higher tier of employment for home care workers—involving higher status, greater variety of work, higher compensation and full-time employment—it is possible to improve the job satisfaction and performance of the workers involved, and to encourage other workers to view their jobs as offering possibilities for advancement and professional development.

The intervention was to consist of the appointment of up to twenty employees (five in Milwaukee and fifteen in Syracuse) as "staff aides," who would be full-time workers on the administrative payroll of each agency and who would be eligible, therefore, for vacation, sick leave, retirement, and health insurance benefits identical to those accorded regular office staff. Specifically, the benefits consisted of ten days of paid vacation, six paid sick days, three paid personal days, and subsidized health insurance. Each local office director would select a group of employees eligible for the staff aide position by virtue of their training, experience, and performance on the job. The research team would then randomly select about half of the group to be program participants; the rest would be controls.

Among the duties outlined for the staff aides were providing relief for regular home aides during vacations or other absences, providing staff relief to area health facilities, working alternate weekends at the discretion of the agency, serving difficult cases or cases in difficult-to-reach areas, serving short-notice or short-hour (one- to two-hour) cases, and performing community education/public relations functions such as recruiting workers or speaking to incoming home aides. Because the staff aide position would entail more responsibility than the routine aide assignment, staff aides would receive $.50 per hour more than they would as a home health or personal care aide. The project budget included funds for the wage differential, the benefit package, and for 10 percent unbillable time (three to four hours per week) for each staff aide.

PROGRAM IMPLEMENTATION

The first meeting of the Quality Care CEO, corporate staff, and the project management and research teams took place in October 1985. The letter of agreement authorizing the project was signed in April 1986, and the process of collecting baseline data and selecting staff aides began almost immediately.

Selecting Program Participants

Both agencies employed the same general criteria for selecting staff aides. At each site those eligible for the staff aide position were required to have the requisite state training for home health or personal care aide. In addition, workers were selected on the basis of experience, reliability, and perceived willingness to take on challenging tasks.

Beyond shared criteria, however, the selection process differed somewhat at each agency. The Milwaukee agency conceived the position as a "step up the career ladder" for a small group of deserving employees. The manager did not publicize the staff aide program until she and her staff had identified and contacted potential program participants, narrowing an initial pool of fifty candidates down to fourteen workers, all from the noncertified branch. In contrast,

Table 9.2
Proportion of Quality Care Aides Who Agreed to Participate

	Syracuse	Milwaukee
Agreed	15 (83%)	3 (60%)
Refused	3 (17%)	2 (40%)
	18 (100%)	5 (100%)

the Syracuse agency conceived the position as a promotion for deserving workers but also as a motivating force for other employees and a marketing device to recruit new aides. Accordingly, Syracuse sent out fliers to its employees and posted notices about the staff aide opportunity. The Syracuse office also spent several thousand dollars on large display advertisements that ran for several Sundays in the Syracuse metropolitan area newspapers. These advertisements announced the opening of the staff aide positions and prominently mentioned the forty-hour workweek and associated benefits. The response to all of these efforts was small, however, and disappointing to the office manager. She and her staff ultimately enlarged the pool of candidates by personally contacting a number of employees, of whom thirty-five (nineteen from the main office and sixteen from the agency's three satellites) agreed to be formally considered for the demonstration.

Each of the agencies provided the research team with a list of potential program participants roughly double the projected size of the staff aide group. From these lists, the researchers randomly selected approximately equal numbers of participants and controls. Then the respective agencies notified the program participants of their selection. As Table 9.2 indicates, 83 percent of the Syracuse group and 60 percent of the Milwaukee group agreed to become staff aides when offered the opportunity.

Program Dropouts

The number of workers who dropped out of the staff aide program was significant. Within two weeks of the start of the demonstration, four (27 percent) of the Syracuse staff aides dropped out because they found the forty-hour workweek too onerous, because they did not want to accept the cases they were assigned, or because they had transportation or babysitter problems. These workers did continue in their regular aide assignments. The agency replaced the four dropouts with four new staff aides also randomly selected by the research team in the same manner as the original group. Subsequently, however, one of the replacements, along with three other staff aides, dropped out of the program. Of all nineteen Syracuse workers who agreed to be staff aides during the course of the project, eight (42 percent) dropped out of the program for various reasons. None of them left the agency when they dropped out, although two terminated within six months of leaving the program. (For more detailed follow-up, see Tables 9.6-9.9.)

Within the first two weeks of the demonstration, one of the Milwaukee aides also dropped out of the staff aide program. By that time the Milwaukee agency was experiencing a major decline in business as the result of a statewide cutback in Blue Cross coverage, so the office manager decided not to replace the dropout. Thus the Milwaukee demonstration consisted of only two staff aides, not a large enough group in itself to allow for meaningful statistical analysis. Table 9.3 summarizes the program status of the potential and actual staff aides selected at each agency.

Full-time Work

The intent of the Quality Care demonstration was that staff aides would work a guaranteed forty-hour week, and the assumption was that on average about 10

Table 9.3
Program Status: Syracuse and Milwaukee

	Syracuse	Milwaukee
Total population of potential Staff Aides	36	14
Agency decided not to offer* the position	0	2
Offered but refused	3	2
Prog. Participants	19	3
(drop outs)	(8)	(1)
Controls	14	7

*From the 14 names submitted by Milwaukee, the research team selected 7 program participants, and the agency offered the staff aide position to 5. One of the two "rejects" left the agency before she was offered the position; the other was serving a long-term live-in case that would have been difficult to fill with another aide, so the agency decided not to offer her the position.

percent of this time would be unbillable because it was spent in traveling between clients, on sick leave, or on vacation. In fact, at the outset of the demonstration the gap between hours paid and hours billed was substantially larger. During one week monitored by the research team in September 1986, the Syracuse staff aides worked only 307 billable hours (77 percent) out of the 480 "target" hours they were paid. Between the start of the project in June and the end of October 1986, four months into the demonstration, billed hours attributable to the staff aides were only about 80 percent of hours paid.

According to the Syracuse office manager, the problem was that staff aides were failing to call in for assignment on a regular basis and were refusing to accept early morning, evening, and weekend fill-in assignments. All the staff aides had been made aware of their responsibility to accept forty hours of work when they agreed to participate in the project, and individual staff aides had been contacted since to improve their performance. Yet cooperation was still inadequate. The manager pointed out that some of the staff aides were working more than the required forty hours, while some were working considerably fewer hours. She questioned whether all of the staff aides shared the middle-class work ethic underlying a commitment to a forty-hour workweek.

Among the staff aides, on the other hand, four complaints surfaced: (1) the field staff supervisors weren't coordinating assignments; thus workers were bothered by needless phone calls; (2) the supervisors were overscheduling the staff aides—that is, requiring them to work too many cases to fulfill the forty-hour obligation; (3) supervisors were asking the aides to drive long distances on occasion—an imposition some of the aides resented; (4) some assignments called for the aides to provide staff relief at nursing homes or hospitals—a change in environment that also caused resentment among some of the workers.

After a series of monthly meetings where the supervisors and the staff aides aired their problems and discussed possible solutions, the agency manager instituted a variety of program changes. She allowed the aides to drop their commitment from forty to thirty hours per week, retaining their benefits but losing the guarantee of forty hours of pay. Two of the staff aides chose this option but were then dropped from the program when they subsequently failed to meet the thirty-hour obligation (these are included as dropouts in Table 9.3). To facilitate coordination, the manager assigned each field supervisor a team of staff aides for whom she would be responsible. This arrangement minimized the number of phone calls to any individual worker. To address the overscheduling issue, the supervisors assigned all staff aides to some permanent cases to fill twenty to thirty hours of time each week. The remaining ten to twenty hours per worker were then available for temporary short-term assignments.

The mix of long-term and short-term assignments relieved some of the daily pressure on staff aides, and they appreciated the opportunity to maintain ongoing relationships with a group of their clients. The supervisors also liked the mixed arrangement, in part because it eased their problems in scheduling workers who lacked telephones or transportation necessary for flexible, short-term assignments. Furthermore, they had concluded that there simply were not enough short-notice cases or fill-ins to occupy fifteen staff aides for forty hours each week.

As a result of these program adjustments, unbilled hours at the Syracuse agency fell to 12 percent of hours paid, close to the 10 percent budgeted, and remained at around 10 percent throughout the rest of the demonstration period. In Milwaukee, unbilled hours were about 17 percent of paid hours in the first six months of the demonstration and about 20 percent for the remainder of the demonstration period. However, because only two staff aides were involved and the budgetary implications were much less significant than in Syracuse, management apparently did not perceive the relatively high rate of unbilled hours as a problem.

Group Meetings and Staff Morale

In Milwaukee, the two staff aides met individually and periodically with the office manager and supervisory staff. They were conscious of their special status in the agency and pleased to receive full-time work and associated benefits. However, the small size of the demonstration program precluded the kind of group identity that was to emerge in Syracuse.

At Syracuse Quality Care the meetings devoted to resolving the full-time work issue forged a new sense of group identity among the staff aides. They requested special uniforms and pins, which they ultimately declined when the agency asked them to share the cost. They asked for regular meetings with the agency manager and the field supervisors—an activity that was not routine for other aides. The manager responded positively, and meetings—both informational and social—continued more or less monthly throughout the demonstration period.

Among other things, the meetings afforded the staff aides and the supervisors an opportunity to discuss their feelings about the program. At one meeting, both the aides and their supervisors talked about what aspects of the program were most important to them. Two of the staff aides emphasized the importance of benefits. One said: ''The best part about the staff aide program is the opportunity to receive benefits; the negative aspect is that it sometimes makes the job harder because I can't refuse to go on jobs since I am responsible for a full 40-hour week.''

Another staff aide said:

> Probably the biggest advantage of the staff aide program is the fact that benefits are made available, even though I haven't taken advantage of them personally. I also like the variety of patients I care for. But sometimes it is difficult to get 40 hours in, and I don't like working every weekend in order to fill the 40-hour week.[5] Overall, I think there are more advantages than disadvantages, and I think the program should continue.

A third staff aide emphasized the importance of the forty-hour week: ''The biggest benefit of the program is the 40-hour week because I need to work 40 hours to get by. I do seem to be in demand a little more than I want in my off hours. And I feel a stronger bond with Quality Care.''

A fourth staff aide praised the program but thought there should be another raise in pay because of the greater demands made on her.

As for the field staff supervisors, they generally praised the program and the credibility it built with contracting agencies. One of the supervisors said: ''One of the biggest advantages of the program is having many aides available to call on short notice. Also now that the community is aware of the program, people at VNA and DSS [the county Department of Social Services] tend to ask specifically for staff aides. Sometimes, though, it is difficult to fill each aide for 40 hours.''

Another supervisor noted that patients were pleased to have workers who were higher status and were therefore perceived to provide better service: ''This idea has been favorably received. We are more credible as a company. In addition, if it is necessary to substitute with a staff aide, she is always readily accepted by the patients.''

Job Responsibilities and Job Enhancement

As the quotes from the staff aides imply, the major changes in their daily work life came from the forty-hour work commitment and from the pressure they felt to accept short-notice cases, ''fill-ins'' for other workers, and weekend work. Those who stayed with the program obviously felt that the psychological and tangible benefits, the support of their peers, the improved communication with office staff, the incremental wage, and the predictability of a forty-hour paycheck were worth the additional work pressure they experienced. The short-notice cases, the fill-ins, and occasional assignments to provide staff relief in local health facilities meant greater—but not always welcome—variety in the staff aides' schedules and work environment than prior to the demonstration. However, the tasks they performed on the job were essentially the same as those performed by ordinary home aides. The ''community education/public relations'' functions outlined in the initial job description were the only departure from routine home care duties anticipated at the start of the demonstration, and they never materialized.

Management Perspectives

Eight months through the demonstration, the Syracuse office manager, the Quality Care CEO and several of his corporate staff, the project management team, and the research team met at Quality Care corporate headquarters to assess the progress of the project. At that meeting the Syracuse manager cited eight advantages of the program: (1) increased loyalty to Quality Care among the staff aides; (2) higher morale among the staff aides because they felt superior to the rest of the aide work force; (3) staff aide appreciation of the health benefits, although only seven of nineteen signed up for the insurance and no one signed up for family coverage; (4) acceptance of ''fill-in'' staff aides by clients, who felt they were getting ''preferential care''; (5) improved quality of service, defined as ''more consistent care provided more reliably''; (6) increased confidence on the part of contractors that they could begin cases more quickly; (7) marketing advantages, because the staff aide program set the agency ''apart''; and (8) a marginal increase in business, resulting from calls to contractors indicating free staff aide hours. The manager emphasized, however, that a 10 percent volume increase she had hoped to achieve as a result of the staff aide program had not occurred. The staff aides were not quite the mobile Green Beret force she and corporate headquarters had hoped for, nor could the agency generate 600 hours of new business each week to occupy fifteen staff aides for forty hours each.

A major disadvantage of the program cited by the office manager was the amount of administrative time it consumed. Distributing and collecting questionnaires as part of the project's research agenda was only one element of time involved. In addition, the program required ''strict controls, separate schedules, constant auditing, monthly after-hours meetings by the entire staff, weekly staff meetings, extra paperwork involved in admitting and discharging staff aides, and extra record-keeping on the benefits used by each of the staff aides.'' Furthermore, staff aide salaries were reported along with the salaries of other office staff on the monthly profit and loss statements, thus falsely inflating one of the office manager's performance indicators—the ratio of office salaries to sales.

According to the manager, most staff aides did not feel their new position differed much from their former position, inasmuch as they maintained twenty to thirty hours per week of more or less permanent assignments to fill the forty-hour requirement. Sick leave and vacation pay were clearly important to the staff aides, but, according to the manager, the aides took advantage of these benefits in ways that were not intended and that disrupted the weekly office routine. Specifically, she observed, the staff aides would use ''all benefits all the time'' as soon as they were accumulated. In effect, they used the benefits to fill out the forty-hour week without actually working forty hours. In contrast, she had anticipated that, like other salaried staff, the staff aides would accumulate the benefits and use them only periodically. Finally, the office manager reported that she was disappointed that the staff aide program seemed to lack broad applicability to the work force and had not been an effective recruiting device. Although she had advertised for the staff aide position in local newspapers, no one had responded to the advertisements, and inquiries from within the agency's existing work force often came from aides who lacked either a car or a telephone and were therefore least likely to be able to fulfill the requirements of fill-ins, short-notice cases, and the like.

After visiting the Syracuse office and listening to the report of the office manager at this meeting, the Quality Care CEO expressed skepticism about the likely impact of the project. He noted that the staff aides were a special, pre-selected, and perhaps elite corps of workers, who were not typical of the aide work force and whose experience could not be generalized to the aide work force. He said that originally he thought 30 to 40 percent of the work force might become staff aides, but on the basis of the Syracuse experience, he had drastically reduced his estimate. More likely, he thought, offices with a large volume would decide to have a few staff aides each. Furthermore, he expressed skepticism over the value of the forty-hour week and the benefit package as a recruitment device, and he suggested that higher hourly wages combined with specified wage increases for merit or longevity might be more effective overall in recruiting and retaining workers. In the end, said the CEO, decisions about continuing the staff aide programs in Syracuse and Milwaukee or instituting new programs in other offices would be made at the local level, taking into consideration the implementation problems involved, the costs, and the effects on turnover that were yet to be reported.

PROGRAM COSTS

The direct cost of the Quality Care demonstration was approximately $2,500 per program participant. Of this amount, approximately 40 percent went toward unbilled hours, one-third went toward the $.50 per hour wage differential, 20 percent went toward the subsidized health insurance, and 7 percent went toward vacation and sick leave benefits. If this $2,500 were spread across a year (assuming the worker worked forty hours per week for fifty weeks), it would have amounted to $1.25 per hour—30 percent of the aides' average hourly wage of $4.13 or 17 percent of the agencies' $7.50 per hour billing rate for home aide services. If unbilled hours had been cut in half, this move would have resulted in a saving of $500 per worker, lowering the hourly costs of the program (spread over a year) to $1.00 per hour per worker—still a substantial increase over existing labor costs.

PROGRAM EFFECTS

The explicit objectives of the staff aide project were to improve the job satisfaction and performance of the workers involved by offering five quality of work life improvements: (1) higher status (especially through "promotion"), (2) higher compensation, (3) better benefits, (4) full-time employment, and (5) greater variety of work. As implemented, the program did offer these "improvements" to staff aides—although not all were perceived as improvements by all program participants. However the program components may have been perceived, Tables 9.4 through 9.9 indicate that the impact on turnover—the "performance" measure selected for study—was substantial, significant, and lasted for at least six months after the formal end of the demonstration. At that eighteen-month follow-up point, the staff aides were still receiving their $.50 per hour wage increment and the forty-hour work guarantee. However, the Syracuse agency, experiencing declining revenues, had dropped the vacation, sick leave, and retirement benefits when the demonstration funding ended.

The impact of the program on job satisfaction per se, as distinct from turnover, is more difficult to assess because of potentially biased baseline data on the staff aide group and because of missing data on controls (see Methodological Appendix). Nevertheless, from the data that are available, it seems that the major impact of the program was on staff aides' satisfaction with benefits, opportunities for advancement, and hours worked.

The following section of this chapter presents brief summary data on the Milwaukee program, which because of its small size did not lend itself to detailed statistical analysis. The next section then presents more detailed data and discussion of the Syracuse demonstration.

Milwaukee

As described in the section on program implementation, the Milwaukee staff aide program started out with three staff aides. One of the three dropped out of the program within the first two weeks but continued to work at the agency throughout the demonstration and follow-up period. The other two remained staff aides throughout the demonstration period, although one reverted to regular aide status at the end of the demonstration.[6] Because the two remaining staff aides also continued to work throughout the demonstration and follow-up period, the percentage of working program participants remains the same, whether or not the dropout is included.

Table 9.4 shows that one year after the start of the Milwaukee demonstration, 100 percent of the original staff aides were still working, compared to only 43 percent of the controls, a 57 percent difference. Table 9.5 shows that at the eighteen-month follow-up, again all of the original staff aides were working, while only one (14 percent) of the controls was still on the job, a difference of 86

Table 9.4
Quality Care Milwaukee: 12-Month Follow-up, Work Status of Program Participants and Controls Including Program Dropouts

	Staff Aides	Controls	Difference
Working	3 (100%)	3 (43%)	57%
Inactive	0	4 (57%)	
	3 (100%)	7 (100%)	

Table 9.5
Quality Care Milwaukee: 18-Month Follow-up, Work Status of Program Participants and Controls Including Program Dropouts

	Staff Aides	Controls	Difference
Working	3 (100%)	1 (14%)	86%
Inactive	0	6 (86%)	
	3 (100%)	7 (100%)	

percent. Because the numbers in the Milwaukee program are so small, tests of statistical significance are not presented.

Syracuse

The Syracuse demonstration started out with fifteen staff aides, four of whom dropped out within the first two weeks of the program's start. The four dropouts were replaced by four newly selected staff aides. One of the four replacements subsequently dropped out, along with three of the original aides—two of whom were dropped because of unwillingness to work at least thirty hours per week (see Table 9.3 and section on "Full-time Work"). Thus altogether there were nineteen participants at one time or another in the Syracuse staff aide program, of whom eight became dropouts. Tables 9.6 and 9.7 present turnover data comparing all nineteen program participants, including dropouts, to the fourteen controls.

As can be seen from Table 9.6, nearly three-quarters of all workers who were staff aides, even for a short period of time, were still on the job twelve months after the start of the demonstration, compared to only 29 percent of controls. Because the absolute numbers of workers involved are small, cautious interpretation is necessary. Nevertheless, the 45 percent difference between the two groups was quite substantial and statistically significant. Furthermore, the difference held at the eighteen-month follow-up (see Table 9.7) even though by that time eight of the original program participants were no longer staff aides and the remaining staff aides were receiving a reduced benefit package.

Tables 9.8 and 9.9 present similar follow-up data but exclude from the staff aide group the "two-week dropouts" and include only those program participants who were staff aides for at least six months. In this analysis, the impact of the program is basically the same, but a bit stronger. The proportion of staff aides still on the job at twelve months rises to 80 percent, and the difference between program participants and controls rises to 51 percent. At the eighteen-

Table 9.6
Quality Care Syracuse: 12-Month Follow-up, Work Status of Program Participants and Controls Including Program Dropouts

	Staff Aides	Controls	Difference
Working	14 (74%)	4 (29%)	45%
Inactive	5 (26%)	10 (71%)	
	19 (100%)	14 (100%)	

Chi square = 5.4 with 1 degree of freedom; $p < .02$.

Table 9.7
Quality Care Syracuse: 18-Month Follow-up, Work Status of Program Participants and Controls Including Program Dropouts

	Staff Aides	Controls	Difference
Working	13 (68%)	3 (21%)	47%
Inactive	6 (32%)	11 (79%)	
	19 (100%)	14 (100%)	

Chi square = 7.2 with 1 degree of freedom; $p < .01$.

Table 9.8
Quality Care Syracuse: 12-Month Follow-up, Work Status of Program Participants and Controls Excluding 2-Week Dropouts

	Staff Aides	Controls	Difference
Working	12 (80%)	4 (29%)	51%
Inactive	3 (20%)	10 (71%)	
	15 (100%)	14 (100%)	

Chi square = 7.6 with 1 degree of freedom; $p < .01$.

Table 9.9
Quality Care Syracuse: 18-Month Follow-up, Work Status of Program Participants and Controls Excluding 2-Week Dropouts

	Staff Aides	Controls	Difference
Working	11 (73%)	3(21%)	52%
Inactive	4 (27%)	11 (79%)	
	15 (100%)	14 (100%)	

Chi square = 8.0 with 1 degree of freedom; $p < .01$.

month follow-up, the proportion of staff aides still on the job is 73 percent, compared to only 21 percent of controls, a 52 percent difference. Again, these differences are large and statistically significant.

To understand more fully the impact of the staff aide program, a survey of participants at the one-year follow-up was designed to find out what the most and least important aspects of the program were to them and what the impact of the program was on their earnings, schedules, and career opportunities. Of the fourteen program participants still working at the agency either as staff aides or as regular home aides, only eight (57 percent) responded to the written survey, and all were still staff aides. Once again, the small numbers mean that caution should be exercised in interpreting the findings cited below.

Asked to choose the most important part of the program, seven of the eight workers who served as staff aides for the duration of the demonstration chose the forty-hour guarantee, while one chose the health insurance (see Table 9.10). The overwhelming importance of the guaranteed hours may help explain why the program's impact on these workers lasted beyond the end of the demonstration and the cessation of the demonstration's more generous benefit package (although the guarantee cannot be a factor in explaining the retention of program dropouts). Asked to choose the least important part of the program, four chose the staff aide meetings, two the retirement contribution, one the incremental pay, and one the health insurance. None of the staff aides cited the guaranteed hours, the vacation pay, or the sick leave as "least important" aspects of the job.

Table 9.11 shows that six of the eight staff aides found their schedule more predictable under the staff program and that six of the eight perceived the staff aide position as a "step up the career ladder." Half of the group thought they "made more money" under the staff aide program than they had before, and only one was sorry for having agreed to participate in the program.

To assess attitude changes associated with participation in the staff aide program, we compared staff aide responses to the twelve-month follow-up

Table 9.10
Most and Least Important Program Aspects: Remaining Staff Aides

What was the most important part of the Staff Aide Program to you?

	No. of votes
Guaranteed 40 hours	7
Health insurance	1
Vacation pay	0
Sick leave	0
$.50 per hour wage increment	0
Retirement plan	0
Staff aide meetings	0
Total	8

What was the least important part of the Staff Aide Program to you?

	No. of votes
Guaranteed 40 hours	0
Health insurance	1
Vacation pay	0
Sick leave	0
$.50 per hour wage increment	1
Retirement plan	2
Staff aide meetings	4
Total	8

Table 9.11
Other Attitudes toward the Program: Remaining Staff Aides

	Agree	Disagree	Neutral	Total
I made more money under the Staff Aide Program than before	4 (50%)	1 (12.5%)	3 (37.5%)	8 (100%)
My schedule was more predictable	6 (75%)	1 (12.5%)	1 (12.5%)	8 (100%)
Being a Staff Aide was a step up the career ladder	6 (75%)	1 (12.5%)	1 (12.5%)	8 (100%)
I'm sorry I agreed to participate in the Staff Aide prog.	1 (12.5%)	7 (87.5%)	0	8 (100%)

survey (N=9) with responses to the baseline survey (N=14). The twelve-month follow-up revealed a major increase in satisfaction with benefits and smaller increases in satisfaction with opportunities for advancement, hours worked, treatment by the company, and treatment by the supervisor (see Table 9.12). The smaller increases, in particular, should be viewed with caution because a difference in the attitudes of one or two workers could alter the direction of change over time. On the other hand, the differences reported in Table 9.12 might actually be understated insofar as baseline answers were affected by respondents' knowledge that they had been selected as program participants (see Methodological Appendix). Overall job satisfaction among staff aides—extremely high at the baseline measurement point—was similarly high at the twelve-month follow-up. At both points, 100 percent of respondents reported that overall they were slightly or very satisfied with their job. Again, satisfaction at baseline may be overstated insofar as respondents knew they had been chosen as program participants. Staff aides responding to the twelve-month follow-up were slightly less likely to report they would look for a new job in the coming year than those who responded to the baseline survey.

Two findings that ran counter to expectation were those on satisfaction with pay and on loneliness. Although staff aides were paid a $.50 per hour increment, they were proportionately more dissatisfied with pay at the twelve-month follow-up than at baseline. Perhaps, like the staff aide quoted in this chapter's section on staff morale, others responding to the follow-up questionnaire viewed the wage increment as inadequate to their increased responsibilities. A second "negative" finding was that proportionately more staff aides reported feeling lonely on the job at the twelve-month follow-up than at baseline. Whereas all fourteen staff aides submitting the baseline questionnaire disagreed with the statement "I feel lonely on the job," only six out of nine submitting the follow-up disagreed. One inference is that moving from client to client—even if only part of the job involved temporary short-term assignments—was more isolating than serving fewer clients on a more long-term basis.

Overall, caution should be exercised in drawing firm inferences from the data in Table 9.12 because the numbers of baseline and follow-up respondents are small and there are no comparative data on controls, who could conceivably also have become more satisfied over the course of the twelve-month follow-up period. Nevertheless, the data are suggestive in that they show the strongest improvements in job satisfaction on three of the five dimensions directly affected by the demonstration—that is, benefits, hours, and opportunity for advancement.

PROGRAM POSTSCRIPT

The Quality Care demonstration came to an end in June 1987, one year after its start. Of the two program participants in Milwaukee, one remained a staff aide with the same pay and benefit package she had received during the demonstration. The other lost her staff aide status because she worked full-time, 9 to 5,

Table 9.12
Syracuse: Differences in Job Satisfaction Among Staff Aides Comparing Baseline* and 12-Month Follow-up**

	Satisfied (Slightly or Very)			Dissatisfied (Slightly or Very)		
	Baseline	12-Mos.	Diff.	Baseline	12-Mos.	Diff.
Pay	36%	33%	-3%	35%	44%	+9%
Benefits	0	66%	+66%	100%	22%	-78%
Advancement	57%	88%	+31%	29%	0	-29%
Hours	79%	100%	+21%	21%	0	-21%
Treatment (Company)	86%	100%	+14%	0	0	0
Treatment (Supervis.)	93%	100%	+ 7%	0	0	0
Overall Satis.	100%	100%	0	0	0	0

Intend to look for a new job:

Agree			Disagree		
Baseline	12-Mos.	Diff.	Baseline	12-Mos.	Diff
14%	11%	-3%	50%	66%	+16%

I feel lonely in this job:

Agree			Disagree		
Baseline	12-Mos.	Diff.	Baseline	12-Mos.	Diff
0	11%	+11%	100%	66%	-34%

*Baseline respondents: N=14
**Follow-up respondents: N=9

at another job, and the Milwaukee agency found it could not provide her with forty hours of work during evenings and weekends. Early in the project year, business at the Milwaukee office had declined precipitously as a result of reductions in Blue Cross home care coverage. Amidst declining sales, the office manager left in October 1986, and there was no reason for her successor to expand the staff aide program. The new manager stayed a bit more than a year, then left shortly after the project's end. As Medicaid began to fill the gaps created by Blue Cross reductions, sales volume at the Milwaukee office gradually rebounded. Despite the recovery, however, there were no immediate plans to expand the staff aide program. The office was without a manager and all systems were on hold pending merger with the local Kimberly home care office.

In Syracuse, the office manager decided to continue the staff aide program in a modified form. She suspended the time-consuming monthly staff aide meetings but continued the $.50 per hour wage increment and the forty-hour workweek guarantee. The agency issued checks to the staff aides for any unused vacation and personal time and for retirement benefits accumulated during the demonstration period. Starting July 1987, however, the staff aides lost the nineteen days of combined vacation, sick leave, and personal time that were accorded salaried staff and that had been funded by the demonstration.[7] They also lost their subsidized health insurance; if they wanted to continue coverage under the company plan, they would have to pay $70 per month for an individual or $157 for a family plan. The office manager assigned one of her office staff with knowledge of local health insurance options to help the staff aides explore cheaper alternative coverage, including Medicaid.

One of the staff aides left the Syracuse program almost immediately after the demonstration ended to take a full-time position with benefits at a local hospital. However, she remained on the Quality Care roster, serving clients at home in her off-hours. Another staff aide left in November 1987 to take a full-time office job, and she too continued to serve Quality Care cases in her spare time. By December 1987, eighteen months after the start of the demonstration, there were six staff aides in the Syracuse office.

The reduction in staff aide benefits at the end of the demonstration was partly attributable to declining agency revenues. During the course of the project, Quality Care had announced its intention to apply for Medicare certification and thereby compete with the Syracuse VNA for Medicare business. The VNA subsequently canceled its contract with the agency and transferred its business to other noncertified agencies in the area. As a result, sales at Quality Care fell for a period of months, and the office manager dismissed some of her office staff in an effort to cut fixed costs. Having taken that painful step, she felt she couldn't justify extending the costly staff aide benefit package in light of declining service volume.

In part, too, the benefit reduction reflected the office manager's discomfort with the way in which the staff aides had used their benefits while the demonstration was in effect. To the extent that the aides had used their vacation, sick leave, and personal days to shield themselves from the forty-hour work requirement, the benefits had undermined one of her basic reasons for instituting the experiment—to increase the volume of service provided by the agency. Furthermore, the frequent and unpredictable use of leave time interfered with the scheduling of assignments carried out by the field staff supervisors.

Reviewing the experience of the staff aide program six months after its end, the Syracuse office manager drew four conclusions: (1) the rich benefit package was unaffordable and counterproductive; (2) the work guarantee should be for thirty rather than forty hours—this change would impose fewer demands on the aides and create less stress for the supervisors responsible for scheduling; (3) improved communication between the supervisory staff and the aide work force was critical; and (4) amenities such as dinners, parties, Christmas presents, and the like were an important part of any effort to retain valued workers and ought to be recognized as a legitimate budget item by corporate headquarters. By this time, the Syracuse office volume had begun to rebound, and revenues were pulling ahead of the previous year. Medicare certification was imminent, the office manager was planning a major marketing initiative to local hospitals, and staff aides figured prominently in her plans for serving Medicare patients. She no longer saw the staff aide option as a ''magic bullet,'' but she was convinced there would always be a need for the services of a special corps of highly responsible, mobile, more or less full-time workers.

The Quality Care CEO didn't disagree, but he concluded that the Syracuse office could have received higher return by investing resources in capturing the local IV therapy market, or some other high technology segment, than by spending its time organizing and supervising the staff aide effort. Meanwhile, his own resources were devoted to implementing the Kimberly Quality Care merger announced in the summer of 1987. For the time being, issues of aide recruitment and retention would take a backseat to the multiple tasks involved in consolidating national, regional, and local operations of the new home care giant.

NOTES

1. Until September 1986, Wisconsin Blue Cross wrote supplemental Medicare policies that covered 365 home care visits—including both skilled and ''unskilled'' care—per year for each subscriber. Claiming major financial losses, however, the insurer announced that starting September 1986, those who wished home care coverage would have to pay an extra premium. In addition, eligibility criteria were tightened, and custodial care was limited.

2. This incentive plan replaced an earlier plan, whereby the manager and staff could periodically earn the equivalent of a half or full paycheck for meeting established volume quotas.

3. Upjohn Company's 300-office home care subsidiary and Medical Personnel Pool's 220-office home care operation were larger.

4. Quality Care was most eager to launch the demonstration in New York State, where recruitment problems were particularly salient. The project team pressed for an additional site in the Midwest to add greater geographical diversity to the project.

5. The guidelines for the program said that workers would be required to work alternate, not consecutive, weekends. However, this staff aide apparently did work consecutive weekends.

6. The latter held a regular full-time job at a local health care facility and had fit her staff aide responsibilities into evenings and weekends. When it became difficult for the agency to schedule forty hours of work in those ''after-hours'' periods, she lost her staff aide position but continued on at the agency.

7. Vacation benefits reverted to those accorded regular home aides—a maximum of forty hours per year based on average number of hours worked per week in the prior year and payable only at year's end.

Part III

Overview of Work Life Programs

10

Overview: Adopting and Implementing Work Life Changes

One of the main objectives of the demonstrations was to assess the potential for introducing work life improvements into the home care industry. As the case studies in Part II attest, each of the demonstration sites provided a wealth of information on organizational management and priorities, on work force characteristics, on local market conditions, and on the political and economic environment of the participating agencies. This chapter presents an overview of how these factors affected the adoption and implementation of the various work life programs. Then it discusses the broader implications of these findings.

MOTIVES FOR ADOPTING WORK LIFE IMPROVEMENTS

The design of the demonstrations was such that the project management and research teams solicited the local sponsors and implementing agencies rather than vice versa. Although these organizations had to formulate plans for the work life programs they wished to implement, they were, on the whole, responding to an outside stimulus rather than acting on their own initiative. Why had they not previously taken such initiative, and why did they agree to institute the various work life changes when approached by outsiders?

Large public bureaucracies, enmeshed in established rules and procedures, are notoriously slow to change. The New York City Human Resources Administration, informal sponsor of the Long Life and Independent Living demonstrations, was—and is—the proverbial bureaucracy. Smaller organizations, such as HRA's vendor home attendant agencies, may be less rule-bound and more innovative. However, the vendor agencies were creatures of HRA, established for the sole purpose of providing HRA-funded services and tightly bound by the provisions of their HRA contracts. Thus they were unlikely to alter employment conditions without the encouragement and approval of that large bureaucracy.

Compared to public organizations, private organizations often have greater flexibility to alter their operations. Furthermore, economic theories of the firm suggest that for-profit enterprises canvass the environment in pursuit of profit-raising and cost-cutting opportunities (Caves, 1964). According to this view, if work life improvements could reduce turnover, increase worker productivity, expand service volume, and lower the ratio of fixed costs to revenue, profit-minded employers would be motivated to invest in them. Presumably, for-profit companies like Remedy and Quality Care would institute such improvements without inducements from foundations or other third parties if the benefits outweighed the costs.

One problem with the theory, of course, is the uncertainty about costs and effects. How can a firm know whether a given intervention will yield the desired results at an affordable cost, and why should it risk the effort to find out, if other less uncertain profit-enhancing options are available? Behavioral—as distinct from purely economic—theories of the firm suggest that avoiding uncertainty is a major goal of many organizations—public or private, nonprofit or for-profit. The small to negative profit margins achieved by Remedy and Quality Care (and typical of others in the industry as well, as discussed in Chapter 5), price competition in the quest for county contracts, and price sensitivity on the part of private pay clients made these companies risk-averse when it came to adopting work life changes. Because neither company invested much in its home aide work force, the direct costs of turnover were relatively small. In contrast, the costs of efforts to reduce turnover could be substantial and the outcomes uncertain. Furthermore, both companies functioned in part as temporary help agencies and were therefore accustomed to an impermanent work force.

In their avoidance of uncertainty and their adherence to standard operating procedures, Remedy and Quality Care resembled many other organizations that postpone decisive action until confronted by specific problems or perceived gaps in performance (Cyert & March, 1963; Mouzelis, 1972). In such organizations, emerging problems that cannot be dealt with by traditional procedures provide the principal impetus for change.

The major inducement offered by the project to local sponsors and implementing agencies was outside funding to minimize the financial risks entailed in improving employment conditions. The amounts of money available were minuscule (approximately $50,000 to $150,000 per demonstration) compared to the multi-million-, even billion-, dollar budgets of the corporate and governmental sponsors. The strategic importance of these funds was probably greater than the dollar amounts would suggest, especially at the New York City and San Diego sites, where the public budgeting process left little slack for innovation.[1] Nevertheless, the proffered funds would not have been sufficient to enlist the cooperation of any of the organizations in the absence of other motives.

The case studies reveal five additional factors that influenced decisions to adopt the work life changes: (1) perceived performance gaps, (2) perceived competitive advantages, (3) politics, (4) prestige, and (5) personal goals and values. Some of these motives originated from intrinsic work life problems and solutions. Others, especially prestige, were associated primarily with the extrinsic advantage of participating in a national demonstration.

Perceived Performance Gaps

Perceptions of an emerging "performance gap" in recruiting entry-level aides and keeping them in the work force were a critical motivating factor. These perceptions first appeared at the agency level, then caught the attention of corporate leadership or public officials. Quality Care was probably the most acutely sensitive to labor shortage issues. Responding to local alarms, regional staff in the company's home state had recently formed a New York State "Recruiting Task Force" to consider ways of attracting new workers, and work life improvements were prominent among the options considered. Recruitment was less problematic for agencies in San Diego and New York City, in part because of a fairly plentiful supply of new immigrants and illegal aliens. With passage of the Immigration Reform and Control Act of 1986, however, the threat of worker shortages began to loom in these areas as well.

High turnover was a perceived problem at all sites. Remedy estimated 45 percent annual turnover among homemakers employed by the San Diego office. Neither Quality Care nor Long Life and Independent Living computed turnover statistics (although turnover rates for selected groups of workers were later calculated by the research team), but they acknowledged high turnover, especially among new workers. All attributed unwelcome recruitment costs, discontinuities in care, and client dissatisfaction to turnover problems. Of particular concern in New York City was discontinuity in care for difficult clients with intensive social and psychological needs.

The emerging performance gap in New York City extended beyond both recruitment and turnover. The city's home attendant program, administered by the Human Resources Administration, had been remarkably free of scandal after moving from an individual provider to a contract system in 1980. Nevertheless, the program's rapid growth, huge expenditures, vulnerable clients, and minimally trained workers were beginning to attract critical attention from groups as disparate as the tabloid newspapers and the city's philanthropic foundations. The potential for crisis or scandal was increasingly salient to HRA officials[2]—hence their willingness to experiment with work life changes that might improve service.

Perceived Competitive Advantages

Most home care agencies compete for workers, contracts, and clients.[3] In tight labor markets competition for workers theoretically provides an incentive to offer increased wages, stable employment, benefits, and/or other perquisites. The case studies illustrate, however, that the supply of home aides in some labor markets (e.g., inner-city areas heavily occupied by poorly educated minority women and recent immigrants—sometimes illegal) is more plentiful than area-wide unemployment rates might suggest. Competition for home care contracts and for referrals from local hospitals, physicians, and social welfare agencies also provides an incentive to promote work life improvements, insofar as they are thought to be associated with quicker or better service. However, price competition built into systems like San Diego's, where the low bidder gets the exclusive right to serve public home care clients, generally overshadows government's concern for quality. Price also constrains quality concerns among private pay clients and their families, who often have limited resources to pay for home care. In any case, the link between work life improvements and better service is not well established.

Despite these constraints, the major competitive advantages that came from adopting the work life improvements were the opportunities to provide quicker response and to claim superior service as a function of better trained and better paid workers. Both for-profit sponsors of work life interventions—Quality Care and Remedy—were eager to pursue these advantages. As pointed out in the Quality Care case study, a major objective of the Syracuse office was to capture a larger share of the local home care market by using staff aides to serve short-notice and difficult cases, thereby increasing flexibility and expanding service capacity. The Syracuse staff aide program would also feature prominently in efforts to persuade local referral sources—for example, the county Department of Social Services, the Visiting Nurse Association, hospital discharge planners, and area physicians—that Quality Care could provide more responsive service and more capable workers than its local competitors. As pointed out in the San Diego case study, one of the major attractions of the project to Remedy was the belief that adopting work life improvements would make the company a stronger competitor for county contracts. Other things being equal, evidence of worker satisfaction and reduced turnover could be valuable assets in the competitive bidding process.

Politics

Perceptions of political advantage were more subtle than perceptions of competitive advantage but were a motivating factor as well. Politics broadly defined was probably a latent motive underlying Remedy's participation. Decisions on competitive contracts to deliver In-Home Supportive Services were generally made by bureaucrats in county departments of social service but approved by county boards of supervisors—political bodies sensitive to the relationships among employment conditions in public programs, reliability of service, and constituent voting. Furthermore, general policy decisions on conditions of work and conditions of IHSS awards were made by the state legislature. Establishing a reputation as a beneficent employer and a responsible service provider could only further Remedy's ends in the political arena.

Political considerations were also latent in the decision of the New York City HRA to endorse the project. As pointed out above and in the Long Life/Independent Living case study, the New York City demonstration was launched during a period of growing media and public concern over conditions in the city's home care industry. That concern had a political dimension, illustrated by the fact that David Dinkins, then Manhattan Borough president, allied himself with the home care unions in campaigning for improved working conditions in the city's home attendant program. In consenting to upgrade a portion of the home aide work force, HRA was in part anticipating the emergence of this issue on the city's political agenda.

Prestige

Prestige derived from participation in a national demonstration was part of the competitive and political advantage expected from the work life programs. Although local sponsors—Remedy and Quality Care, in particular—sought and obtained guarantees of confidentiality from the project management and research teams, the desire to gain favorable publicity sometimes overcame the desire for confidentiality. Quality Care corporate headquarters actually issued a press release describing its role in a new national demonstration aimed at upgrading the home care work force, and the Syracuse office publicized its staff aide program in marketing its services. When their home attendants graduated from the special training program that was part of the demonstration, Long Life and Independent Living got local press coverage prominently citing their innovative training. The Remedy demonstration did not attract press coverage, but informal communication made state and local decision makers aware of the company's work life efforts. Thus the sponsors and the implementing agencies found public relations value in supporting the work life improvements.

Personal Goals and Values

Finally, the personal commitment of key actors at each site was an important motivating factor. For convenience and brevity, throughout this book Remedy, Quality Care, Independent Living, Long Life, and HRA have been referred to as if the organizations themselves rather than the people within them made the critical decisions affecting adoption and implementation of the various demonstration programs. Obviously, however, the decisions were made by individuals acting for their organizations, not by some disembodied abstraction—"the organization."

At each of the demonstration sites, individuals in positions of authority with a concern for the work force and a desire to innovate were key in deciding to adopt work life changes. As described in the case studies, the key person at Remedy was the son of the founder and was vice chairman of the company; the key person at Quality Care was the founder of the company and chairman of the board. Each of these men expressed a strong personal commitment to upgrading home care employment within the constraints of a profit-making enterprise. At New York City HRA, the person responsible for moving the project forward was the head of the Medicaid program and former head of the home care office. Her personal concern for the long-term viability of the city's home care program and her personal endorsement of the project were key to obtaining approval from city hall and cooperation from the home attendant agencies.

None of the sponsors would have forced an agency director to participate against his or her better judgment. All of the directors expressed support for upgrading the home aide's job and participating in the demonstration project, but their personal enthusiasm for the project varied. Almost certainly, none would have undertaken a work life improvement program of the demonstration's magnitude without an adequate financial cushion and encouragement from corporate management or, in the case of Long Life and Independent Living, from the bureaucracy that provided their sole financial support. Indeed, enhancing their standing with corporate or bureaucratic sponsors was probably one of the main reasons the agency directors agreed to implement the work life changes. The combination of foundation funding and corporate or bureaucratic support gave them the rare luxury of undertaking a relatively risk-free effort that would possibly redound—materially or symbolically—to their credit with workers, clients, and patrons.

FACTORS AFFECTING IMPLEMENTATION

To institute work life changes successfully, the participating agencies had to shift from the relatively passive role they played in the site selection process to an active role in implementing change. This role sometimes strained their organizational capacity and clashed with their operational goals. The resulting tension had a critical impact on the work life programs. Other factors affecting the programs were local fiscal, political, and market conditions and the cooperation of the home aide work force itself. The sections that follow describe the organizational and environmental factors that affected implementation. Worker cooperation is discussed in Chapter 11.

Operational Goals and Capacity of the Implementing Agencies

The implementing agencies shared two main operational goals: (1) to provide services to clients and (2) to meet the performance standards established by corporate headquarters and/or by other organizations (e.g., county and city departments of social services, local Visiting Nurse Associations, etc.) that contracted for their services. Instrumental to these goals were three others: (1) to achieve a degree of organizational autonomy within the constraints imposed by the environment; (2) to ensure stable or growing revenues and/or profits; and (3) to avoid, insofar as possible, disruption of existing operating procedures and routines. Although outside funding minimized the financial risks attendant on adopting work life changes, implementation entailed a variety of costs and potential conflicts with these operational goals.

Some of the conflicts were attributable to the scarcity of managerial and staff resources at the agency level. At the corporate level, Quality Care and Remedy had substantial management capacity. However, at the agency level, resources for carrying out innovative programs were thin. Managerial capacity was also strained at the two independent agencies involved in the project—Long Life and Independent Living. At Remedy, Long Life, and Independent Living, constraints on management and staff capacity derived largely from the tight administrative cost limits imposed by the public agencies that contracted for service. Neither Quality Care Syracuse nor Quality Care Milwaukee labored under quite as tight reimbursement limits, but both agencies took pride in lean and efficient management. Furthermore, managerial and staff bonuses available under Quality Care's corporate incentive program were contingent upon meeting net profit targets that were sensitive to administrative costs.

Whatever the cause, the scarcity of organizational resources meant that implementation of some of the work life changes required either the diversion of staff from routine operations or the enlistment of outside help. All the guarantees of full-time work, for example, depended on coordination and scheduling by in-house staff, who were considerably strained by the commitment. On the other hand, all the training and support activities relied on outside institutions and consultants, whose priorities were sometimes different from those of the implementing agencies. Both strategies were somewhat disruptive to agency operations, but diverting staff from routine operations was more so. Thus program components that required the commitment of "in-house" resources were most at risk.

Clashes between implementing work life changes and maintaining routine agency operations occurred in several key areas, some more compromising than others. One area of conflict was scheduling of training and support components. A second was implementation of the "guaranteed hours" or full-time work components. A third was assignment of specially trained workers (in the Long Life and Independent Living demonstration) to difficult clients.

Training and Support. None of the agencies had the internal staff resources to develop or implement the training and support components. Thus where training and support were required, they were provided by outside consultants. The major advantage of using outside consultants was the experience and expertise they brought to the task. Furthermore, in all of the demonstration sites where they were employed, the outside consultants also provided technical assistance to the supervisory staff to enable them to carry on at least some of the training and support functions after the consultants withdrew. The major disadvantage of using outside consultants was the lag in start-up caused by personnel changes and other problems at the consulting organizations. As noted in the San Diego case study, long delay in implementing support groups, especially for Spanish-speaking workers, seriously undermined the impact of the support component.

Scheduling of training and support sessions created other problems for the implementing agencies. Scheduling of these sessions threatened to disrupt agency operations in two ways: (1) scheduled sessions might conflict with the client assignments of participating home aides and (2) the process of notifying aides and, if necessary, finding substitute workers to take their cases might divert the attention of supervisory staff from more pressing scheduling and assignment problems. The agencies preferred to convene classes and worker support groups on weekends and evenings, leaving aides' weekday client schedules intact. This policy minimized disruptions in service to clients and relieved office staff of the need to locate substitute workers or "fill-ins." It also imposed an extra burden on the workers. Attending the training and support programs—however satisfying or beneficial—meant longer hours on the job and disruptions in the personal lives of those who attended.

As the case studies note, the agencies reached different compromises. At Remedy, classes and support groups were scheduled for weekday mornings. First the homemakers attended these sessions; then they went to their regular client assignments. The training and support were still add-ons to the workers' job responsibilities, but weekends and evenings were left free for personal pursuits. At Long Life and Independent, the initial training sessions were scheduled for Saturdays, but follow-up sessions alternated between weekdays and weekends. These compromises represented some "slippage" in the objectives of the interventions—the idea, after all, was to ease the burden of work on the participating home aides, not to intensify it. However, the relatively high attendance rates at these sessions and the satisfied comments of the home aide participants suggest that the sacrifice in personal time was perceived as worthwhile.

Guaranteed Hours and Full-time Work. A second, more critical area of conflict between agency operations and work life improvements was the "guaranteed hours" component. Scheduling of home aides was a nonmechanized, labor-intensive task that required administrative staff to take into account linguistic and personal compatibility between aides and clients; the geographical accessibility of clients; the mode of transportation available to aides; travel time between assignments; and the time-based needs of clients, such as early morning help in rising and dressing or early evening help in preparing for bed. Because scheduling was integral to the agencies' operations, it could not be delegated to outside consultants. Yet the scheduling of full-time work for anywhere between fifteen and fifty-five home aides participating in the Remedy and Quality Care demonstrations was sufficiently complex and time-consuming that it interfered with the routine scheduling operations of the supervisory staff.

The demonstration at Quality Care Syracuse called for scheduling forty hours of work each week for fifteen workers; the Remedy demonstration called for scheduling thirty-five hours of work each week for about fifty-five workers (thirty-four "current" workers and twenty-one "new" workers, all of whom had participated in the training programs). Neither agency had sufficient administrative staff to dedicate specific supervisors to implement the full-time work guarantee. Furthermore, even if they could have freed up the necessary staff time, there were other disincentives to implementing this component. As noted in the case studies and discussed below, changes in local market conditions led to declines in the demand for service. In the face of service contractions, assigning individual program participants full-time work could have required cutting the hours of other home aides and disrupting existing client-worker relationships—both counter to the operational goals of the agencies. Finally, also discussed in the case studies and in the next chapter, the program participants themselves sometimes rejected client assignments or cited transportation or other problems interfering with their ability to accept thirty-five or forty hours of work. Given these obstacles to implementation, it is not surprising that there was considerable slippage—particularly at the larger and more ambitious Remedy demonstration—in the objective of achieving full-time work for all demonstration participants.

Assignment of Program Participants to Difficult Clients. Another, smaller area of slippage was assignment of specially trained program participants at the two New York City home attendant agencies—Long Life and Independent Living—to the behaviorally and psychologically difficult clients whom they were trained to serve. The home aides who graduated from the training program received a $.30 per hour wage increment for continuing to serve difficult clients. However, during the course of the demonstration some of these clients were institutionalized or died, and their cases were closed. The objective of the project was to reassign the specially trained aides to other difficult cases when such events happened, but the agencies' field coordinators could not always find an available difficult case at the appropriate time.

Unless there were obvious problems with the status quo, the coordinators preferred not to remove an untrained worker from a difficult assignment to make room for a program participant, for to do so would conflict with established client-aide relationships and established agency routines. Furthermore, they wanted to avoid penalizing and possibly losing program participants by leaving them without work and unpaid until an appropriate reassignment could be made. So they assigned some program participants to routine cases (ineligible for the wage increment)—to some degree "wasting" the special training and invalidating the pay raise built into the demonstration. In such cases, the implementing agencies judged that the immediate benefits of maintaining existing service and employment arrangements outweighed any long-term benefits that might have accrued from adhering more closely to the objective of matching program participants to difficult clients.

The Impact of Local Fiscal, Political, and Market Conditions on Work Life Improvements

The preceding discussion illustrates how the organizational goals and capacity of the implementing agencies affected the implementation of the work life programs. Forces in the external environment were also critical to implementation, inasmuch as they constrained the range of acceptable changes and affected the capacity of the agencies to put acceptable options into practice. Those agencies that served solely public clients—that is, Remedy in San Diego and Long Life and Independent Living in New York City—were most constrained by the regulatory and fiscal policies of bureaucrats and politicians responsible for local home care programs. Those agencies that served a mix of public and private clients—that is, Quality Care Syracuse and Quality Care Milwaukee—were somewhat more insulated from local political and fiscal conditions. At the same time, they were more vulnerable to local market conditions and to changes in the policies of private third-party payers or other organizations that contracted for their services.

As noted in the case studies, state and local bureaucrats and politicians imposed major constraints on the work life changes implemented in San Diego and New York City. The San Diego County Department of Social Services, informal sponsor of the Remedy demonstration, vetoed a wage increment proposed by Remedy and the union because it did not want to be responsible for funding the increment beyond the life of the demonstration. It also vetoed a proposal to give the homemakers an expanded role in the client assessment process, fearing encroachment on the territory of county caseworkers. After approving a more modest demonstration plan offering guaranteed full-time work but no wage increment, the county then proceeded with business as usual and began to cut back on the number of cases and hours assigned to the Remedy contract—a tack it periodically took to avoid exceeding budgeted home care expenditures. The resulting decline in demand for Remedy services impeded efforts of the supervisory staff to assign full-time work to all program participants. Lastly, the competitive bidding process mandated by the state and employed by the county to award the exclusive In-Home Supportive Services contract stipulated no minimum employment package for the homemakers. The process thereby rewarded the bidder who trimmed wages, benefits, and other work life enhancements to submit the low bid. When Remedy lost the IHSS contract to the low bidder in December 1987, the training, support, and full-time work guarantee provided under the demonstration fell by the way.

Political and fiscal conditions also had a profound effect on the implementation of work life improvements in New York City. As the Long Life/Independent Living case study shows, state regulators objected to an initial proposal that would have created a new category of "senior" home attendant, specially trained and paid to perform a variety of medical tasks that were prohibited under existing regulations. The state explained that it was in the process of developing regulations for just such a worker (called a Level 3 worker in New York parlance), and the demonstration effort would be redundant or conflicting. The city Human Resources Administration and the participating agencies then developed and got permission to implement an alternative plan, providing special training and wage increments for home attendants serving behaviorally or psychologically difficult clients. That intervention—successfully implemented at Long Life and Independent Living—was acceptable to state regulators because it did not touch upon the medical responsibilities of the workers. Ironically, well after the demonstration ended, the state was still mired in political controversy over the tasks to be performed by Level 3 workers. Nursing groups, on one side, fought to limit the scope of home attendant practices, while advocates for the disabled, on the other, sought to expand the sphere of allowable aide activities. Meanwhile, implementation of the policy was stalled.

Despite political impediments to regulatory reform, for reasons described in the case study, the New York political climate during the period of the demonstration was generally conducive to proposals for improving employment conditions in the city's massive Medicaid-financed home attendant program. In the spring of 1988, the city and the state agreed to increase Medicaid reimbursement to cover a union-management settlement providing a nearly 40 percent wage increase over a one and a half year period, as well as greatly expanded health insurance benefits. Furthermore, the city included in its fiscal 1988-1989 budget funds to expand to roughly 7 percent of the caseload a special training and compensation program for workers serving behaviorally difficult or medically complex cases.[4] Because it bore the public stamp of approval of the unions, the home attendant agencies, the city's Human Resources Administration, the mayor, the governor, and the state Department of Social Services (whose Medicaid budget would supply the necessary funds), the precedent established by the wage and benefit package approved in 1988 was far more certain and secure than the outlook for the work life improvements embodied in the demonstration program.

Unlike Remedy and the New York City home attendant agencies, the Quality care agencies participating in the project derived their revenues from a mix of public and private payers, including individual elderly clients and their families. The Syracuse office benefited from New York State's relative largesse in financing home care, although county social service departments in the Syracuse area were far more conservative in authorizing home care expenditures than was New York City. Subcontracts with other private agencies, most notably the local Visiting Nurse Association, were also an important part of the Syracuse agency's business mix. When the VNA canceled its contract, the resulting decline in Quality Care's revenues forced a cut in office staff. After the end of the demonstration period, the Syracuse office manager also cut the vacation, sick leave, and health insurance benefits of the remaining program participants as part of the agency's general effort to reduce overhead in the face of declining service volume.

In Milwaukee, the Quality Care demonstration was never intended to be as large as in Syracuse. Even so, it was nipped in the bud as a result of changes in Blue Cross reimbursement that occurred just as the demonstration was getting underway. In August 1986, Wisconsin Blue Cross, which had the most generous home care payment coverage of virtually any private insurer in the United States, announced it was losing money and would reduce the number of covered home care visits from 365 per year to 40, while eliminating coverage for most custodial care. The financial impact on Quality Care Milwaukee was temporarily devastating, and only two home aides were enrolled in the Milwaukee demonstration for most of the demonstration period. While the agency eventually expanded its Medicaid business and recovered from the loss of Blue Cross revenues, major expansion of the staff aide program was not anticipated.

IMPLICATIONS

Four major findings on the adoption and implementation of work life improvements emerge from the case studies and the overview in this chapter. First, a variety of incentives, both positive and negative, motivated local sponsors and implementing agencies to look favorably upon upgrading the home aide's job. Second, despite interest in work life improvements, several major obstacles impeded their adoption. Third, the incentives motivating work life improvements were not powerful enough in themselves to overcome major obstacles to change. All significant work life changes were instituted in response to external stimuli. Fourth, extended support for work life changes was dependent on supportive conditions in the local environment.

The implications of these findings for the home care industry at large are (1) that home care providers will likely be responsive to future proposals for work life improvements, (2) that forces external to industry management may, nevertheless, provide the major impetus for change, and (3) that substantial and sustained improvements in employment conditions will require changes in the procurement and payment policies of government, private third-party payers, and others that contract for home care services.

Factors Facilitating Work Life Improvements

The local sponsors and implementing agencies had a variety of motives for supporting work life improvements. Occupants of key managerial roles at the corporate and agency level supported change and believed that upgrading employment conditions would help in recruiting workers and holding them acountable for delivering reliable service. Home care providers saw the potential for competitive advantages associated with a well-paid, full-time, mobile work force and gained prestige from acting as responsible employers. Occasionally, politicians saw the advantage of allying themselves with unions, workers, and management in support of better wages and benefits. Performance gaps created by worker shortages in some areas, by high turnover, and by mounting media criticism also created a climate conducive to change. At the outset of the project, however, none of these incentives had been sufficient to lead to major work life improvements at any of the demonstration sites.

Factors Impeding Work Life Changes

Working against change in the industry were risk aversiveness among corporate and agency managers, uncertainty about the costs and effects of work life improvements, limited capacity to implement any improvements that required substantial inputs of managerial and administrative resources, and significant financial dependence on government, private third-party payers, and other agencies that contracted for home care services. Adherence to low bid contracting in the California in-home services system imposed a tight constraint on possibilities for job enhancement. However, even state and local governments that used cost-based payment systems were disinclined to finance costly increases in wages or benefits unless, as in New York City, they were compelled to do so by the force of political events. One of the few private third-party payers—Blue Cross of Wisconsin—that generously funded home aide services, instead of financing industry improvements, sought to escape from its obligations after experiencing financial difficulties attributable to its home care coverage. Given the substantial costs involved in instituting work life improvements (ranging from about 6 percent to 17 percent of the agencies' billing or reimbursement rates in the three demonstrations), this reluctance to increase payment rates to upgrade employment conditions was a formidable obstacle to change.

The Role of External Forces in Promoting Change

Two sets of work life changes are reported in this book. The first set consists of the various job enhancements embodied in the demonstration programs. The second set consists of the substantial wage and benefit increases approved by New York City and state officials in 1988. Both sets of changes were instituted in direct response to external stimuli. The demonstration programs at Remedy, Quality Care, Long Life, and Independent Living were all a response to the offer of outside funding in exchange for instituting work life improvements. The changes in New York City were a response to the vigorous political and media campaign launched by the home attendants' unions.

Although the demonstration agencies were clearly interested in upgrading home care employment, none would have incurred the risks and costs of far-reaching work life improvements in the absence of outside funding. Moreover, none of the demonstrations continued in their original form after demonstration funding expired. The Remedy training, support, and guaranteed hours program collapsed after the county awarded the exclusive In-Home Supportive Services contract to Remedy's low-bidding competitor. At Quality Care, the Syracuse office withdrew the costly vacation, sick leave, and health insurance benefits that had been part of its staff aide demonstration. In New York City, Long Life and Independent Living stopped paying the $.30 per hour wage increment to specially trained demonstration participants, pending the appropriation and authorization of additional Medicaid funds by the city and the state. The loss of incremental wages was immediately apparent to the workers, who had received their supplemental pay in separate checks throughout the demonstration period. However, they could take consolation from the news they received in the spring of 1988 that city and state officials had approved a wage increase of $1.25 per hour along with substantial improvements in benefits.

The experiences of the demonstration agencies in Syracuse, Milwaukee, and San Diego, as well as in New York City, illustrate both the limits and the potential for significant and lasting work life reform in an industry where prices and revenues are tightly constrained by third-party payers and also by the limited resources of the typical self-paying client. However responsive the demonstration agencies were to opportunities for instituting work life improvements, the fate of such improvements ultimately lay in the hands of state and local policy makers, private insurers, and other organizations that purchased the bulk of home care services and indirecty paid the wages and benefits of much of the home aide work force.

Private insurers and purchasers of service—for example, Blue Cross or local VNAs—were, in turn, primarily concerned with their own solvency and their own competitive position in the community. They were not completely indifferent to quality of work life issues for the home aide work force, but such issues were not of high priority. Like private third-party payers, local policy makers were also primarily concerned with the fiscal implications of their purchase of service and payment policies, but fiscal considerations sometimes gave way to work life improvements when politics intervened.

Where, as in San Diego, state contributions to local home care expenditures were clearly circumscribed, where the supply of home aides was more or less sufficient, where the political culture was relatively conservative, and where publicly financed home care generally received little media attention, fiscal considerations tended to dominate policy making, and the short-term prospects for funding major work life improvements seemed dim. New York City and New York State, on the other hand, provided evidence that political forces could converge to create support for substantial work life improvements. Whether the popular support engendered by the coalition of unions, providers, and prominent politicians would be temporary or long-standing, it was clearly instrumental in achieving major gains for the home aide work force in New York City in 1988.

At the same time, similar alliances of advocacy groups, providers, and responsive politicians—concerned about the availability of home care workers and the quality of services provided—showed signs of emerging and capturing media attention in other areas, such as Boston, Los Angeles, New Jersey, northern Virginia, and Washington, D.C. (*Boston Globe,* 1987; County of Fairfax, 1988;

District of Columbia, 1988; Loth, 1987; *Record,* 1987; Weinstein, 1988). The emergence of these alliances fueled public concerns about employment conditions in the home care industry and offered additional evidence of the potential for political action to build support for work life improvements.

NOTES

1. Outside funding was a more important inducement to the implementing agencies than to the sponsors because it represented a more substantial portion of the agencies' budgets.
2. In September 1986, just as the New York City demonstration was getting underway, the police arrested a former home attendant in the murder of two elderly, handicapped women she had previously served. The home attendant subsequently pleaded guilty and admitted helping a man rob and kill the women to support a crack habit. The case received a good deal of publicity (McFadden, 1987).
3. To some extent, home attendant agencies in New York City are an exception to this statement. They do compete for workers in the low skilled labor market. There is some competition for HRA contracts, but HRA awards contracts to more than one agency in a given service area. Given the demand for home attendant services, the agencies don't need to compete for clients; there seem to be more than enough clients to fill each agency's caseload each week.
4. As of September 1988, however, plans for implementing this expanded program—based in part on the demonstration model—had not been formulated.

11

Overview: Worker Participation, Turnover, and Continuity of Care

Chapter 10 noted that one of the factors impeding adoption and implementation of work life improvements in the home care industry is uncertainty about their impact. This chapter attempts to reduce that uncertainty by providing an overview of the outcomes of the work life demonstrations. The effects of each are detailed in the three case studies (Remedy, Long Life/Independent Living, and Quality Care) presented in Part II of this book. This chapter summarizes those case study findings and discusses their implications.

The three major findings on worker participation and program effects are:

1. A significant proportion of home aides were either unwilling or unable to participate in the work life programs
2. A portion of those who did elect to participate subsequently dropped out—presumably because, contrary to expectation, the changes did not improve the quality of their work lives
3. Despite those who dropped out, the work life changes had a significant and apparently lasting impact on turnover among program participants

This chapter begins with a discussion of workers' decisions about whether or not to participate in the work life programs when offered the opportunity. Then it proceeds with a discussion of the factors that may have affected their decisions to drop out of the programs once enrolled. In both situations the full-time work component was a critical factor:

- Contrary to expectation, for a sizable portion of workers not already working full-time, the full-time work component was either a deterrent to program participation or a reason for dropping out. This suggests that a forty-, thirty-five-, or even thirty-hour week was not necessarily a work life improvement from the perspective of many in the work force.

After discussing participation and dropout rates, the chapter goes on to discuss program impacts. Even taking into account dropouts, the work life programs did have a significant impact on worker turnover and on continuity of care. The most important program outcomes (discussed in greater detail within the chapter) are the following:

- Each of the work life programs significantly reduced worker turnover. Depending on the site, program participants were 11 to 44 percent more likely to be on the job one year after the start of the demonstrations than their relevant control groups. Across all sites, there was a significant 16 percent difference in one-year turnover between program participants and controls.
- Continuity of care significantly improved in the one work life program that directly aimed to increase it. Program participants were 16 percent more likely than controls to be serving the same client at the one-year follow-up as at the start of the demonstration.

The final section of the chapter discusses findings relevant to the choice of target groups and components of work life programs. The most important findings of this section are the following:

- The effects of basic training and support (such as that provided by the Remedy program) were greatest for workers who worked twenty to twenty-nine hours per week (four to six hours per day). Basic training and support apparently had relatively little impact on the turnover of workers who worked more than thirty or fewer than twenty hours per week.[1]

  An important implication is that focusing such efforts on workers with a moderate work attachment (i.e., four to six hours per day) might have yielded greater benefits in terms of increased job commitment and reduced turnover.
- The one program that included new workers produced a 19 percent reduction in their turnover relative to controls. Nevertheless, the turnover of new worker program participants was higher than that of either current worker participants or controls. Thus the program's impact on new workers, while significant, was limited.
- The most comprehensive program had the highest acceptance rate among workers selected for participation and the greatest impact on the turnover of program participants. An important implication is that more comprehensive work life interventions aimed at the areas of greatest worker dissatisfaction may have the greatest overall impact.

WORKER PARTICIPATION IN THE WORK LIFE PROGRAMS

Each of the work life programs addressed one or more problems identified by management, union representatives, and the home aides themselves. These problems included deficiencies in training and support, pay and benefits, opportunities for advancement, and hours of work. Given the isolation of the home aide work force and evidence of their dissatisfaction with these aspects of the job,[2] the expectation was that there would be a high participation rate in the work life programs. In fact, the workers' response was mixed. Table 11.1 shows that the proportion of contacted workers who agreed to participate in the demonstrations ranged from a low of 25 percent of current workers at Remedy to a high of 78 percent of those contacted at Quality Care.

The difference at Remedy between current workers (i.e., those on the job for several months or more) and new workers (those who had worked no more than six weeks) was striking. Only 25 percent of current workers, compared to 64 percent of new workers, agreed to participate in the Remedy program. Perhaps the current workers had adapted to the status quo by taking on other jobs or lowering their job expectations, while new workers may have been more sanguine about the opportunities offered by the demonstration and freer to pursue them. The most salient features of the Remedy program were the training—specially geared to the experience of current or new workers—and the guaranteed thirty-five-hour workweek. About 35 percent of each group declined for reasons explicitly pertaining to the thirty-five-hour week—that is, conflict with another job, conflict with school, child care problems, and simply the wish not to work thirty-five hours per week (see Table 7.4 in the Remedy case study).

Table 11.1
Proportion of Workers Contacted Who Agreed to Participate

	Agreed	Declined	Total
Remedy			
Current workers	25% (34)	75% (100)	100% (134)
New workers	64% (21)	36% (12)	100% (33)
Total Remedy	33% (55)	67% (112)	100% (167)
Long Life & Independ. Living*	67% (100)	33% (50)	100% (150)
Quality Care* **	78% (18)	22% (5)	100% (23)

*Long Life, Independent Living, and Quality Care demonstrations included only current workers.

**Includes both Syracuse and Milwaukee workers.

Another 13 to 17 percent declined because they didn't want to participate in the training component. The remaining 50 percent or so cited a variety of reasons, including transportation problems, illness or death in the family, lack of interest, inconvenience, etc. Thus, despite the fact that more than two-thirds of Remedy current workers responding to the baseline survey said they would like to work thirty-five hours or more per week, only a quarter of those actually offered the opportunity chose or were able to take advantage of it.

The acceptance rates at Long Life/Independent Living and at Quality Care[3] were much higher. The work life program at Long Life/Independent Living neither offered nor required longer hours on the part of participating home attendants. Except for training and support sessions scheduled for a series of Saturdays, the program did not interfere with other job, school, or personal time commitments the home attendants might have. It did offer special training to deal with the problems of difficult clients—problems that were probably quite salient to the workers, who were already assigned to such clients. Furthermore, the demonstration provided a $.30 per hour wage increment for continuing to serve difficult clients after "graduation." Unless the worker had difficulties in attending the training sessions, she could hardly go wrong by agreeing to participate in the demonstration.

The highest proportion (78 percent) of workers agreeing to participate was at Quality Care. However, two qualifications to this statement are in order. First, the Syracuse office manager had sent out fliers, posted notices, and paid for newspaper advertisements describing the staff aide program, its forty-hour workweek, and its generous vacation, sick leave, and health insurance benefits. She had anticipated an enthusiastic response but received few inquiries. Second, those finally offered the staff aide positions were randomly drawn from a preselected group chosen by the office manager and her staff on the basis of experience, reliability, and perceived willingness to take on challenging tasks. Thus they represented a small portion of the Syracuse home aide work force rather than the typical worker.

Notwithstanding these qualifications, the Syracuse program might have been expected to elicit the most positive worker response, inasmuch as it combined improvements in the four work life areas generally cited as the source of greatest worker dissatisfaction—pay, benefits, opportunities for advancement, and hours of work.[4] Of these four areas, the Remedy program addressed hours and, to a lesser extent, benefits; the Long Life/Independent Living program addressed pay and opportunities for advancement; but only the Quality Care program offered higher pay, better benefits, promotion, and full-time work.

PROGRAM DROPOUTS

Program participants became program dropouts in two ways—by dropping out of either the training or the guaranteed work component. Table 11.2 summarizes dropout data for the two programs with training components. Only one of thirty-

Table 11.2
Training Program Dropouts

	Graduates	Dropouts	Total
Remedy			
Current workers	97% (33)	3% (1)	100% (34)
New workers	67% (14)	33% (7)	100% (21)
Total Remedy	85% (47)	15% (8)	100% (55)
Long Life & Independ. Living	100 (100)	0 (0)	100% (100)
Quality Care		Not Applicable	

four participants dropped out of Remedy's training program for current workers, but a third of the twenty-one new workers dropped out of the training program designed for them. Thus, although current workers were less willing to participate in the first place, they were much more likely to stick with the training program once they had committed themselves to participating.

The training program implemented at Long Life/Independent Living was extremely successful in terms of worker participation. Virtually all of the participants attended virtually all of the sessions, even though many were on weekends, and all of the participants graduated. The promise of a $.30 per hour wage increment contingent upon graduating was a tangible incentive undoubtedly contributing to the 100 percent completion rate.

Long Life and Independent Living training graduates were also loyal program participants throughout the course of the demonstration. The Long Life/ Independent Living program did not entail a full-time work requirement, although the overwhelming majority of program participants—like most other workers at those agencies—worked at least thirty-five hours per week. The training graduates could have dropped out of the program by declaring they no longer wanted to serve difficult clients, but none did. Instead, some asked to change to another client, citing a variety of reasons for their requests. In some cases these home attendants were assigned to difficult clients and remained eligible for the wage increment; in other cases, they were assigned to a routine case and became ineligible for the increment until reassigned to another difficult case. Of one hundred program graduates in total and twenty-one who changed clients during the demonstration year, only four actually requested the change (see Table 8.3, Long Life/Independent Living case study). The rest changed cases because of case closings or client requests.

In contrast, the full-time work components of the Remedy and Quality Care programs were a major source of dropouts. Table 11.3 summarizes data on Remedy and Quality Care participants who left those programs because of inability or unwillingness to meet the thirty-five- or forty-hour[5] full-time work requirement.

Although all program participants at each site had agreed in advance to work thirty-five or forty hours per week on a regular basis in exchange for a guarantee of full-time pay, a number subsequently declined to accept the full complement of client assignments. At Remedy, three months after the end of training, 23 percent of training graduates (eleven out of forty-seven) had decided they did not want to work thirty-five hours per week (see Table 7.6, Remedy case study).[6] These workers never formally dropped out of the program, and Remedy never labeled them dropouts; they kept their special uniforms and identification badges and were simply paid for the hours they worked. However, for the purposes of this analysis, they are included in the dropout category to illustrate the extent of worker inability or unwillingness to adhere to the full-time work commitment.

The number of Remedy training graduates who found it difficult to adjust to the thirty-five-hour week may have been even greater than the eleven workers cited above. As the case study indicates, a full fifteen months after the end of training, there were an additional five homemakers who reportedly wanted to

Table 11.3
Number and Percent Dropouts from the Full-time Work Requirement

	Dropouts
Remedy	
All training graduates (Total 47)	23% (11)
Quality Care	
Both sites (Total 22)	41% (9)
Remedy & Quality Care (Total 69)	29% (20)
Long Life & Independ. Living	Not Applicable

work thirty-five hours per week but were assigned fewer hours by Remedy and paid only for the hours they worked (see Table 7.6, Remedy case study). It is possible that Remedy supervisors were demonstrating bad faith in distributing client assignments. However, the supervisors reported that these workers could not be assigned the full complement of hours because they couldn't be contacted when needed or because they declined assignments, citing transportation, child care problems, and the like. Thus, even though these workers may have wanted to work full-time, they may have acted otherwise.

Adhering to the full-time work requirement also proved problematic for a number of program participants at Quality Care. Five participants at the Syracuse and Milwaukee agencies dropped out of the staff aide program in its first two weeks—all citing problems with the work schedule. During the course of the demonstration, the Syracuse office manager lowered the work requirement from forty to thirty hours per week, but four more dropped out of the Syracuse program—either voluntarily or at the request of the agency—because they could not work the required number of hours. In the Quality Care demonstration, workers lost the wage increments and the benefits that accompanied staff aide status when they dropped out of the program. Thus they incurred a substantial penalty for falling below thirty hours of work per week. Nevertheless, nine staff aides in total (41 percent of program participants at the two agencies) made the decision not to work full-time (see Table 11.3).

The sizable portion of Remedy and Quality Care workers for whom the full-time work commitment was either a burden or a deterrent to program participation suggests that, at least in the short run, a forty-, thirty-five-, or even thirty-hour week was not necessarily a work life improvement from the perspective of many in the home aide work force. These workers may have wanted full-time work. Indeed, some of them were already working full-time by taking additional part-time jobs to supplement the hours worked at their primary place of employment. Perhaps if the opportunity for full-time work had been presented before they had made other commitments, they would have taken it. Others were coping with personal or family problems that interfered with a full-time work schedule. Some workers, reliant on public transportation, preferred to work fewer hours rather than travel lengthy distances between clients on a daily basis.[7] Still others, especially those aides who were expected to serve weekend, short-hour, and short-notice cases, found working full-time to be extremely stressful. As the Quality Care case study shows, the additional stress and responsibility associated with their promotion to staff aide status led some of the Syracuse program participants to feel increased dissatisfaction with their pay, despite the fact that the staff aide job carried a wage increment of $.50 per hour in addition to expanded benefits (see Table 9.12, Quality Care case study). The fact that six of the eight Syracuse dropouts continued to work for the agency after leaving the program suggests that they were grateful for the opportunity to experiment with full-time work but preferred a less demanding schedule.

THE IMPACT OF WORK LIFE CHANGES ON TURNOVER AND CONTINUITY OF CARE

Each of the work life programs had a significant impact on worker turnover, even taking into account the experience of dropouts. Table 11.4 summarizes follow-up data (including all program dropouts) presented in each of the case studies. It shows that, depending on the demonstration site, program participants

Table 11.4
Turnover Analysis—One-Year Follow-up, All Demonstration Sites

	Program Participants	Controls	Percent Difference
Remedy			
Current workers			
On the job	82% (28)	71% (24)*	11%
Inactive	18% (6)	29% (10)*	
New workers			
On the job	38% (8)	19% (7)	19%
Inactive	62% (13)	81% (30)	
Current & new workers combined			
On the job	65% (36)	44% (31)	21%
Inactive	35% (19)	56% (40)	
[Chi Square = 6.0; p <.02.]			
Long Life/Independent Living			
On the job	84% (84)	73% (104)	11%
Inactive	16% (16)	27% (38)	
[Chi Square = 4.0; p <.05.]			
Quality Care **			
On the job	77% (17)	33% (7)	44%
Inactive	23% (5)	67% (14)	
[Chi Square = 8.4; p <.01.]			

*Matched controls--see discussion in Remedy case study
**Includes both Syracuse and Milwaukee workers

were 11 to 44 percent more likely to be on the job one year after the start of the work life programs than their relevant control groups.

Perhaps the most striking finding of Table 11.4 is the greater difference between program participants and controls achieved by the Quality Care program compared to the other interventions. One factor contributing to the greater reduction in turnover at Quality Care may have been that turnover was somewhat higher to begin with. Only 33 percent of the Quality Care controls were on the job at the one-year follow-up point, compared to 44 percent of combined current and new worker controls at Remedy and more than 70 percent of controls at Long Life and Independent Living. The one-year turnover rates of Quality Care and Remedy controls (new and current workers combined) were close to the popularly cited industrywide turnover rate of 60 percent (Surpin, November 1987), while the turnover rate of Long Life and Independent Living controls was far lower. A second factor may have been the small size and relatively high degree of attention accorded the Quality Care program participants. With only three staff aides in Milwaukee and no more than fifteen at one time in Syracuse, program participants had the opportunity for closer personal contact with each other than did participants in San Diego or New York City. Furthermore, the office manager herself met regularly with the Syracuse staff aides, while program participants at the other sites rarely if ever had personal contact with the agency director. A third factor contributing to the greater reduction in turnover at Quality Care may have been that the Quality Care program embodied a more comprehensive set of work life changes than the other demonstrations. Because the numbers of workers involved in the Quality Care programs are small, cautious interpretation of the turnover data is necessary.

Table 11.5 aggregates the one-year follow-up data for all of the sites and shows a 16 percent difference overall between all program participants and all controls. The combined control groups at all demonstration sites had a one-year turnover rate of 39 percent, compared to a rate of only 23 percent for all

Table 11.5
Turnover Analysis—One-Year Follow-up, Aggregate Data—All Demonstration Sites

	Program Participants	Controls	Percent Difference
On the job	77% (137)	61% (142)	16%
Inactive	23% (40)	39% (92)	

[Chi Square = 12.9; $p<.001$.]

program participants. As can be seen from the table, this difference is statistically significant at the .001 level.

Eighteen-month follow-up data are available for only two of the three sites—Remedy and Quality Care. These data, presented in Table 11.6, show a sustained effect in turnover on all but the Remedy new worker group, whose turnover had steeply increased by the end of eighteen months. (Possible reasons for increased turnover among new workers are discussed in the section on new workers.) At the eighteen-month follow-up point, the Remedy demonstration was still in effect insofar as the training graduates were still eligible for full-time work and support groups were still meeting informally (see the Remedy case study). As described in the Quality Care case study, the staff aide program was also still in effect, although the Syracuse program had been trimmed. At the eighteen-month follow-up point, the Syracuse staff aides were still eligible for

Table 11.6
Turnover Analysis—18-Month Follow-up, Two Demonstration Sites

	Program Participants	Controls	Percent Difference
Remedy			
Current workers On the job	74% (25)	56% (19)*	18%
Inactive	26% (9)	44% (15)*	
New workers On the job	14% (3)	11% (4)	3%
Inactive	86% (18)	89% (33)	
Current & new Workers combined On the job	51% (28)	32% (23)	19%
Inactive	49% (27)	68% (48)	
Long Life/Independent Living	Not Available		
Quality Care ** On the job	73% (16)	19% (4)	54%
Inactive	27% (6)	81% (17)	

*Matched controls--see discussion in Remedy case study
**Includes both Syracuse and Milwaukee workers

full-time work and were still earning the $.50 per hour wage increment, but they no longer received the generous vacation pay, sick leave, and health insurance benefits they had received during the twelve-month demonstration period. Given these modifications in the program, the lasting effects of the demonstration are all the more remarkable.

Table 11.7 aggregates the eighteen-month follow-up data for Remedy and Quality Care and shows a 28 percent difference in turnover between program participants and controls. Thus the aggregate impact of the two demonstrations was even stronger at the eighteen-month point than at the one-year follow-up, despite the declining impact on the Remedy new worker group.

A major assumption underlying all the work life programs was that reduced turnover would improve continuity of care for clients insofar as stable workers tended to stay with the same cases over time. The Long Life/Independent Living program actually tested this proposition by measuring—in addition to turnover—the rate of client reassignments among program participants and controls. A prime objective of the program was to improve continuity of care for the difficult clients who were the focus of the training component. At the one-year follow-up point, the program had proved effective in achieving this objective: 63 percent of program participants, compared to only 46 percent of controls, were still serving the same difficult client to whom they had been assigned a year earlier—a 17 percent difference (see discussion in Long Life/Independent Living case study and Table 11.8). Furthermore, more than 60 percent of the program participants who changed clients during the period of the demonstration did so because the clients were institutionalized or had died and/or because the case was closed—all conditions pretty much beyond the control of the home attendants. In contrast, nearly two-thirds of the controls changed cases because either they or their clients requested a change (see Table 11.9). An important inference is that the controls were much more likely than

Table 11.7
Turnover Analysis—18-Month Follow-up, Aggregate Data—Two Demonstration Sites*

	Program Participants	Controls	Percent Difference
On the job	57% (44)	29 % (27)	28%
Inactive	43% (33)	71% (65)	

[Chi Square = 13.4; $p<.001$.]

*Remedy and Quality Care (Remedy matched controls)

Table 11.8
Long Life and Independent Living, Continuity of Care Among Program Participants and Controls at One-Year Follow-up

	Participants	Controls	Difference
Same Client	63 (63%)	66 (46%)	17%
Different Client	21 (21%)	38 (27%)	6%
Inactive	16 (16%)	38 (27%)	11%
Total	100 (100%)	142 (100%)	

(Chi Square = 6.9, p <.05 with 2 degrees of freedom.)

Table 11.9
Reasons for Changing Clients: Comparison of Program Participations and Controls at One-Year Follow-up

	Participants	Controls	Difference
Client died/hospitalized/ case closed	13 (62%)	13 (34%)	28%
Change requested by Client or Home Attendant	8 (38%)*	25 (66%)**	
	21 (100%)	38 (100%)	

[Chi Square = 4.1, p <.05 with 1 degree of freedom.]

*Of these, 4 changes were requested by home attendants, and 4 by clients.
**Of these, 14 were requested by home attendants, and 9 by clients.

program participants to have changed clients because of circumstances that could have been addressed had they benefited from the training, support, and wage differential for serving difficult clients.

What happened to the program participants who did change clients? Because they were specially trained to serve difficult cases, the expectation was that if their original case closed, they would be reassigned to another difficult case.

Contrary to expectation, however, this reassignment occurred little more than half the time. As described in the case study, one obstacle to reassigning program participants to difficult cases was that supervisory staff did not always have another difficult case available when a program participant needed reassignment. Rather than risk losing skilled and reliable workers by putting them "on hold" (without pay) until more appropriate difficult cases could be found, the supervisors preferred to reassign them to routine cases. One implication is that the availability of transitional funds to pay program participants until appropriate reassignments could be made might have facilitated the matching process.

Use of such a transitional mechanism might also have reduced turnover. Both program participants and controls with open cases were about 10 percent more likely to be on the job at the one-year follow-up than their counterparts whose cases had closed. The implication here is that reductions in turnover among seasoned workers—whether or not specially trained—might have been achieved by providing transitional pay to home attendants who found themselves out of a job because their clients died or experienced a decline in health, sending them to a hospital or a nursing home.

TARGET GROUPS AND PROGRAM COMPONENTS

Some of the project's findings have implications for "targeting" programs and for combining various program components. The outcome data available from the Remedy program suggest (1) that basic training and support programs may be most effective when focused on workers with a moderate job attachment (four to six hours per day) and (2) that programs focused on new workers can be effective in reducing turnover among this high turnover group. Comparison of outcomes across the demonstrations suggests that comprehensive interventions may be more effective than those that address more limited aspects of work.

Job Attachment

The Remedy work life program had a selective impact on workers, depending on how many hours per week they worked. "Moderate hours" workers—those homemakers who worked an average of twenty to twenty-nine hours per week (four to six hours per day)—were the ones most affected by participation in the program. Homemakers who averaged thirty or more hours per week had very low turnover rates regardless of whether or not they participated in the demonstration; homemakers who averaged fewer than twenty hours per week had relatively high turnover rates—again regardless of whether or not they participated in the demonstration. A nearly full-time schedule (i.e., thirty hours or more per week) was apparently more important than training and support in influencing turnover. Furthermore, at the opposite end of the full-time/part-time continuum, the training and support apparently did little to mitigate the effects of very part-time work.

In contrast, program participation made a big difference for workers in the twenty- to twenty-nine-hour group. Table 11.10 shows that 88 percent of program participants in this group were still on the job at the eighteen-month follow-up, compared to only 55 percent of matched controls—a 33 percent difference. An important implication is that focusing training and support efforts on workers with a moderate work attachment (i.e., four to six hours per day) may yield the greatest benefits in terms of increased commitment and reduced turnover.

New Workers

The Remedy data on new workers (see Tables 11.2, 11.4, and 11.6) indicate the magnitude of the turnover problem among these workers and the difficulty of designing effective programs for them. However, the data also provide evidence that high turnover in this group can be reduced.

Table 11.10
18-Month Follow-up, Remedy Program Participants and Matched Controls: Hours of Service During Demonstration Period

Medium Hours*

	Program Participants	Matched Controls	Difference
Working	14 (88%)	6 (55%)	33%
Inactive	2 (12%)	5 (45%)	
	16 (100%)	11 (100%)	

[Chi Square = 3.6; p <.1.]

*Medium hours = 20-29 hours per week on average.

	High Hours** Program Participants	High Hours** Matched Controls	Low Hours*** Program Participants	Low Hours*** Matched Controls
Working	8 (80%)	8 (100%)	3 (38%)	5 (33%)
Inactive	2 (20%)	0	5 (62)	10 (67%)
	10 (100%)	8 (100%)	8 (100%)	15 (100%)

[Chi Square = 1.8; p <.3.] [Chi Square = 0.]

**High hours = 30 hours per week or more on average.
***Low hours = fewer than 20 hours per week on average.

As described in the case study, one-third (seven) of the twenty-one new workers dropped out before the training program ended, and all had terminated by the six-month follow-up point. These may have been individuals who were simply not suited to the work, and after making that discovery, they left. If so, an argument can be made that their seven training slots were wasted and that it would have been far more efficient to screen them out of the program in the first place. The problem is that no screening criteria existed.

Forty-three percent of the new workers (six out of fourteen) who finished the training program left during the following year—all before the delayed start-up of their relevant English- or Spanish-speaking support group (see the case study, Chapter 7). It is possible that the immediate availability of a support group for training graduates, unaccustomed as they were to the job, might have averted some of their turnover.

Nevertheless, durng the one-year follow-up period the program had a discernible impact even in the absence of the support component. Including the dropouts in the analysis, the difference in one-year turnover between participants and controls was 19 percent (see Table 11.4). If the dropouts are excluded and only training graduates are considered, the difference is twice as large (38 percent) and quite significant. Table 11.11 shows that at the one-year follow-up, 57 percent of new worker training graduates were on the job, compared to only 19 percent of new worker controls.

An optimistic interpretation of these data would emphasize that the reduction in turnover for new training graduates (38 percent) was 27 percent greater than the reduction for current worker training graduates (11 percent) (see Table 11.4).[8] A negative interpretation of the data would emphasize that the 43 percent turnover rate among the new worker training graduates was still a great deal higher than the 18 percent turnover rate among current worker training graduates and higher even than the 29 percent turnover rate among the current worker matched controls (see Table 11.4). Thus the program's effect on new workers' turnover was clearly limited.

During the subsequent six-month follow-up period, the turnover rate of the

Table 11.11
Remedy New Workers: Training Graduates Only, Turnover Analysis—One-Year Follow-up

	Program Graduates	Controls	Percent Difference
On the job	57% (8)	19% (7)	38%
Inactive	43% (6)	81% (30)	

[Chi Square = 5.5; p<.02. Chi Square was corrected for small cell size.]

new worker training graduates increased dramatically. Table 11.12 shows that by the eighteen-month follow-up point, only 21 percent of the training graduates (three out of fourteen) were still on the job. Their turnover rate had increased to 79 percent, just 10 percent lower than the 89 percent rate of the new worker controls. This 10 percent difference was smaller than the 18 percent difference between current training graduates and controls at the eighteen-month measurement point.

As noted in the Remedy case study, it is difficult to interpret these findings in the absence of exit interview or questionnaire information about leavers' reasons for leaving. One explanation for the falloff in program effects on new workers after the one-year follow-up may be that the benefits of training and support attenuated over time.[9] If that explanation were the case, however, they should have attenuated for current workers as well, and that result apparently didn't happen.

Another explanation may be related to the work schedules of the new workers. Those training graduates who left the job during the eighteen-month follow-up period worked an average of only thirteen hours per week before they left, while those who stayed on the job were working an average of thirty-four hours per week (see Table 11.13). However, this explanation is also problematic. On the one hand, working relatively few hours per week may have undermined the job commitment of the program participants—in particular, because they had been promised thirty-five hours per week of work—and therefore contributed to their turnover. On the other hand, it is possible that these program participants started out with (or subsequently developed) a relatively weak commitment to the job and that their short workweek was a result of their desire to leave rather than a cause.

Piecemeal versus Comprehensive Work Life Programs

A final implication, based on data from all the demonstrations, is that more comprehensive work life programs and programs aimed at the areas of greatest

Table 11.12
Remedy New Workers: Training Graduates Only, Turnover Analysis—18-Month Follow-up

	Program Graduates	Controls	Percent Difference
On the job	21% (3)	11% (4)	10%
Inactive	79% (11)	89% (33)	

[Chi Square = .5; not significant. Chi Square was corrected for small cell size.]

Table 11.13
Remedy New Workers: Average Weekly Hours of Service During Demonstration Period

	Training Graduates	Controls
Working at 18 mos.	Mean = 34 hrs. Median = 40 hrs. N = 3	Mean = 25 hrs. Median = 31 hrs. N = 4
Inactive at 18 mos.	Mean = 13 hrs. Median = 16 hrs. N = 11	Mean = 14 hrs. Median = 11 hrs. N = 33

worker dissatisfaction might have increased the impact of the programs overall. The job satisfaction data collected from the home aide surveys indicated three major and two minor sources of employee dissatisfaction. The three major worker concerns were pay, benefits, and opportunities for advancement. A third to a half of all survey respondents expressed dissatisfaction with these aspects of the job. The two minor areas of concern were hours of work and training and support. Fifteen to 20 percent of the respondents expressed dissatisfaction with these. As implemented, the Remedy program primarily effected changes in training and support and secondarily in hours of work and benefits. Thus, it really addressed just one of the three major sources of worker dissatisfaction and only marginally at that. The Long Life/Independent Living program provided better pay, an opportunity for advancement, and special training and support. Thus, it addressed two of the three major sources of dissatisfaction. Only the Quality Care program provided better pay, better benefits, promotion, and full-time work. Thus, it addressed all three of the work life issues identified by the home aide work force as major sources of dissatisfaction.

A review of the data on worker participation in the three demonstrations (Table 11.1) shows that the Remedy program had the lowest acceptance rate among workers contacted and Quality Care the highest—a finding consistent with the notion that the most attractive program was the one offering the greatest change in the areas of greatest worker concern. A review of the data on program dropouts (Tables 11.2 and 11.3) shows that Quality Care also had the highest overall dropout rate—almost certainly because the full-time work schedule was more rigorously implemented than at Remedy. Finally, a review of the data on program effects (Table 11.4) shows that despite its relatively high dropout rate, the Quality Care program had a far greater impact on worker turnover than either of the other two work life programs. Turnover among Quality Care program participants was 44 percent lower than among Quality Care controls, while the comparable differences at Remedy and at Long Life and Independent

Living were 21 percent (combined Remedy current and new workers) and 11 percent, respectively.

As discussed above, several factors may have contributed to the greater impact at Quality Care, including a higher level of turnover in the first place. However, at least some of the difference may have been attributable to the comprehensive and powerful set of work life changes implemented at Quality Care. Given the relatively low one-year turnover rates of 29 percent among current worker controls at Remedy and 27 percent among controls at Long Life and Independent Living, the fact that the less comprehensive programs at those sites reduced turnover even further is quite remarkable. Had more comprehensive or more potent changes been implemented at either of those sites, quite possibly the overall impact of the work life programs would have been greater than the 16 percent reduction in turnover across all sites (see Table 11.5).

NOTES

1. Basic training is distinguished here from specialized training, such as that provided by the Long Life/Independent Living demonstration. The latter demonstration, devoted to developing and rewarding special skills for serving difficult clients, reduced turnover and increased continuity of care among program participants who generally worked thirty-five hours a week or more, usually on a single case.
2. See Chapters 4, 7, 8, and 9 for discussion of workers' attitudes toward their jobs.
3. Both demonstrations included current workers only.
4. See Chapter 4 for survey data on worker attitudes.
5. Full-time work was defined as thirty-five hours per week at Remedy and forty hours per week at Quality Care.
6. At the end of three months, an additional 17 percent (eight) of the forty-seven training graduates had become inactive. These workers are counted in the turnover statistics but are not classified as dropouts.
7. All Remedy workers and all of the staff aides at Quality Care were paid for time spent traveling between clients. However, in many, if not most, home care agencies, workers are not paid for travel time. Thus to receive pay for eight hours of work, they might have to spend as many as ten or more hours on the job, depending on the number and location of clients they served. This fact could be a major deterrent to agreeing to full-time work.
8. Table 11.4 presents data on all thirty-four current worker program participants, including the one program dropout. If the dropout is excluded to make the analysis comparable to the analysis of new worker training graduates, the number of current worker training graduates becomes thirty-three and the number of those active becomes twenty-seven. The turnover rate of this group remains the same—82 percent. The outcome data remain the same at the eighteen-month follow-up.
9. Remedy did continue to convene informal support groups throughout the demonstration period, but these were neither as frequent nor as focused as those conducted by the UCSD Medical Center consultants.

PART IV

Recommendations and Policy Implications

12

Summary

Previous chapters have identified the critical factors affecting working conditions and job satisfaction among the home aide work force, discussed the feasibility of work life programs for these workers, and assessed their impact. In preparation for the final chapter of recommendations for managers and policy makers, this chapter briefly summarizes the book's major findings about the work force, the job, the home care industry, and the feasibility and impact of work life programs designed to reduce worker turnover and improve continuity of care.

MAJOR FINDINGS

Workers and Working Conditions

The data amassed in Chapters 2 and 3 graphically illustrate the effects of labor market segregation in the home care industry. Typical of women in gender-segregated jobs, the workers responding to the home aide survey were almost entirely (98 percent) female, disproportionately minority (56 percent), poorly educated (nearly 40 percent had not graduated from high school), single (nearly 60 percent), primary providers for their family (65 percent), and low income (45 percent reported family income under $10,000 in 1985).

The home aide's job, like most jobs in the secondary labor market, is generally part-time and offers low wages, few benefits, minimal training, little job security, and little opportunity for advancement. Although the job allows the worker to feel personally responsible for her work, provides feedback, and is believed to be intrinsically meaningful and worthwhile (see Chapter 3), employment conditions are poor. Work life problems documented by the home aide survey and by the case studies (see Chapters 2, 7, 8, and 9) include low wage levels and lack of wage parity (median hourly wage was about $4.30 in 1985, below the wage of aides in institutions); part-time, episodic work (more than half the workers worked fewer than thirty-five hours per week, and nearly 40 percent worked fewer than twenty-five); inadequate benefits (fewer than 20 percent of survey respondents, for example, had health insurance coverage through their employer or union); minimal training and support (none of the demonstration agencies and few of the comparison agencies provided sixty hours of training for home aides, as recommended by the national accrediting body, nor did any of the agencies provide significant organizational support for the workers, who often had to deal with physically and/or emotionally demanding clients).

Factors Affecting Job Satisfaction and Turnover

With the survey of more than 1,200 workers in five cities, it has been possible to document what heretofore have been anecdotal descriptors of factors affecting home aide satisfaction and turnover. The models described in Chapter 4 indicate that youth, loneliness, and dissatisfaction with pay and benefits were the major determinants of aides' intent to turnover. As has been found in other studies, younger workers were more likely than older workers to express intent to leave. Aside from lower job mobility in general, which seems to be associated with increasing age, older workers may have lower job expectations, lesser financial needs, or greater investment in the job.

Another principal determinant of intent to leave—a finding unique (though not unsurprising) to the study of home aides—was loneliness. The home aide lacks organizational support (e.g., a facility in which she regularly works, colleagues she regularly sees, supervisors who regularly provide instruction and feedback). Thus, loneliness or feeling isolated on the job appears to be one of the structural or inherent conditions of home care. Nevertheless, feelings of isolation were directly impacted by perceived training adequacy (or inadequacy). Apparently, agencies can mitigate workers' perceptions of loneliness—an important finding for managers and one borne out by the success of the work life demonstrations.

The third major determinant of intent to leave was dissatisfaction with pay and benefits. Consistent with other studies of worker turnover, monetary rewards and other material aspects of the job significantly affected the turnover intentions of survey respondents. Improvements in this area ought to contribute to a more stable work force, and the demonstrations provide sound evidence that this result is the case.

With regard to factors affecting workers' job satisfaction, positive attitudes about pay and benefits, supervisor supportiveness, and task variety all had significant positive and direct effects. Furthermore, in all the explanatory models of workers' satisfaction and intent to leave (see Chapter 4), supervisor supportiveness had both direct and indirect effects—making this component of the job an extremely important one for agency managers concerned with the quality of work life.

Finally, the impact of race on worker perceptions was found to have important—and disturbing—implications. Findings from the survey indicate that black workers were more likely to perceive the job as monotonous, were less closely bonded to their clients, were more likely to perceive pay inequities, and were less satisfied with their work than were white workers. The data suggest that black workers may experience particular difficulties on the job and that some may be "stuck" in home care for reasons of discrimination or lack of skills, education, or opportunity.

Financial Conditions in the Industry

Addressing work life problems requires the investment of resources in better training and supervision, higher compensation, adequate benefits, redesign of jobs to enhance worker satisfaction, and development of opportunities for advancement. However, the financial data presented in Chapter 5 indicate that the home care industry itself is not in strong financial health and is therefore unlikely to invest much in work life improvements without support from outside sources. Of ten publicly owned for-profit companies, for example, only three indicated consistently positive profitability over a multiyear period.[1] The analysis pointed to the combined forces of public policy cost containment, frail elderly poverty, and overly rapid, poorly capitalized expansion as factors constraining the financial capacity of the industry.

Feasibility and Impact of Work Life Programs

The work life demonstrations were designed to assess the potential for improving employment conditions at the bottom of the home care hierarchy. In this respect, they were a clear success. As the case studies (Chapters 7, 8, and 9) and the two overview chapters (Chapters 10 and 11) attest, each of the demonstrations effected change in one or more key aspects of work life—(1) training and support, (2) wages and benefits, (3) hours of work, and (4) status and promotion. Furthermore, each of the demonstrations had a significant impact on the turnover of participating workers. The demonstrations provide a wealth of evidence that the potential exists for instituting effective work life changes in the home care industry—changes that will improve quality of work life and continuity of care. At the same time, the case studies make abundantly clear that to realize this potential will require overcoming substantial organizational, financial, and political barriers.

Feasibility One factor common to all the demonstrations was the agencies' relatively passive role—that is, all the agencies responded to outside stimuli, rather than initiating work life changes of magnitude on their own. Major inducements to participate included outside funding, the potential to reduce worker turnover, the potential to increase service volume (and therefore revenues), possible competitive advantages (vis-à-vis other home care agencies), favorable publicity, political considerations, and altruistic concern for the workers (Chapter 10). Working against change were risk aversiveness among corporate and agency managers and uncertainty about the costs and effects of work life changes.

To implement the work life demonstrations successfully, the agencies had to shift from their passive role in the site selection process to an active role in promoting work life changes. A second factor common to the demonstrations was the strain this active role imposed on organizational resources and the conflict it sometimes engendered with operational goals (Chapter 10). None of the agencies had internal staff with both the time and the experience to run the training and support components. They had to rely on outside consultants or subcontractors to provide these services. Even so, the training and support components interrupted the daily work flow of the agencies and as a consequence were burdensome to both managers and workers. Scheduling full-time work and matching specially trained aides to appropriate clients also strained the agencies' staff resources.

The third factor common to all the demonstrations was the vulnerability of the work life changes to conditions in the local environment. Those agencies that exclusively served public clients were most vulnerable to the regulatory and fiscal policies of bureaucrats and politicians responsible for local home care programs. State licensing policies affected the definition of the home aide's job and constrained efforts to expand and upgrade the scope of work (San Diego and New York). State and local funding policies determined whether or not wage differentials could be implemented as part of the demonstrations (yes in New York and no in San Diego) and whether or not they would be extended beyond the life of the demonstration (no in New York, at least in the short run). Fiscal constraints also produced periodic cutbacks in service that, in addition to affecting clients, limited the ability of employers to assign full-time work to program participants. Even where workers were unionized, the contract between agencies and government payers (not the labor-management contract) was the ultimate determinant of the wage and benefit package. Where political conditions fostered fiscal conservatism (e.g., in California), the short-term prospects for work life improvement seemed dim. On the other hand, where political conditions fostered an alliance of labor, management, advocacy groups, and public officials concerned over access and quality (e.g., in New York), significant upgrading took place.

Those agencies that served a mix of public and private clients (the Quality Care agencies) were somewhat more insulated from local political and fiscal conditions than those agencies completely reliant on public funds. However, they were more vulnerable to local market conditions and to changes in the policies of private third-party payers or other organizations that contracted for their services. At the Syracuse agency the loss of a private contract to local competitors reduced volume and revenues, creating pressure to reduce overhead by eliminating the richer benefit package instituted as part of the demonstration. At the Milwaukee agency the severe loss in volume experienced when Blue Cross radically cut its home care benefit forced a cut in employment and in the size of the demonstration. Moreover, the effects of the Blue Cross change in benefit policy had reverberations throughout the state.

In all cases the effects of the external environment were most decisive at the point where demonstration funding ended and the local agencies or their sponsors had to decide whether or not to continue to fund the work life programs. The changes implemented during the demonstration period entailed substantial costs relative to the low wages and low payments that characterized the implementing agencies. The per participant costs of the programs ranged from about 6 percent of the $6.50 per hour county reimbursement rate in San Diego to about 17 percent of the $7.50 per hour billing rate for home aide services at Quality Care Syracuse. During the demonstration period, the availability of outside funding protected the work life programs from the constraints imposed by available payment sources. Afterwards, the programs at the two publicly funded agencies were abandoned (in San Diego because the county awarded the home care contract to a competing low bidder at a rate that allowed little or no job enrichment; in New York City because the Medicaid budget did not provide for an extension, although funds were budgeted for the following fiscal year). The program at Quality Care continued with the full-time work guarantee and the $.50 per hour wage increment but without the costly vacation, sick leave, or health insurance benefits.

Impact on Turnover and Continuity of Care While the work life programs were in place (and up to six months after the end of the demonstration period), their impact was significant (Chapter 11). Each of the demonstrations significantly reduced worker turnover. Depending on the demonstration site, program participants were 11 to 44 percent more likely to be on the job one year after the start of the demonstrations than their relevant control groups. Across all demonstration sites, there was a 16 percent difference in one-year turnover between program participants and controls. Moreover, these differences were as great or greater at the eighteen-month follow-up point for the two demonstrations where eighteen-month data were collected.

Second, in the program that focused on continuity of care, workers involved in the demonstration were significantly more likely to be with the same client a year later than were workers in the control group: 63 percent of program participants, compared to only 46 percent of controls, were still serving the same difficult client—a 17 percent difference. Furthermore, program participants who changed clients did so mainly because of circumstances outside their control—the client died or was institutionalized, or the case was closed for some other reason. In contrast, controls generally changed cases because they or the client requested a change—circumstances that presumably could have been addressed had they been part of the program.

Target Groups and Program Components

Some of the work life demonstrations yielded findings relevant to the choice of target groups and program components. The Remedy San Diego program showed that basic training and support components had their greatest effect on workers with a moderate job attachment—that is, those working twenty to twenty-nine hours per week (four to six hours per day). Training and support had relatively little impact on the turnover of workers who worked thirty hours or more per week or fewer than twenty hours per week. The former were highly likely (80 to 100 percent) to remain on the job regardless of whether or not they were included in the demonstration, while the latter had turnover rates above 60 percent—again, regardless of whether or not they were in the demonstration.

The Remedy work life program also demonstrated that training and support components aimed at new workers could yield a short-term reduction (nearly 20 percent) in turnover among new employees. (The reduction in turnover was even greater—38 percent—among those new workers who made it through the training program.) However, the program's impact evidently eroded at the end of eighteen months. Furthermore, the turnover of new worker program participants was higher than that of either current worker participants or controls—suggesting definite limits on the effectiveness of programs focusing on new workers.

Finally, the Quality Care demonstration—combining full-time work with promotion to staff status, better pay, and better benefits—suggested that comprehensive work life programs may have a far greater impact than more piecemeal efforts to reduce turnover and improve continuity of care. (The Quality Care program produced a 44 percent reduction in turnover, compared to 11 percent at the combined New York City agencies and 21 percent for Remedy current and new worker program participants.) While the numbers involved were small and the baseline (i.e., the controls') turnover rate at Quality Care was higher than at the other demonstration agencies, at least some of the difference may have been attributable to the more comprehensive and therefore presumably more powerful set of interventions implemented. None of the other demonstrations addressed all four work life issues—wages, benefits, opportunities for advancement, and hours of work—cited as the greatest source of worker dissatisfaction in the home aide survey.

Worker Participation and Dropout Rates

As discussed above, the overall impact of the work life programs was clearly positive. However, two important qualifications should be noted: first, as measured by participation rates, a sizable number of aides were either unwilling or unable to take advantage of the opportunities offered by the demonstration programs; second, a portion of those who did elect to take part in the demonstrations subsequently dropped out—presumably because, contrary to expectation, participation did not improve the quality of their work lives.

The proportion of contacted workers who agreed to participate in the programs ranged from a low of 25 percent to a high of 78 percent,[2] depending on the agency and whether the workers were current workers or new workers. In the one demonstration where it was possible to analyze separately new workers (64 percent participation rate) and current workers (25 percent participation rate), the new workers were much more likely to agree to participate. Perhaps the current workers had adapted to the status quo by taking on other jobs or lowering their expectations, while new workers may have been more sanguine about the opportunities offered by the demonstration and felt freer to pursue them. Combining data from all the demonstrations, the overall participation rate was about 50 percent of workers directly offered a place in one of the programs.

A portion of those who did elect to take part in the work life programs subsequently dropped out. The dropout rate was much higher among new workers than among current workers.[3] The full-time work components of the demonstrations that included them were a major source of program dropouts. Many of the dropouts apparently experienced personal or family problems, transportation problems, and/or stress associated with filling the thirty-five- or forty-hour quota by serving weekend, short-visit, or short-notice cases—all deterring them from keeping their original commitment. At Quality Care Syracuse, where vacation benefits conferred by the program were relatively generous, many of the program participants "filled" their forty-hour week by taking vacation hours to equal the difference between hours actually worked and forty.

What are the implications of these findings for managers and policy makers? The next chapter presents a series of recommendations applicable to home care employers, then follows with a discussion of policy options to support work life improvements.

NOTES

1. Wisconsin data released after this financial analysis was completed underscore the financial constraints on the industry. Among all 157 agencies that applied for home health licensure in that state in 1987, there was a negative 2 percent margin. Deficits were 13 percent among governmentally sponsored home health agencies and 6 percent among nonprofits. The proprietary home care sector in Wisconsin earned a 4 percent profit margin (Wisconsin Department of Health and Social Services, September 1988).

2. For reasons described in the Quality Care case study, the 78 percent acceptance rate at that agency is probably overstated.

3. This finding is based on the fifty-five Remedy program participants. Remedy was the only demonstration that explicitly included new workers and therefore allowed separate analysis of new and current workers. The dropout rate among new worker participants at Remedy was 33 percent; the dropout rate among current worker participants was 3 percent.

13

Management Strategies and Policy Options for Ensuring a Sufficient and Reliable Home Aide Work Force

The U.S. home care system confronts multiple and competing demands. Consumers expect home care providers to deliver reliable, quality service to meet the growing demands of those frail elderly and disabled persons (and their families) who could not otherwise remain at home. They also expect government and private insurers to subsidize services for those who cannot afford them. Providers expect public and private third-party payers to compensate their services at a level sufficient to recruit and retain workers, expand their markets, and maintain financial health. Workers expect a living wage, a reliable income, benefits commensurate with those of workers in institutional settings, and opportunities to advance beyond the unskilled entry-level job. Policy makers look to home care as a less expensive alternative to hospital or nursing home care and seek to constrain home care expenditures through a variety of cost control measures aimed at both unit cost and service volume. At the same time, they face increasing pressure to expand home care entitlements and to ensure quality and reliability of service. To meet these demands will require changes in both the delivery and financing of home care.

This concluding chapter discusses both management strategies and policy options for upgrading home care employment and ensuring a sufficient and reliable supply of home care workers. The underlying assumptions are that additional investment in the home aide work force will be necessary to meet the demands of a growing elderly population and that investments in work life programs ultimately can and should be funded through reforms in service delivery and financing. Such reforms should be designed to integrate financing of services, to allow trade-offs between institutional and home care, and to reward efficiencies in service delivery.

Presented first are a number of recommendations for managers of home care agencies. Some of the recommendations are derived directly from the home aide survey and the work life demonstrations, while others are derived from the literature in the field and from the authors' more general experience.[1] After discussing managerial strategies, the chapter outlines a range of both short- and long-term policy options for bringing about change in the home care system.

Given increasing demand for the essential services provided by the home aide and mounting concern over insufficient supply, labor leaders, managers, and government officials have begun to move work life issues to the public agenda. The authors' hope is that the information and the recommendations presented throughout this book will enlighten the ensuing debate over appropriate work life improvements and necessary policy changes.

RECOMMENDATIONS FOR HOME CARE EMPLOYERS AND MANAGERS

The recommendations discussed in this section are organized in six categories: (1) worker recruitment and screening; (2) worker training and support; (3) pay, benefits, and other rewards; (4) hours of work; (5) opportunities for advancement; and (6) political action. Categories 1 through 5 consist of specific work life changes that the demonstrations showed to be effective or that the survey data suggest should be effective. These changes can, by and large, be implemented at the discretion of employers,[2] given sufficient resources. Category 6 discusses political strategies useful to employers in garnering resources to support selected work life improvements.

Although they are presented and discussed separately, the changes embodied in the work life demonstrations were implemented in various combinations so that particular program components could reinforce each other. For example, training was followed by support; specialized training received incremental pay; and full-time work made the home aide eligible for expanded benefits and/or higher wages. Furthermore, the experience of the demonstrations indicates that the most comprehensive work life program was the most effective. Thus, for maximum effect employers should consider combining the various components to respond to the particular problems of their workplace and the particular concerns of their work force.

Worker Recruitment and Screening

1. *Employers should focus their recruiting efforts on "mature" workers.* The importance of age as a predictor of turnover suggests that management should focus efforts to recruit aides on older workers, who because of life circumstances, temperament, or lower employment aspirations, seem more inclined to stay on the job. Anecdotal evidence collected during the course of the project suggested that young women were less happy than older women in the job of home aide. That evidence was substantiated by the survey data and the turnover

models. The median age of the survey respondents was forty-four years, and nearly 35 percent were fifty years or older. Thus the home aide work force is not a young one. One implication of the turnover models is that recruiting a younger work force—as would be the result, for example, of efforts to place welfare mothers in home aide jobs (Enns, Bell, & Flanagan, 1987)—would exacerbate the turnover problems of the industry.

2. *Employers should develop and apply better mechanisms for screening potential employees.* The extremely high turnover rate among new workers (and their high dropout rate from the Remedy training demonstration) suggests that management could do much more to screen potential employees. Screening was quite limited at most of the agencies visited during the course of the project. The focus was on the minimum requirements of citizenship or legal resident status, references, a physical examination (where required by state or county), and a quick and superficial assessment of personal characteristics, such as overtly aggressive or bizarre behavior. Interviews rarely took more than ten minutes. Informal screening mechanisms mentioned by managers included reliance on long-term agency aides to recruit like-minded workers, use of waiting lists or waiting periods between the time a potential employee was interviewed for the job and the time she actually entered training or employment, and warnings to new workers that they would be assigned to difficult cases or cases with unpopular hours (e.g., weekend cases). The latter two devices were intended to discourage all but the most dedicated (or desperate) job applicants. Only one agency (not one of the demonstration agencies) had a fairly sophisticated screening process, using three agency employees to interview the prospective worker and applying explicit rating criteria.

The problem with using more sophisticated and selective screening devices, of course, is that given worker shortages, many agencies find it necessary to accept minimally qualified workers in order to meet the demand for service. Furthermore, given scarce administrative resources, even those inclined to be more selective lack sufficient staff to devote significant time to screening. Nevertheless, an hour spent on screening an applicant might save one of the two or three hours spent in finding a replacement for her after she quit or failed to appear for a client assignment. The data indicate that in the screening process, agencies ought to pay careful attention to evidence about the applicant's ability to work independently, her feelings about working alone, and the value she places on socializing with coworkers.

Worker Training and Support

1. *Employers should allocate training resources to (a) reinforce and supplement basic training and (b) develop special skills and career tracks within the home aide work force.* The work life demonstrations included both kinds of training, and both were successful (in combination with other components) in reducing turnover and/or improving continuity of care. In addition to imparting

technical skills and information to participants, the training programs gave workers an extended and intensive opportunity to get to know each other, to get to know their supervisors, and to identify themselves with the agency. One of the training programs also explicitly dealt with stress on the job and with mechanisms for coping with loneliness and boredom.

The models of job satisfaction and intent to turnover described in Chapter 4 indicate how and why such training would prove effective in reducing turnover. The models pointed to supervisor support as an important component of job satisfaction and to loneliness as a major determinant of inclination to leave the job. In addition, the survey data indicated that training could mitigate feelings of loneliness: workers who perceived their training to be adequate were significantly less likely to report feelings of isolation and therefore significantly less likely to report intent to turnover.

These findings suggest that three important functions of in-service training for home aides—as important as the function of imparting information—should be to develop mechanisms for coping with isolation on the job, to foster relationships with supervisors, and to foster relationships among peers. A corollary of this statement is that training courses should minimize didactic teaching methods, maximize interactive techniques, and emphasize role-playing and other hands-on methods for building worker confidence and competence. Furthermore, to develop peer support among workers, managers should establish cohorts of home aides who regularly participate together in in-service training and ongoing support groups. In both demonstration training components, meeting together in small groups on a regular basis was an important factor in fostering supportive relationships among workers and between workers and supervisors.

2. *Specialized training programs should focus on the skills required to deal with categories of clients or cases particularly problematic to workers and therefore to managers.* One of the perverse incentives evidently operating in home care agencies is to reward long-term, valued employees by giving them "easy" cases and to relegate difficult cases to new employees, sometimes rationalizing this procedure as a test of their commitment to the job. Such assignments are understandable in an industry where flat pay scales and undifferentiated tasks offer few opportunities to reward deserving workers. The effect of this perverse reward system, however, is to exacerbate turnover among new workers, who are already the most vulnerable to turnover, and to subject the neediest clients to the least experienced aides.

Identifying categories of problem clients or problem cases, developing training programs aimed at those problems, offering valued employees the opportunity to gain special skills in working with those clients, and compensating them with appropriate pay provide a way of both overcoming perverse incentives and also rewarding deserving employees and relieving some of the administrative burden associated with problem cases (see recommendations on "Opportunities for Advancement" below). This approach was the successful tack taken by the New York City (Long Life and Independent Living) home attendant demonstration, which trained workers to serve psychologically and behaviorally difficult clients—clients whose "problem behaviors" were a source of discontinuities in care and worker turnover. Other problem cases that might be the target of special training and compensation programs include clients with more intense or complex medical needs and technology-dependent clients.[3]

3. *Employers should ensure that there is an organizational support system to assist the aide in dealing with problems on the job, as well as with endemic isolation. In the interest of both career development and quality assurance, employers should explore the feasibility of training and promoting a select group of aides to serve as field support staff fulfilling this function.* Most supervision of home aides is carried out by case coordinators (schedulers), who spend most of their time in the office and much of their day on the telephone and who rarely visit the aide in the home. The case coordinator's large caseload generally requires that she devote most of her energy to logistical concerns—for example, is the case covered, will it be covered tomorrow? Much of her remaining time is spent responding to noncritical complaints, which she attempts to address with the limited resources at her disposal. Less frequently, she must respond to a more serious complaint or a real emergency—again with relatively scant information and few resources. Little time is left for substantive supervision or feedback to workers in the home.

Substantive decisions about the care of the client are usually made by the agency nurse (or sometimes by a nurse employed by a different organization with jurisdiction over the case). In contrast to the coordinator, the nurse spends much of her time in the field. However, in many agencies, her caseload is so large that she may visit a given home only three or four times a year. Furthermore, the client, not the worker, is the focus of the nurse's attention: "The staff nurse who monitors the patient's care often acts as if the paraprofessional has nothing to do with the patient's health unless she/he has neglected to do a task on the plan of care or is doing it improperly" (Surpin, November 1987:26).

New field support staff are needed who can visit the homes on a more frequent basis, have a consistent set of cases, and work on a team basis with the aide assigned to the case, the case coordinator, and the nurse. The new field staff would provide support to the aide in the home and report back to the agency on the progress of the case, the aide's performance, problems encountered, and needs for additional training or supervision. These field support staff might well be "senior home aides"—a position that does not formally exist in most agencies and is certainly not recognized by third-party payers. This new position is discussed below under "Opportunities for Advancement."

4. *Training and support components should pay special attention to the problems of new workers, black workers, and members of other racial and/or linguistic minority groups. Where resources are scarce, they should focus on workers with a moderate job attachment—that is, those workers who work four to six hours per day.* Given the inexperience and vulnerability of new workers and the perverse incentive system (described above) that assigns them the least desirable

and most difficult cases, these workers should be the focus of more intensive training and support efforts. Experience with new work training and support at Remedy in San Diego suggests the efficacy of intensive training for new workers in the early months of employment and the need for immediate support following training. To build on early training, to develop ties to the agency, and to develop commitment to the job, new workers, for example, might be accorded first priority in receiving visits from field support staff under the proposed organizational support system outlined above.

Given the impact of race on perceptions of job monotony, pay inequity, worker-client relations, satisfaction, and intent to turnover, problems experienced by racial and linguistic minorities should also receive careful attention in training and support programs.

> Being alone with the patient in the home often creates a situation in which the worker is treated and/or talked about as the ''maid'' by the patient. This most often happens when the race and class expectations of white middle class patients are acted out with black and Latin home care workers who are seen as domestic service workers rather than providers of health care (Surpin, November 1987:14).

Training and support need to help workers deal with such difficult situations, and managers need to take additional action where necessary.

To maximize efficient use of scarce management resources, a third group of workers who should be the focus of in-service training and support activities consists of those with a moderate attachment to the job—as evidenced by working between four and six hours per day. Analysis of turnover data in the Remedy demonstration indicated that the effects of training and support were greater for these workers than for those who had a very limited number of assignments or a very heavy work schedule. Allocating scarce resources to workers willing to work less than half-time may not be a prudent expenditure for the agency. On the other hand, if sufficient resources are available, providing in-service training and support to workers with a strong job attachment (more than six hours a day in direct service) may be justified on the grounds of equity or quality assurance, even though it may not do much to reduce turnover (because turnover in this group tends to be so low in the first place).

Pay, Benefits, and Other Rewards

1. *Employers should strive toward parity wages and benefits between home aides and aides in the institutional (i.e., hospital and nursing home) sector.* The demonstrations did not directly test this proposition, in the sense that none instituted an across-the-board increase in wages and/or benefits—that is, one that was not tied to special skills or promotion to an upgraded position. However, the survey data indicate the major importance of satisfaction with pay and benefits in determining the aide's inclination to leave the job. Furthermore, there is a

massive literature stressing the importance of both compensation and opportunity for advancement (discussed below) in workers' decisions to leave the job or stay (Price & Mueller, 1986). Turnover aside, considerations of equity between institution and home-based workers performing similar tasks and of social priorities favoring increased use of home versus institutional care provide a strong rationale for increasing wages in the home care sector to match those in nursing homes and hospitals.

The problem is that, unlike most other employers, home care agencies are quite limited in their capacity to improve compensation. In most industries, employers experiencing labor shortages and excess demand for services or products would raise workers' wages and increase prices to cover costs. As noted in Chapter 5, however, home care prices and wages are artificially constrained by third-party payers. To reach wage and benefit parity with institutional employers will require changes in third-party payment for home care. Hospitals and nursing homes are also constrained by third-party payment—the difference is that their workers unionized and won significant wage and benefit concessions in the 1960s and 1970s, when third-party payment was less constraining and the impetus for cost control was less compelling.

2. *Employers should use wage differentials, expanded benefits, and visible status symbols—such as uniforms, badges, and employee awards—to reward home aides for length of service, reliability, responsibility, and the acquisition of advanced skills.* Tangible rewards for performance were a part of all three demonstrations. They figured most prominently in the Quality Care work life program, where program participants (relatively long-term employees) received both incremental pay and expanded benefits as full-time staff aides. These rewards were also an important part of the New York City (Long Life/Independent Living) program, where longtime home attendants received a wage increment after completing special training and while serving difficult clients. Remedy San Diego would have liked to include a wage differential in its demonstration, but the county Department of Social Services vetoed the idea. Instead, Remedy workers received expanded health insurance, uniforms, and badges while participating in the demonstration. By all accounts these rewards were extremely important to program participants—all the more so, because they were such a rarity—and, without doubt, they contributed to the overall impact of the demonstrations.

Common sense suggests that employers should seek to reward, with wage increases and fringe benefits, length of service to the agency. "It is difficult to see how turnover can be significantly reduced unless seniority is substantially rewarded by pay. If this recommendation is implemented, then the cost of quitting for the employee will be high" (Price & Mueller, 1986:215). Similarly, willingness to undergo specialized training, to serve longer hours, or to assume additional job responsibilities ought to rewarded, on the simple principle of "positive reinforcement" for desirable work behavior (Price & Mueller, 1986:211).

3. *Transitional pay should be made available to valued workers to tide them over between case closings and reassignment to appropriate clients.* One of the problems of the home aide work force—addressed by full-time work guarantees implemented in two of the three demonstrations—is the episodic nature of work. Generally, when a client goes to the hospital, enters a nursing home, or dies, the worker goes without pay until a new assignment can be made. In the absence of guaranteed full-time work (discussed below), employers may find the use of transitional pay for selected workers (e.g., those with special skills or long tenure) both affordable and effective. This idea was not tested in the demonstration but arose from the Long Life/Independent Living program, where the rush to reassign program participants after case closings because of client institutionalization or death interfered with the matching of specially trained workers to difficult cases. Case closings were also closely associated with worker turnover for both program partipants and controls—suggesting that some means of bridging the financial gap between a case closing and a reassignment could lead to higher proportions of workers remaining with the agency.

Hours of Work

1. *Employers should look upon full-time, year-round employment as a goal to be achieved for that portion of the work force willing to make the necessary commitment of time, energy, and responsibility.* Guaranteed full-time work would be a more comprehensive and presumably more effective antidote to the episodic nature of the home aide's job than would the selective application of transitional pay discussed above. The desirability of full-time work is almost always a prominent feature of discussions of quality of work life in the home care industry. Advocates of work life reform have estimated that only 20 to 30 percent of the aide work force want "limited, flexible hours, sometimes referred to as 'mother's hours' . . . and not the great majority" (Surpin, November 1987:30). The home aide survey data are generally consistent with this view: about 30 percent of the respondents expressed the wish for twenty-five or fewer hours of work per week, while 60 percent reportedly wished to work thirty-five hours or more. Observations such as these have led reform advocates to make recommendations like the following: "State regulations should require that each agency have a core paraprofessional work force, either through direct provision or sub-contractors, with salaried positions based on a 40 hour workweek. A minimum of 65 percent of the work force should be working on this basis" (Surpin, November 1987:36).

In agencies where a high proportion of the caseload consists of clients receiving four or more hours of service per day (as in New York City), this goal may be workable. The experience of the project's two guaranteed hours demonstrations (Remedy and Quality Care), however, suggests that agencies with a high proportion of "short-hour" or "short-visit" cases will have difficulty moving toward a large full-time work force. The Remedy and Quality Care experience suggests that—at least in the short run—the proportion of the workers who are willing or able to take on full-time aide's work in any given home care agency is a good deal less than the proportion of workers who express the desire for such work. If we take into account both those workers who declined to participate in the demonstrations and those who dropped out, the proportion of workers who stayed with the guaranteed hours programs was only about 30 percent (a much larger percentage stayed on at the agencies, but as less than full-time workers).

Those who declined to participate or subsequently decided not to adhere to the full-time work commitment may have wanted full-time work. Indeed, some of them were already working full-time by taking additional part-time jobs to supplement the hours worked at their primary place of employment. Perhaps if the opportunity for full-time work had been presented before they had made other commitments, they would have taken it. Perhaps, too, if they had better understood the associated benefits (e.g., more vacation time or expanded health insurance coverage), or if the offer had been permanent rather than tied to a one-year demonstration, more workers would have accepted it. Others turned down the opportunity or later gave it up because of transportation difficulties and personal or family problems. Still others dropped the full-time commitment, citing stress associated with the weekend, short-visit, and short-notice cases that were a required part of the forty-hour workweek. This onerous aspect of full-time home aide work should not be underestimated, inasmuch as agencies would almost inevitably have to draw on "inconvenient" cases to fill thirty-five or forty-hour schedules for significant numbers of full-time workers. Stress would be exacerbated, moreover, in agencies that did not count travel time between clients toward the thirty-five or forty-hour schedule. (This situation was not the case at the demonstration agencies, but it is prevalent in the industry.)

The demonstrations also showed that the full-time guarantee—sometimes onerous to the worker—posed difficulties for managers as well. While managerial expectations were that full-time workers would be a mobile force of Green Berets who could help in difficult situations, fill in on short notice, and increase the volume of services provided, in reality the workers were less mobile than anticipated, and the difficulties of scheduling them were considerable.

Given the practical difficulties experienced by both workers and managers, transition to a generally salaried full-time aide work force does not seem realistic in the near future. Nevertheless, the importance of the full-time work guarantee for those who were able to participate and their subsequent favorable turnover experience indicate that this guarantee is a viable and effective way to reward and reinforce positive performance on the part of a select group of workers.

2. *As a corollary, where full-time work entails serving weekend, short-notice, and/or short-visit cases, workers should receive incremental compensation.* The idea that full-time work is necessarily a reward in itself is contradicted by the above discussion of problems attendant on the thirty-five- or forty-hour per week schedule. One of the more surprising findings of the project was that Quality Care staff aides who received a $.50 per hour increment for committing to full-

time work were actually less satisfied with their pay at the end of the demonstration year than they had been at the outset of the demonstration. One implication is that full-time work, however desirable, is not a substitute for pay and benefits commensurate with responsibilities and competitive with similar jobs in other organizations.

Opportunities for Advancement

1. *Employers should develop two promotional tracks for home aides. One would be a "clinical" track with special training and compensation geared to serving particular categories of cases or clients. A second promotional track would be "administrative"—with special training and compensation for assuming increased staff responsibilities (e.g., in field support or quality assurance).* The literature on worker turnover strongly supports the importance of advancement opportunities as a determinant of job satisfaction and the decision to stay on the job. Dissatisfaction with opportunities for advancement was second only to dissatisfaction with pay and benefits among the respondents to the home aide survey. The perception that participating in the work life program was a promotional opportunity was strong among the participants, even in the Remedy demonstration, where the opportunity to participate was determined entirely by random selection (the other two demonstrations combined special selection criteria with randomization). This perception almost certainly contributed to the positive impact of the programs.

The New York City (Long Life/Independent Living) demonstration is a good example of developing a clinical track for promoting the home aide. As discussed earlier, by training and compensating workers to deal with psychologically and behaviorally difficult clients, the program simultaneously—and successfully—addressed a burdensome management problem for the agency while providing advanced skills and better payment for a valued group of workers.

Viewed retrospectively, the Quality Care staff aide program was in a sense a hybrid between the clinical and administrative tracks. From the perspective of the workers it was a clinical track, for their sole function was to provide direct client service. (Although initially the agency director thought some quality assurance or marketing functions might be included, they were not.) From the perspective of the director, however, there were some important administrative goals that were, as it turned out, imperfectly achieved. These included increasing the mobility of the work force, shortening the response time in filling client assignments, and increasing agency volume—none of which were explicitly explained to the staff aides. Perhaps if the hybrid nature of the staff aide track had been better understood at the outset, the participants could have been better prepared to deal with the administrative objectives implicit in their role.

The senior home aide or new field staff position described above as part of a recommended organizational support system more clearly exemplifies an administrative track for promoting home aides. Like the clinical track, it could simultaneously accomplish several objectives—strengthening supervision of workers in the field both to reduce turnover and to improve quality of care, while providing promotional opportunities for accomplished workers. Furthermore, it would tap and develop for managerial purposes the talents and experience of the people who are most knowledgeable about the job of the home aide—the home aides themselves.

Such an experiment was implemented in six New York City home attendant agencies in the fall of 1988, with evaluation results projected for the spring of 1990. That experiment, funded by a special city budget appropriation, established three or four "field support liaison" positions at each of the participating agencies. The liaisons were promoted from the agencies' home aide work force, were accorded staff salaries and benefits, and received special training and supervision to help them carry out the field support role. Spending the equivalent of approximately three days each week in the field and two in the office, each of the liaisons was expected to be able to visit about fifteen home aides a week, with repeat visits scheduled on a regular basis. The hope was that these visits would enrich the work life of both the liaisons and the aides they visited, thus reducing turnover and absenteeism and improving quality of care.

Political Action

1. *Home care employers should work together to lobby state and local governments and private insurers for sufficient reimbursement to provide decent jobs and adequate compensation for the home aide work force. In this quest, employers should seek alliances with unions and with consumer groups, which stand to benefit from improvements in worker satisfaction and quality of service.* To implement successfully the quality of work life improvements recommended above, managers will have to commit significant managerial resources and substantial sums of money. These will not likely be found in most home care agencies, with their modest profits or operating deficits. Nor can the elderly who make use of home care services very easily pay for such efforts out of their own pockets. If meaningful and long-lasting work life improvements are to be made, they will have to be paid for by government purchasers of service (and financed out of public tax monies) or by private insurers (and financed out of consumer premiums). In either case, public or private policy makers will have to be persuaded to allocate the necessary dollars.

Wresting higher reimbursement from third-party payers will not be as easy for the home care industry as it has been for hospitals and nursing homes. Health care cost control is a far more salient issue today (and will likely be even more salient in the future) than it was when hospital workers won competitive wages in the 1970s. Much of the improvement in their conditions of work occurred in the era of cost-based reimbursement. Nursing home workers, too, benefited from improved wages and benefits funded by reimbursement based on costs.[4]

Home care paraprofessionals are the last large group of health care workers to seek adequate wages and benefits and they are doing so at a time when financial resources are quite scarce. Further, they work in a relatively new, highly fragmented system that has not yet been fully integrated into the health care mainstream. They also have lacked, until recently, the collective voice, resources and power of the health-related unions that have enabled paraprofessionals in hospitals and nursing homes to take for granted what home care paraprofessionals most desire (Surpin, November 1987:29).

To win better conditions for their workers, employers will need to make their case on its merits. Through task forces, study commissions, conferences, and, above all, media coverage, they will need to make the public aware of labor shortages that threaten access to service and substandard working conditions that threaten quality of care. They have already begun this process, and they have struck a responsive chord in areas with the most severe worker shortages.

Making the case on its merits, however, is rarely sufficient to change public policy or move private insurers. In addition to their own lobbying efforts, industry leaders need to educate and enlist the support of powerful "elder" lobbies and consumer groups at the state as well as the national level. These groups have already mobilized to protest premature hospital discharges and arbitrary denial of Medicare home health benefits; campaigning against insufficient home care for the elderly who are chronically ill and against inhumane conditions for their caretakers must be made to seem a logical extension. Finally, to strengthen their cause further, home care employers (particularly those who are nonunionized) need to overcome their fear of unions and ally themselves with labor, particularly in areas where labor has a strong political voice. With management, labor, and consumers all articulating the plight of the worker, politicians will likely respond.

POLICY OPTIONS

What changes in public policy would support the work life improvements necessary to move home aide employment from marginal to mainstream? This final section of the chapter outlines a range of policy changes that individually or in combination would constitute progress toward ensuring a sufficient and reliable home aide work force to meet the escalating demand for care. First are relatively modest changes that could be implemented within the existing home care financing system. Second are changes that would expand existing third-party financing. Third are innovations in delivery and financing. These changes are presented as options rather than as recommendations, for their appropriateness and feasibility depend upon a host of other considerations, peripheral to work life issues but fundamental to long-term care reform.

Changes Within the Existing Home Care Financing System

Of $3 to $4 billion spent on unskilled home services in the United States in 1985, Medicaid and other local public funding sources paid 40 to 50 percent.

(Medicare paid 15 to 20 percent, while individuals and their families paid roughly 30 to 40 percent; see Chapter 5.) Given the dominant role of state and local governments, their financing, reimbursement, and regulatory policies are obviously critical to support for work life improvements. Six relatively modest policy changes implemented at the state and local level could have a positive impact:

1. *States could change licensing laws to allow aides to assume more responsibility.* Most states have "nurse practice acts" and other regulations that specify the domains of various professional and paraprofessional workers. These regulations generally prevent home aides from performing medically related services reserved for nurses, and the nursing community has been adamant in seeking to protect its domain (see Chapter 8 for discussion of the debate in New York State). If state officials and professional experts were to reexamine established territorial boundaries, they would almost certainly find areas where home aide responsibilities could be expanded to facilitate job redesign and the development of clinical tracks such as those discussed under "Recommendations for Employers."

2. *States and localities could phase out or substantially reduce so-called individual provider programs and contract with vendor agencies to provide the bulk of publicly funded home care services.* Nearly a dozen states still rely on individual providers ostensibly employed by the client though paid by the government to provide in-home services. California and Michigan have the largest IP programs, employing more than 100,000 workers in that capacity. The states and localities take little responsibility for these workers beyond issuing paychecks (for wages even lower than those paid to agency-employed home aides) and withholding taxes. Worker training and oversight are virtually nonexistent. If the client is senile, demented, or otherwise mentally impaired, the IP system can lead to problems of quality for the client and liability for the state.

Moving toward greater reliance on vendor agencies in these states would create identifiable and accountable employers—an advantage to public officials worried about administrative and substantive oversight of the services they fund. Such a move would also, undoubtedly, facilitate unionization, inasmuch as unions cannot easily identify or contact individual providers, let alone negotiate contracts with each of the IPs' individual "employers." Vendorization would therefore almost certainly put more organizational and political clout behind efforts to improve employment conditions—a situation many policy makers admittedly wish to avoid.

Aside from the desire to avoid unionization and to purchase home aide services as cheaply as possible, policy makers in states with IP programs must also answer to self-help lobbies for the disabled, who argue strongly that "self-directing" clients ought to be able to employ their helpers directly. There is also increasing concern among advocates for the elderly in giving the latter direct responsibility for their care givers to enhance feelings of control and associated life-satisfaction.[5] To address these legitimate concerns, states and localities could maintain ''mixed mode'' programs, where some fraction of total services was still provided by workers employed directly by their clients.

3. *Where states and localities contract for services through a process of competitive bidding, they could specify minimum compensation requirements for all bidders, to avoid low bids based on substandard wage and benefit packages.* Assuming these minimum requirements reflected prevailing practices, this policy would tend to reinforce existing wages and benefits, as well as underlying union-management agreements in vendor agencies that were unionized. In its absence, unionized vendors are at a relative disadvantage in the bidding process insofar as nonunion agencies can submit low bids based on ''poorer'' packages for the work force. A progressive state or county could also use this mechanism to promote higher wages and benefits by specifying minimum requirements richer than prevailing practice.

4. *States and localities could selectively fund work life improvements based on criteria such as need, cost, efficacy, etc.* Given existing variations in local labor market conditions and existing variations in employment conditions across agencies within any one market area, policy makers may wish to support work life improvements selectively, depending on the relative supply of available workers, the merits of individual proposals, or the resources required to implement them. Selective funding of work life interventions could be carried out through a ''request for proposal'' (RFP) process, similar to one recently instituted in Massachusetts, whereby home care agencies submit plans to the state Rate Setting Commission for approval (Shark, 1987). Funding of such proposals could be based on competition among agencies for a limited pool of supplemental resources or on regulatory criteria awarding funds to all proposals that met specified standards.

5. *States and localities could approve across-the-board increases in publicly funded home care programs to make wage and benefit packages competitive with those in nursing homes and hospitals.* Although unlikely to take such action unilaterally, bureaucrats and politicians may acquiesce to the demands of labor/management/consumer alliances (like those advocated under ''Recommendations for Managers'' above), particularly if a recent or impending crisis in access or quality affords an opportunity to claim credit for solving a serious public problem. Mounting evidence of worker shortages across the country suggests that major improvements in employment conditions such as those recently approved in New York City (and those approved in Massachusetts over the last few years) may be possible in other communities as well. Even in New York and Massachusetts, however, working conditions for aides in the home care industry are still generally inferior to those of aides employed by hospitals and nursing homes.

6. *State and local governments could take the initiative in fostering more efficient modes of service and committing a portion of efficiency gains to upgrading home aide employment.* Experience with ''shared aide'' programs suggests that in some areas more efficient deployment of the work force could serve

current client caseloads—at equal levels of satisfaction—with many fewer hours and significantly lower costs. For example, shared aide programs implemented in Monroe County, New York, served clusters of "heavy care" clients in apartment complexes and elderly housing developments at costs that were 30 to 50 percent lower than prior to implementation of the programs. The savings in hours and costs were achieved by clustering clients, organizing work around tasks rather than visit hours, and forming worker teams that allowed aides to share clients, specialize, and cover for each other. Such restructuring, however, is a complex undertaking. Among the ingredients necessary for success are (1) a critical mass of geographically proximate clients, (2) assignment of those clients to a single home care provider (in many communities multiple agencies serve clients in any one building or neighborhood), (3) valid, reliable, and common client assessment tools to determine appropriate services, (4) adequate worker training, on-site supervision, and quality assurance, and (5) altered billing procedures and payment mechanisms to reflect the task versus visit orientation of the system.

The team approach offers the prospect of reduced worker isolation, increased worker productivity, greater service reliability for the client, and, in some cases, greater flexibility as well. On the other hand, without adequate compensation, support, and supervision, shared care might intensify the burden for the worker, reduce access for the client, and impair the worker-client relationship.

If indeed it is possible to save dollars by restructuring the home aide's job (in geographical and physical settings conducive to shared work) without impairing either worker or client satisfaction, it should be possible to channel some of the savings into both work life improvements and expanded client caseloads. For this reason, policy makers ought seriously to consider encouraging experimentation with more efficient service modes. They could do so by consolidating geographically proximate cases under common vendors, offering technical assistance and support to agencies willing to implement shared aide programs, and offering incentives for innovation (e.g., allowing agencies to keep part of their savings). Such actions could produce substantial payoffs in the form of greater resources to meet the challenge of providing reliable service and meeting growing demand.

EXPANSION OF THIRD-PARTY FINANCING AND DEVELOPMENT OF INNOVATIVE DELIVERY SYSTEMS

Third-party payment that is "low and slow" is a major deterrent to service quality and adequate worker supply in the home care sector. It is not nearly as great a deterrent, however, as the absence of third-party payment altogether. In 1980, more than half of single persons aged 75 and older—those most likely to need long-term assistance from a "formal" care giver, usually a home aide—had income below $6,000, including annuitized nonhousing assets; more than 80 percent of this group had income under $12,500. These incomes did not leave much discretionary income to pay for home care services out of pocket, where the average reported out-of-pocket payment was $164 per month (Chapter 5). Were the cost of service increased to move home aides above their $7,000 median annual income, the already heavy burden on the elderly poor and near poor would likely be intolerable, and some would almost certainly go without services critical to their survival.

Experts on long-term care generally agree on the need for expanded home care services and on the array of services, ranging from transportation and chore services to skilled nursing care, necessary to enable the frail elderly and disabled to function independently in the community (Rowland, 1987). Few of these services, however, are covered by insurance—private or public. Private long-term care insurance, while expanding, covered only an estimated 200,000 policyholders nationwide in 1986, and these policies provided very limited home care coverage (GAO, May 1987). Because of limited coverage under Medicare as well, Medicaid has become the predominant third-party payer of long-term care (GAO, September 1986). But Medicaid requires that the elderly impoverish themselves before becoming eligible for coverage, and, in any case, Medicaid programs (with the exception of New York State) are much more likely to cover nursing home care than care at home. According to the GAO (September 1986), Medicaid spending on home care represented less than 2 percent of total Medicaid expenditures in 1983, with New York accounting for nearly 80 percent of that amount. Given this paucity of third-party payment for long-term care in general and home care in particular, the relatively modest policy options discussed as possible changes within existing financing mechanisms can have only limited effect. To have a major impact on the home care industry will require major long-term care reform.

The most prominently mentioned approaches to reform are (1) promoting private initiatives to increase savings or to expand the private long-term care insurance market, (2) providing public long-term care insurance (e.g., through expanding Medicare or Medicaid), and (3) developing innovative delivery systems to make long-term care more affordable and accessible (Davis & Rowland, 1986; Rivlin & Wiener, 1988; Rowland, 1987). Any one of these reforms would likely bring more dollars into the home care industry, some of which would go to pay for home aide services. Of the three, however, the development of innovative delivery systems seems most likely to result in upgrading and integrating the job of the home aide into the rest of the health care system.

The assumption underlying proposals for delivery system reform is that "as an underpinning for improved financing, the long-term care system needs restructuring to improve the coordination and provision of services, especially in non-institutional settings, and to assure a continuum of health and social services." (Rowland, 1987:237). The principal elements of proposed delivery system reform are (1) *channeling* clients through a single entry point for service delivery, (2) *case management* (providing an in-depth assessment of the services required by the client and arranging for those services to be delivered), and (3) *integrated financing* of services. Examples of this approach include social health maintenance organizations (SHMOs), which extend the concept of prepayment for acute care to include prepayment for certain long-term care services, for which the SHMOs are also at financial risk[6]; life care communities, where housing, food, social services, home help, and chronic long-term care are provided to residents of a retirement community in exchange for fixed entrance fees and fixed monthly payments; and "life care at home," offering services similar to those of life care communities and on similar prepaid terms, but allowing the elderly to remain in their own homes rather than move to a retirement community.

These innovative systems could be financed privately (e.g., through employer retirement plans, religious or other nonprofit associations, or for-profit enterprises); publicly (e.g., through government grants, vouchers, or third-party payments); or through various public-private partnerships. Whatever their source of financing, they would differ significantly from the traditional home health delivery system in the financial principles on which they were founded, their integration, coordination, and greater reliance on nonmedical home care support.

In that context, home aides, rather than being temporary, part-time, underpaid workers in a fragmented system, subject to weak supervision, often provided by nurses employed by another agency, could instead become valued members of an interdisciplinary team. Adequate pay scales and equitable working conditions for these workers at the base of the service hierarchy would be of much greater importance to managers at risk for the financial outcomes of the care delivered. Thus the biggest step toward improving the availability and quality of basic home aide services would be to improve the financing and organization of home care. The resulting managerial responsibility and accountability should result in both better quality of work life and better quality of care.

In the absence of work life reform or a major economic recession, the available supply of workers will be insufficient to meet the mounting demand for service. The likely implication is that more and more elderly people will fail to get out of bed, dress themselves, eat, bathe, and take their medication properly. The cumulative effect may take longer to reach the public eye but is even more alarming than what happens to unaided elderly people discharged from hospitals early. Funding higher wages and improved employment conditions should become a priority of public policy, even at the expense of lower volume; for if no one is willing to do the work, volume of service will drop even lower. All the advances in modern medicine that extend life into the "golden years" will seem a cruel joke if society cannot improve upon its current system for delivering care at home.

NOTES

1. This strategy for deriving recommendations is borrowed from Price & Mueller (1986).
2. The terms *employer* and *manager* are used interchangeably in this section to refer to

those who run home care agencies and corporations. The recommendations are geared toward top management in these organizations.

3. See the discussion in the Long Life/Independent Living Case Study of proposals for Level 3 home attendants in New York State to be trained to care for medically complex cases. See also National HomeCaring Council (1987) for a curriculum for serving technology-dependent clients.

4. In some states, such as New York, aides employed by nursing homes receive roughly the same wage and benefit package as those employed by hospitals (Surpin, November 1987). In others, such as Massachusetts, their compensation is below that of hospital employees but, nevertheless, higher than that of home care workers (Commonwealth of Massachusetts, Division of Employment Security, July 1986).

5. Elderly and disabled home care clients do not necessarily relinquish control over aides employed by agencies insofar as they can exercise prerogatives over scheduling of visits and performance of tasks within the home. It is true, however, that clients of publicly funded home care agencies often have very little say over the scheduling of visits.

6. However, as currently being developed, SHMOs focus more on home care related to acute episodes of illness than on home care for chronic care needs.

Methodological Appendix

This appendix includes discussion of methodological issues related to the home aide survey and to evaluation of the individual work life demonstrations. Issues related to the home aide survey include the following: (1) development of the survey instrument, (2) administration of the survey, (3) selection bias among respondents, (4) use of the survey data in developing the models of job satisfaction and intent to turnover, and (5) use of the survey data to measure before and after job satisfaction of participants in the work life demonstrations. Issues related to evaluating the impact of the demonstrations include: (1) random selection of program participants and controls, (2) selection bias among program participants, (3) definitions of turnover, and (4) inclusion versus exclusion of program dropouts from the turnover analysis.

THE HOME AIDE SURVEY

Development of the Survey Instrument

The instrument used to collect information on the attitudes of the home aide work force was a modified version of the Michigan Organizational Assessment Questionnaire (MOAQ) (Cammann et al., 1983). The MOAQ, consisting of a demographic module plus six modules probing workers' attitudes toward their jobs in general as well as toward specific facets of the job, was designed "to [be adapted] to the language and circumstances of any particular organization without losing comparability across organizations where the same issues are important" (Cammann et al., 1983:74).

The MOAQ was modified on the basis of extensive observation in the field. Questions were added pertaining to aspects of the worker-client relationship, work in the home environment, and personal problems that might affect job performance or satisfaction; questions on work group functioning were omitted because home aides do not carry out their tasks in work groups.

Once the MOAQ was modified, it was pilot tested with a small group of home aides to identify unclear, inappropriate, or irrelevant questions. After additional modification, the final questionnaire was also translated into Spanish to facilitate responses from Spanish-speaking workers. Although the instrument was pretested, the amount of missing data for some of the items suggests that language was a problem for a number of the workers.

Administration of the Survey

The questionnaire was administered to home aides employed by seventeen agencies in five cities (Boston, New York City, Milwaukee, San Diego, and Syracuse). With the exception of Boston, all of the cities were selected because they were the site of a demonstration project. Boston was chosen because its close proximity to the research team allowed additional data collection at minimal cost.

In New York City, Milwaukee, San Diego, and Syracuse, a random sample of workers at each demonstration agency received questionnaires (either by mail or at in-service meetings, depending on the agency). In Milwaukee, San Diego, and Syracuse, questionnaires were also administered to workers in "comparison" agencies to achieve a mix of for-profit and nonprofit agency employees in each city. In Boston, seven agencies were randomly selected to represent a mix of for-profit and nonprofit agencies providing a minimum of 50,000 service hours in 1984. The characteristics of the agencies included in the survey are summarized in Table A.1.

A total of 1,284 home aides completed the survey. The response rates of workers who received the questionnaires by mail varied from a low of 10 percent at one Boston for-profit agency to a high of 67 percent at one Syracuse nonprofit agency; response rates at most agencies were in the 45 to 50 percent range. (In a few agencies questionnaires were administered in person and completed by all attendees at in-service training meetings.)

Table A.1
Characteristics of Agencies Participating in the Job Satisfaction Survey

	For-profit	Non-profit	Union	Non-union	Public clients only	Mixed clients
Boston N = 7	2	5	3	4	1	6
New York City N = 2		2	2		2	
Milwaukee N = 2	1	1		2		2
San Diego N = 3	1	2	1	2	1	2
Syracuse N = 3	2	1		3		3
Total 17	6(35%)	11(65%)	6(35%)	11(65%)	4(24%)	13(76%)

Selection Bias Among Survey Respondents

Because home aides are scattered across multiple individual work sites, are rarely required to report in person to agency headquarters, frequently lack telephones or permanent home addresses, and often leave the job after a month or two of service, they are an extraordinarily difficult population to reach. Logistical problems lead, in turn, to the problem of selection bias. Those who can be reached through mail, phone, or on-site contacts may constitute the most stable and possibly most satisfied segment of the worker population. On the other hand, it is possible that those who respond to surveys are motivated to do so because they are the most dissatisfied with their work.

The relatively long job tenure of survey respondents (median years on the job were 3.0, and only 26 percent had been on the job one year or less) and their high levels of overall job satisfaction suggest that the bias was probably in the direction of overrepresenting committed and satisfied workers. Unfortunately, the resources available for the survey were not sufficient to allow contacting of nonrespondents to estimate the selection bias problem.[1]

Development of the Job Satisfaction and Turnover Model

As described in Chapter 4, a theoretical model was developed to explain the relationships among workers' personal characteristics, their perceptions of the work experience, their job satisfaction, and their intent to turnover. Intent to leave the job rather than actual turnover was the dependent variable used for analysis because actual turnover data were not available for most of the workers who responded to the survey.[2]

Based on the theoretical framework, various survey items were selected for inclusion in the analyses. Single-item measures are listed in Table A.2; multiple-item measures are listed in Table A.3. Where factor analyses were used to determine multiple-item

Table A.2
Single-Item Measures

(Items are listed in Chapter 4)

Age
Race
Marital Status
Duration of Job
Training Adequacy
Task Significance
Task Variety
Personal Responsibility
Task Unpredictability
Loneliness
Lock In
Intent To Turnover

Table A.3
Multiple-Item Measures

	Factor Loadings	Cronbach's Alpha
Supervisor supportiveness		
-Sets high standards	.65	
-Lets me know how I am doing	.74	
-Is concerned about me	.73	
-Is available	.61	.86
Worker-client bond (two items: see Chapter 4.)		
Information problems on the job		
-Lack of client information	.76	
-Information on client's care	.86	
-Changes in work assignments	.76	.73
Equipment problems on the job		
-Lack of supplies or equipment	.86	
-Broken equipment	.89	.70
Satisfaction with pay and benefits		
-Pay	.84	
-Benefits	.84	.77
Perceived pay equity		
-All in all, my pay is fair	.82	
-Considering my skills and effort, my pay is fair	.84	.75
Intrinsic job satisfaction		
-Chances to learn new things	.79	
-Chances to do work suited to my abilities	.74	
-Chances to take part in making decisions	.62	
-Chances to accomplish something worthwhile	.76	.80

constructs, factor loadings and Cronbach's alpha (an indication of internal reliability) are listed in the table as well. Because of missing data, means for two of three (or three of four) items were substituted in the constructs. If more than one item in a construct was missing, the entire question was dropped from the analysis. This reduced the overall usable sample to 835 (out of a possible 1,284) respondents.

The statistical method used to estimate the parameters (variables) of the causal model was critical path analysis. Critical path analysis is a method of ordinary least squares (OLS) regression in which groups of determinants are used as independent variables for successive dependent variables. In the causal model shown in Figure 4.1, the demographic factors were taken as the independent variables and ''supervisor supportiveness'' as the first dependent variable in the OLS regression. Next, the demographic factors plus ''supervisor supportiveness'' were taken as the independent variables, with ''training adequacy'' as the second dependent variable in the OLS regression, and so on.

In each regression, standardized betas greater than or equal to +/−.15 are indicative of important effects (the associated p value is less than or equal to .001). These effects can be drawn in an ordered model as shown in Chapter 4. The outcome variable of intent to leave is the end point; each determinant with a direct or indirect effect on the outcome of +/−.15 is then drawn via a backwards chain to the starting point of the regression. Thus, this method allows one to derive a ''path'' linking input determinants with the outcomes of interest.

Models illustrated in Chapter 4 contain only determinants with direct effects greater than 0.10 (and $p<0.01$). (Effects consist of standardized betas in the path regression analysis.) For the two outcomes (intrinsic satisfaction and intent to turnover), explained variance (adjusted R^2) was low—between about 0.30 for intrinsic satisfaction and about 0.20 for intent to leave. As Price and Mueller state, this variance is consistent with other research: ''With individuals as the focus, seldom does one find an explained variance of more than 20 percent and it is common to find studies explaining less than 10 percent'' (1986:203).

Use of Survey Data for Before and After Analysis of Program Participants

An initial purpose of the home aide survey was to collect baseline data on program participants and controls that could be compared to information gathered at a follow-up point a year after the start of the demonstrations. Unfortunately, administration of the questionnaire proved to be a more onerous and time-consuming task than the demonstration agencies had anticipated, so that they did not collect some of the baseline data at all, and some were not collected until after some of the workers had been notified of their participation in the work life programs. This problem vitiated the usefulness of the survey for before and after comparisons.

EVALUATION OF THE WORK LIFE DEMONSTRATIONS

Random Selection of Program Participants and Controls

All of the demonstration agencies agreed in principle to random selection of program participants and controls. Where merit was a criterion for selecting program participants, agencies chose a large enough group of deserving workers that would allow the research team to randomly select both participants and controls from within that ''meritorious'' group.

Several practical problems did, however, interfere with random selection. The most serious problems occurred at Remedy, where—as noted in the case study—the supervisory staff failed to contact 30 percent of current workers and 40 percent of new workers to invite them to participate in the project. In addition, a large proportion of those contacted declined to participate. (Compared to Remedy, the participant selection process at Quality Care, Long Life, and Independent Living was relatively smooth.) These problems suggested that the program participant group might be biased in some way compared to the controls, and, in fact, program participants did have significantly longer work experience than controls (see Chapter 7). We thus needed to address the selection bias issue, as described below.

Selection Bias Among Program Participants

Given evidence of biased selection among the current worker program participants at Remedy San Diego (see Chapter 7), the decision was made to compare their turnover with the turnover of a group of randomly selected controls matched according to prior Remedy service. The matched control group consisted of 34 workers selected from the 450 controls originally identified through random selection. Their mean hours worked at baseline were 1,224, compared to the 1,222 of the program participants. Thus their prior work experience was virtually identical.

Definition of Turnover

Turnover was the main outcome of interest in the evaluation of the demonstrations' impact. In the abstract, turnover is a simple concept, with each employee being either a "stayer" or a "leaver" (Price & Mueller, 1986:48). The turnover rate for a group of workers is the percentage of leavers at a given point in time. In the home care industry, however, turnover can be difficult to measure because the distinctions between stayers and leavers are not always clear. At all the demonstration agencies, a home aide could refuse work for several weeks or pay periods or be unavailable for assignment for some period of time without actually resigning, being fired, or being formally terminated. Or she might declare a leave of absence, then never resume employment.

For the purposes of the turnover analysis, all inactive workers were counted as leavers if they formally resigned, declared a leave of absence, were fired, or missed three consecutive pay periods (six weeks) ending at the six-month, twelve-month, or eighteen-month measurement point.

Agencies routinely kept track of the work status of their employees in order to ensure that clients were served and workers paid. Thus simply by gaining access to payroll and other employee records, it was possible for the research team to collect and analyze turnover statistics at minimal cost and with minimal disruption to agency operations.

Inclusion of Program Dropouts in the Turnover Analysis

In general all program participants, including those who dropped out of training programs or out of the full-time work components of the work life demonstrations, were included in the turnover analyses, on the grounds that to exclude them might bias the results toward a more favorable outcome. In some instances, separate turnover analyses were performed for training graduates only. These instances are clearly indicated in the body of the book.

NOTES

1. At one Boston agency, the research team explored the representativeness of workers who completed the questionnaire at in-service meetings by comparing their demographic characteristics

to a random sample of workers who had not attended the in-service meetings. The two groups did not differ significantly with respect to age, race, education, job tenure, or wage. However, such a comparison provides no indication of whether or how the groups might have differed in attitudes toward the job.

2. At the demonstration agencies, turnover data were collected only for selected demonstration and control workers, many of whom did not complete the questionnaire. Thus, it was not possible to match their attitudes to their actual decisions to leave or stay on the job. Furthermore, other agencies cooperating in the survey agreed to administer the questionnaire to their workers but did not provide access to their payroll or employee registers. Thus, actual turnover data were not collected for many agencies. In any case, intent to turnover has been shown in other research (Arnold & Feldman, 1982) to be strongly related to actual turnover and is therefore a valuable outcome to study.

Glossary of Names and Abbreviations

BLS The U.S. Bureau of Labor Statistics

DSS San Diego Department of Social Services. Responsible for administering the San Diego County In-Home Supportive Services Program

GAO U.S. General Accounting Office

HRA The New York City Human Resources Administration. The large bureaucracy that, among other programs, administers the Medicaid-funded home attendant program in New York City

IHSS The California In-Home Supportive Services Program. A state-county-funded program that finances personal care and homemaking services for the frail elderly and disabled who meet specified income eligibility requirements

Independent Living Home Care Services for Independent Living, Inc. One of the two home attendant agencies that participated in the New York City work life demonstration

IP or IPs Individual providers. Individual home aides who are employed directly by their clients rather than by a home care agency or other organized employer. They may receive payment directly from the state, county, or other governmental agency, but they are hired and fired by the client. The California IHSS program makes extensive use of IPs.

Local 32 B/J A branch of the Service Employees International Union that represents some home attendants in New York City

Local 1199 A branch of the Drug, Hospital and Health Care Employees Union that represents some home attendants in New York City

Long Life Long Life Home Care Services, Inc. One of the two home attendant agencies that participated in the New York City work life demonstration

OECD Organization for Economic Cooperation and Development. An international organization, headquartered in Paris, that supports many economic studies of Western industrialized countries

PPS Prospective Payment System. The Medicare program's hospital reimbursement system

Quality Care Quality Care, Inc., now part of Kimberly Quality Care, Inc. A large national for-profit home care company. Two local Quality Care offices—in Syracuse and Milwaukee—participated in the work life demonstration program.

QWL Quality of Work Life. A term used to describe salient features of the job, such as compensation, health and safety conditions, employment security, opportunities for advancement, etc. (Davis & Cherns, 1975; Walton, 1975)

Remedy Remedy Home and Health Care, Inc. A California-based home care company that contracts to provide services under the state-county IHSS program. Remedy San Diego was the local agency that participated in the work life demonstration program.

SHARP Special Home Attendant Research Project. The acronym applied to the home attendants who participated in the New York City work life demonstration program

UDW United Domestic Workers of America. The homemakers' union in San Diego and many other parts of California

VNAs Visiting Nurse Associations. Long-standing providers of home health care in the United States

References

Abt Associates. 1984. Home Health Services: An Industry in Transition. Home Health Agency Prospective Payment Demonstration. Cambridge, Mass.: Abt Associates.

Afro-American Times. 1987. Brooklyn Home Care Workers Complete Advance Course. March 12.

Arnold, H. & Feldman, D. 1982. A Multivariate Analysis of the Determinants of Job Turnover. *Journal of Applied Psychology,* 67:350-60.

Atkins, B., Meyer, A., & Smith, N.K. 1982. Personal Care Attendants: Attitudes and Factors Contributing to Job Satisfaction. *Journal of Rehabilitation,* July-September, 20-24.

Atkins, G.L. 1985. The Economic Status of the Oldest Old. *Milbank Memorial Fund Quarterly,* 63(2):395-419.

Attorney General. 1985. Opinion of John K. Van de Kamp. California: No. 84-308. July 23.

Beck, B. 1987. Better Home Health Care by Worker-Owners. *New York Times,* June 20.

Bernstein, N. 1987a. The Crisis in Home Care: Health Care Comes Home and Critics Say It's a Ticking Time Bomb. *Newsday,* September 27:5.

Bernstein, N. 1987b. The Crisis in Home Care: Not Dignity, but Desertion. *Newsday,* September 29:7.

Blalock, H. 1972. *Social Statistics.* New York: McGraw-Hill.

Bluestone, B. 1971. The Characteristics of Marginal Industries. In *Problems in Political Economy.* D.M. Gordon (Ed.). Lexington, Mass.: D.C. Heath Company.

Bonnette v. *California Health and Welfare Agency.* 1983. 704 F.2d 1465, 1468-1470 (9th Circuit).

Bonstein, R. & Mueller, J. 1985. Improving Agency Productivity. *Caring,* 4(11):4-9.

Boston Globe. 1987. A Home Care Pay Travesty. April 9.

Brecher, C. & Horton, R. 1984. *Setting Municipal Priorities, 1984.* New York: New York University Press.

Business Week. 1985. Quality Care's Bid to Stand Out in the Crowd. July 22:87.

Butter, I., Carpenter, E., Kay, B., & Simmons, R. 1985. *Sex and Status: Hierarchies in the Health Workforce.* Ann Arbor, Mich.: University of Michigan Press.

California Department of Social Services (DSS). 1988. In-Home Supportive Services Allocations, FY 1984-1987. Sacramento.

California Program Review Board. 1983. Evaluation of In-Home Supportive Services Program. May, Sacramento.

Cammann, C., Fichman, M., Jenkens, G.A., Jr., & Klesh, J.R. 1983. Assessing Attitudes and Perceptions. In *Assessing Organizational Change.* S. Seashore (Ed.). New York: John Wiley & Sons.

Canalis, D. 1987. Homemaker/Home Health Aide Attrition: Methods of Prevention. *Caring,* 6(4):85-89.

Caring. 1988. 7(5) Entire issue.

Caves, R. 1964. *American Industry: Structure, Conduct, Performance.* Englewood Cliffs, N.J.: Prentice-Hall.

Cohen, D., Patrizi, P., Wagner, C., & Brunelle, M. 1984. A Planning Study of Alternative Home Health Ventures That Improve Employment Opportunities for the Homemaker/Home Health Aide. Final Report submitted to the Ford Foundation. Philadelphia: The Wharton School, University of Pennsylvania.

Cole, R. 1988. GrandMet Hotel Sale Indicated. *New York Times,* September 30:D1.

Commonwealth of Massachusetts, Division of Employment Security. 1986. Employment Trends in the Health Care Industry. July. Boston, Mass.: Division of Employment Security.

Community Service Society of New York. 1987. Caring for the Elderly at Home: A Policy Perspective on Consumer Experiences with Publicly-Funded Home Care Programs in New York City. New York: CSS Working Papers.

Conroy, W. 1986. Elderly Consumers Are Victims of Home-Care Industry's Insurance Crisis. *Milwaukee Business Journal,* September 15:6.

Copeman, E. & Weigel, L. 1987. Training Homemaker/Home Health Aides for High Tech Home Care. *Caring,* 6(5):34-37.

Country of Fairfax. 1988. Correspondence with Planning Office, Area Agency on Aging. July 8.

Cronin, M. 1987. Medicaid in New York City: An Analysis of Expenditures, Services, Recipients and Utilization. New York: Human Resources Administration, Medical Assistance Program.

Crowe, K.C. 1988. How Home-Care Workers Won a $315-Million Raise. *Newsday,* May 9:10.

Cyert, R.M. & March, J.G. 1963. *A Behavioral Theory of the Firm.* Englewood Cliffs, N.J.: Prentice-Hall.

Davis, K. & Rowland, D. 1986. *Medicare Policy: New Directions for Health and Long-Term Care.* Baltimore: The Johns Hopkins University Press.

Davis, L. & Cherns, A. 1975. *The Quality of Working Life,* vol. 1: *Problems, Prospects and the State of the Art.* New York: The Free Press.

Deaux, K. & Kite, M. 1987. Thinking About Gender. In *Analyzing Gender:* 92-119. B.B. Hess and M.M. Ferree (Eds.). Beverly Hills, Calif.: Sage Publications.

Dietz, J. 1986. State Home Care Workers Get 11 Percent Pay Raise. *Boston Globe,* June 26.

Dionne, E.J. 1982. Cuomo: The Old Liberalism. *New York Times Magazine.* October 31:22.

District of Columbia. 1988. Correspondence with Chief of Social Services Division, Department of Human Services, August 24.

Donovan, R. 1986. The Health and Social Needs of Home Care Workers, Preliminary Report (Summary of Findings). New York: Hunter College School of Social Work, City University of New York.

Donovan, R. 1987a. Home Care Work: A Legacy of Slavery in U.S. Health Care. *Affilia, Journal of Women and Social Work,* Fall 2(3):33-44.

Donovan, R. 1987b. Poorly Paid Home Health Care Workers Subsidize an Industry. *New York Times,* June 2:31.

Dyckman, Z., Hurwitz, N., Bishop, C., & Cohen, M. 1985. Market Study for Home Health Care Services. Prepared for Health Care Financing Administration, HCFA Contract No. 500-84-0033. Columbia, Md.: Center for Health Policy Studies.

Enns, J., Bell, S., & Flanagan, K. 1987. Evaluation of the AFDC Homemaker-Home Health Aide Demonstrations: Trainee Employment and Earnings. Cambridge, Mass.: Abt Associates.

Federal Register. 1988. June 27, 53(123).

Feldman, P.H. & Sapienza, A.M. 1989. Strategic Management of Quality of Worklife in the Home Care Industry. In *Human Resource Management in the Health Care Sector: A Guide for Administrators and Professionals.* A.S. Sethi and R.S. Schuler (Eds.). Westport, Conn.: Greenwood Press.

FIND/SVP. 1985. The Market for Home Health Products and Services. *Health Industry Today,* February: 46-51.

FIND/SVP. 1987. *Home Health Care Products and Services.* Market Report.

GAO. 1986a. An Aging Society: Meeting the Needs of the Elderly While Responding to Rising Federal Costs. Report to the Chairman, Subcommittee on Intergovernmental Relations and Human Resources, Committee on Government Operations, House of Representatives. September. GAO/HRD-86-135.

GAO. 1986b. Medicare: Need to Strengthen Home Health Care Payment Controls and Address Unmet Needs. Report to the Chairman, Special Committee on Aging, United States Senate. December. GAO/HRD-87-9.

GAO. 1987. Long-Term Care Insurance: Coverage Varies Widely in a Developing Market. Report to the Chairman, Subcommittee on Health and Long-Term Care, Select Committee on Aging, House of Representatives. May. GAO/HRD-87-80.

Garland, S.B. & Fly, R. 1987. Long-Term Care: A Political Time Bomb. *Business Week,* November 30:40.

Gibson, R.C. 1986. Outlook for the Black Family. In *Our Aging Society:* 181-98. A. Pifer and L. Bronte (Eds.). New York: W.W. Norton & Co.

Gillion, C., Schieber, G. & Poullier, J.P. 1985. Measuring Health Care, 1960-1983, OECD Social Policy Studies, number 2, Paris.

Ginzberg, E., Balinsky, W., & Ostow, M. 1984. *Home Health Care: Its Role in the Changing Health Services Market.* Totowa, N.J.: Rowman & Allanheld.

Glenn, E.N. & Tolbert, C. 1987. Technology and Emerging Patterns of Stratification for Women of Color. In *Women, Work, and Technology:* 318-31. B. Wright et al. (Eds.). Ann Arbor, Mich.: University of Michigan Press.

Gotay, C.C. 1983. Home Care for the Dying: Homemakers' Perspectives. *Home Health Care Services Quarterly,* 4(1):55-66.

Grinker, Walker and Associates & Feldman, P., Kane, N., & Sapienza, A. 1985. A Proposal for Improving Employment Conditions of Entry Level Service Workers: Lessons from the Home Care Industry. Proposal submitted to the Ford Foundation, February. Boston: Harvard University School of Public Health.

Gross, J. 1988. Cocaine and AIDS in New York Add to Infant Deaths. *New York Times,* February 13:1.

Hackman, J.R. & Lawler, E.E. III. 1979. Job Characteristics and Motivation: A Conceptual Framework. In *Design of Jobs.* L.E. Davis and J.C. Taylor (Eds.). Santa Monica, Calif.: Goodyear Publishing Co.

Health Care Finance Administration (HCFA). 1987a. Medicaid Medical Vendor Payments by Type of Service and by Region and State, Fiscal Year 1986. Unpublished data. Baltimore, Md.: U.S. Department of Health and Human Services, HCFA, Bureau of Data Management and Strategy, Office of Statistics and Data Management.

Health Care Finance Administration (HCFA). 1987b. Data from the Provider Service File. Baltimore, Md.: U.S. Department of Health and Human Services, Bureau of Data Management and Strategy.

Health Care Finance Administration (HCFA). 1987c. Trends in the Utilization of Medicare Home Health Agency Services: Persons Served, Visits, Charges, & Reimbursements for Selected Years: 1974-1985. Baltimore, Md.: U.S. Department of Health and Human Services.

Health Industry Today. 1985. The Market for Home Healthcare Products and Services. February: 47-51.

Home Care Association of New York State. 1987. Report of the Ad Hoc Task Force on the Human Resource Shortage. Syracuse, N.Y.

Home Care Council of New York City. 1988a. The Care-Givers—Part 1. *New York Times,* March 14.

Home Care Council of New York City. 1988b. The Care-Givers—Part 2. *New York Times,* March 18.

Hoppock, J. 1935. *Job Satisfaction.* New York: Harper & Row.

Human Resources Administration. 1984. Summary Report: Home Care Activity. May. New York: Medical Assistance Program.

In-Home Supportive Services (IHSS) v. *Workers' Comp. Appeals Bd.* 1984. 152 Cal. App. 3d 720, 725-741.

Iverem, E. 1988. New York's Home Health-Care System Facing a Labor Crisis. *New York Times,* January 28:B1.

Joseloff, A. 1986. The Home Health Aide: A Member of the Hospice Team. *Caring,* 5(10):37-38.

Kabanoff, B. 1980. Work and Nonwork: A Review of Models, Methods, and Findings. *Psychology Bulletin,* 88:60-77.

Kahn, R.L. 1980. *Work and Health.* New York: Wiley-Interscience.

Kane, N. 1989. The Home Care Crisis of the Nineties. *The Gerontologist,* 29(1):24-31.

Kavesh, W.N. 1986. Home Care: Process, Outcome, Cost. *Annual Review of Gerontology and Geriatrics.* New York: Springer Publishing Co.

Kaye, L. 1986. Worker Views of the Intensity of Affective Expression During the Delivery of Home Care Services for the Elderly. *Home Health Care Services Quarterly,* 7(2):41-54.

Levit, K.P., Lazenby, H., Waldo, D.R., & Davidoff, L. 1985. National Health Expenditures, 1985. *Health Care Financing Review,* 7:1-35.

Liebman, J. 1986. Rate Setting for Homecare Services in Massachusetts. Boston: Harvard University School of Public Health.

Liu, K., Manton, K., & Liu, B. 1985. Home Care Expenses for the Elderly. *Health Care Financing Review,* 7(2):51-58.

Lohr, S. 1988. The Global Strategy at Grand Met. *New York Times,* October 6:D1.

Long-Term Care Policy Coordinating Council. 1986. Recruitment, Training, and Retention of Home Care Workers in New York State. December. Albany: Department of Health.

Los Angeles Times. 1980. Domestics' Union Makes Gains. November 22.

Loth, R. 1987. The No-Care Zone. *Boston Globe Magazine,* May 31: 14-16, 56-61.

McFadden, Robert D. 1987. Home-Care Attendants Guilty in Murder of 2 Elderly Women. *New York Times,* July 7:B2.

Manton, K.G. 1987. The Interaction of Population Aging and Health Transitions at Later Ages. In *Health Care and its Costs:* 185-221. C.J. Schramm (Ed.). New York: W.W. Norton.

Massachusetts Council for Homemaker-Home Health Aide Services. 1985. Survey of Member Agencies on Personnel Practices, Summer. Boston.

Massachusetts Rate Setting Commission. 1987. The Homebound Elderly: Who Cares? Boston.

Medical and Healthcare Marketplace Guide. 1986. Miami: The International Biomedical Information Service, Inc.

Mitchell, T.R. 1979. Organizational Behavior. *Annual Review of Psychology,* 30:243-81.

Mobley, W.H. 1982. *Employee Turnover: Causes, Consequences, and Control.* Reading, Mass.: Addison-Wesley.

Montgomery, D. 1981. Working in Aging Services: Job Satisfaction, Regulation and Turnover. *Journal of Health and Human Resources Administration,* 4:477-93.

Mootz, A. 1986. Do We Support Standards in the Homemaker-Home Health Aide Field? *Caring,* 5(4):32-33.

Moreno, S. 1987. The Crisis in Home Care: Two Caught in the Fallout. *Newsday,* September 28:7, 32-33.

Moreno, S. 1988. Home-Care Pay Issue Put on City. *Newsday,* January 10:21.

Mouzelis, N. 1972. *Organization and Bureaucracy.* Chicago: Aldine-Atherton.

Murray, W. 1986. A Reporter at Large. *The New Yorker,* December 29:63-75.

National Association for Home Care. 1986. The Attempted Dismantling of the Medicare Home Health Benefit. Washington, D.C.

National HomeCaring Council. 1987. Homemaker-Home Health Aide Services in Support of High-Tech Patients and Their Families: A Trainer's Manual. Washington, D.C.: National HomeCaring Council, a Division of the Foundation for Hospice and Home Care.

National Institute on Aging. 1987. *Personnel for Health Needs of the Elderly Through Year 2020.* September 1987 Report to Congress. Washington, D.C.: U.S. Department of Health and Human Services.

New York State Department of Social Services. 1988. Telephone communication regarding statistics. Albany: DSS Budget Office.

New York Times. 1987. Savings Envisioned in Home AIDS Care. November 20:25.

New York Times. 1988. Home Care Unsung and Underpaid. March 14.

OECD Publication. 1985. The Integration of Women Into the Economy. Paris.

Parks, C. 1986. A Study of Home Care Workers in the Boston Area. Boston: Harvard University School of Public Health.

Paukert, L. 1984. The Employment and Unemployment of Women in OECD Countries. Paris: OECD Publication.

Perspectives. 1986. Hard Times for Home Health. *Medicine and Health,* August 18:40: Supplement. Washington, D.C.: McGraw-Hill.

Pifer, A. & Bronte, L. 1986. *Our Aging Society.* New York: W.W. Norton & Co.

Piore, M. 1975. Notes for a Theory of Labor Market Stratification. In *Labor Market Segmentation:* 125-50. R. Edwards, M. Reich, and D. Gordon (Eds.). Lexington, Mass.: D.C. Heath & Co.

Porter, L. & Steers, R. 1973. Organizational, Work, and Personal Factors in Employee Turnover and Absenteeism. *Psychological Bulletin,* 80:151-76.

Prial, F.J. 1987. Scuffle Seen as Seriously Hurting Hospital Union. *New York Times,* October 11.

Price, J.L. & Mueller, C.W. 1986. Absenteeism and Turnover of Hospital Employees. Greenwich, Conn.: JAI Press.

Raskin, A.H. 1986. A Health-Care Union Returns to Good Health. *New York Times,* May 19:A21.

Record. 1987. A Dearth of Care. February 26. Hackensack, N.J.

Rivlin, A. & Wiener, J. 1988. *Caring for the Disabled Elderly: Who Will Pay?* Washington, D.C.: Brookings.

Roberts, S. 1983. City's Benefit from Upturn is Questioned. *New York Times,* November 28:B1.

Roberts, S. 1987. For Attendants, Poverty at Home and on the Job. *New York Times,* July 20:B1.

Rossi, A. 1986. Sex and Gender in the Aging Society. In *Our Aging Society:* 110-40. A. Pifer and L. Bronte (Eds.). New York: W.W. Norton.

Rowland, D. 1987. Issues of Long-Term Care. In *Health Care and its Costs:* 222-49. C. Schramm (Ed.). New York: W.W. Norton.

San Diego Union. 1982a. Meeting on County Homemaker Service Called Worthwhile. July 30.

San Diego Union. 1982b. Women Protest County's Cut in Pay, Benefits. July 28:B-1.

Scanlon, W.J. & Feder, J. 1984. The Long-Term Care Market Place—An Overview. *Healthcare Financial Management,* 14:18-36.

Scott, G. 1988. Health Workers Get Raise Deal. *Newsday,* April 1:18.

Seashore, S.E. 1975. Defining and Measuring the Quality of Working Life. In *The Quality of Working Life,* vol. 1: *Problems, Prospects and the State of the Art:* 105-18. L. Davis and A. Cherns (Eds.). New York: The Free Press.

Seifer, S. 1987. The Impact of PPS on Home Health Care: A Survey of Thirty-five Home Health Agencies. *Caring,* 6(4):10-12.

Shark, M. 1987. Overview of Proposed Regulation. Letter to Homemaker Task Force, April 15. Boston: Massachusetts Rate Setting Commission.

Shulman, E., Steinberg, G., & Kahn, R. 1987. Senile Dementia: The New Market in Home Health Care. *Caring,* 6(5):58-62.

Silvestri, G.T. & Lukasiewicz, J.M. 1987. A Look at Occupational Employment Trends to the Year 2000. *Monthly Labor Review,* September: 46-59.

Staw, B.M. 1984. Organizational Behavior: A Review and Reformulation of the Field's

Outcome Variables. *Annual Review of Psychology,* 35:627-66.

Stelmach, M., Postma, J., Goldstein, S., & Shepard, K. 1981. Selected Factors Influencing Job Satisfaction of Attendants of Physically Disabled Adults. *Rehabilitation Literature,* 2(5/6):130-37.

Stephenson, P.R. & Cron, W.L. 1986. HIDA. Financial Performance Survey for Homecare/DME Dealers.

Stevenson, M. 1973. Women's Wages and Job Segregation. In *Labor Market Segmentation:* 243-56. R. Edwards, M. Reich, and D. Gordon (Eds.). Lexington, Mass.: D.C. Heath & Co.

Stillman, J. & Gould-Stuart, J. 1988. Quality of Work and Quality of Home Care. New York: Pickman Consulting Group, Inc.

Stockton, M. 1986. Who's Taking Care of You? Hospice Worker Burnout: Its Diagnosis, Prevention and Cure. *Caring,* 6(4):60-63.

Sullivan, R. 1987. New York Shifts its Care for Aged to Their Homes. *New York Times,* May 4:A1.

Surpin, R. 1987. The Recruitment and Retention of Health Care Paraprofessionals. November. New York: Community Service Society, submitted to the Labor-Industry Task Force on Health Care Personnel, New York State Department of Health.

Surpin, R. 1988. Improved Working Conditions Lead to Improved Quality. *Caring,* 7(5):26-31.

Surpin, R. & Grumm, F. 1987. Ending Workers' Hidden Subsidy for Home Care Services. New York: Community Service Society, Worker Cooperative Development Project.

Suzman, R. & Riley, M. 1985. Introducing the "Oldest Old." *Milbank Memorial Fund Quarterly,* 63(2):177-86.

Task Force. 1987. Problems on the Supply Side: The Homemaker Shortage in Massachusetts. March 1987 Task Force Report. Boston: Massachusetts Council for Homemaker-Home Health Aide Services.

Tiagha, H. 1981. Role Analysis of the Position of the Homemaker-Home Health Aide. *Home Health Care Services Quarterly,* 2(4) Winter: 39-56.

Tolchin, M. 1988. House Rejects Bill on Longterm Home Health Care. *New York Times,* June 6.

Trager, B. 1980. Service Definition, *Home Health Care Services Quarterly* 1(2):7-25.

United Hospital Fund. 1987. Home Care in New York City: Providers, Payers, and Clients. New York.

U.S. Bureau of Labor Statistics. 1985. Employment, Hours, and Earnings, 1909-1984. Bulletin 1312-12, vol. 2, March: 698-784. Washington, D.C.: U.S. Government Printing Office.

U.S. Bureau of Labor Statistics. 1985a. Industry Wage Survey: Hospitals, Buffalo-Niagara Falls, N.Y. August. Washington, D.C.: U.S. Government Printing Office.

U.S. Bureau of Labor Statistics. 1985b. Industry Wage Survey: Hospitals, Los Angeles-Long Beach, Calif. August. Washington, D.C.: U.S. Government Printing Office.

U.S. Bureau of Labor Statistics. 1985c. Industry Wage Survey: Hospitals, Milwaukee, Wis. August. Washington, D.C.: U.S. Government Printing Office.

U.S. Bureau of Labor Statistics. 1985d. Industry Wage Survey: Hospitals, New York, N.Y. August. Washington, D.C.: U.S. Government Printing Office.

U.S. Bureau of Labor Statistics. 1986. Occupational Employment Statistics Survey Data.

Washington, D.C.: U.S. Department of Labor.

U.S. Bureau of Labor Statistics. 1987. Industry Wage Survey: Nursing and Personal Care Facilities, September 1985. Bulletin 2275, March. Washington, D.C.: U.S. Government Printing Office.

U.S. Bureau of Labor Statistics. 1987. San Diego, California, Metropolitan Area. Bulletin 3040-55, December. Washington, D.C.: U.S. Government Printing Office.

U.S. Bureau of Labor Statistics. 1988. Occupational Projections and Training Data. Bulletin 2301, April. Washington, D.C.: U.S. Government Printing Office.

U.S. Bureau of the Census. 1984. *Current Population Reports,* Series P-60, No.144, Characteristics of the Population Below the Poverty Level: 1982. Washington, D.C.: U.S. Government Printing Office.

U.S. Bureau of the Census. 1985. *Current Population Survey.* (Employed civilians by detailed occupation, sex, race, and Hispanic origin.) Washington, D.C.: U.S. Government Printing Office.

U.S. Bureau of the Census. 1987. Poverty Level for a Family of Three. Telephone Communication. Boston: U.S. Department of Commerce. Bureau of the Census.

U.S. Congress, Select Committee on Aging. 1987. Black Box of Home Care Quality. Washington, D.C.: U.S. Government Printing Office.

Wallach, S.S. & Tell, E.J. 1986. New Approaches to the Finance and Delivery of Health Care to the Elderly. In *Health Care Cost Management:* 85-94. Brookfield, Wis.: International Foundation of Employee Benefit Plans.

Walton, R. 1975. Criteria for Quality of Working Life. In *The Quality of Working Life,* vol. 1: *Problems, Prospects and the State of the Art:* 91-104. L. Davis and A. Cherns (Eds.). New York: The Free Press.

Weinstein, H. 1988. Organizing Effort by Union Targets Home Care Aides. *Los Angeles Times,* April 19.

Weisman, C. & Nathanson, C. 1985. Professional Satisfaction and Client Outcomes: A Comparative Organizational Analysis. *Medical Care,* 23(10):1179-92.

WHO. 1986. Evaluation of the Strategy for Health for All by the Year 2000, Seventh Report on the World Health Situation, vol. 5, European Region, Copenhagen, DK.

Wisconsin Bureau of Health Care Finance. 1987. Medicaid Expenditures for Home Health Care, Fiscal Years 1982-1986. In *Wisconsin Home Health Agency Utilization: 1986/87.* October. Madison, Wis.: Division of Health, Department of Health and Social Services.

Wisconsin Bureau of Health Care Finance. 1988. Medicaid Expenditures for Home Health Care, Fiscal Year 1987.

Wisconsin Department of Health and Social Services. 1988. A Comparison of Home Health Agencies in Wisconsin. *Health Data Review,* 2(9) September: 1-7.

Wisconsin Office of the Commissioner of Insurance. 1988. Madison, Wis.: Health and Life Section.

Wolff, C. 1987. Health Care at Home: A Mixed Blessing. *New York Times,* October 31.

Woody, B. & Malson, M. 1984. In Crisis: Low Income Black Employed Women in the U.S. Workplace. Working paper number 131. Wellesley, Mass.: Wellesley College Center for Research on Women.

Yu, P. 1987. The Growth of New York City's Medicaid Program, 1981-86. New York: Human Resources Administration, Medical Assistance Program.

Zukas, H., Cone, K., & Leon, J. 1984. Descriptive Analysis of the In-Home Supportive Services Program in California. Berkeley, Calif.: World Institute on Disability.

Index

Absenteeism: and job satisfaction, 13, 41, 42; reduction of, 120
Advancement, opportunity for, 9-10, 18, 42-43, 106, 120, 126, 202-3; and staff aide program, 128-29, 136-42
Agencies. *See* Home care agencies
Aides. *See* Home aides/home attendants
AIDS (acquired immune deficiency syndrome), health care implications of, 6-7, 118
Allied Home Health Association, 86
Alzheimer's disease/dementia, clients with, 12, 14, 35, 36, 109. *See also* Clients, difficult
Attendance. *See* Absenteeism

Bedridden clients, 34-35, 38
Benefits, 9, 26, 106, 126, 144; abuses of, 135, 144, 191; and full-time work, 20, 83, 129; and primary wage earner status, 26; and unions, 13, 80, 82, 104-5, 119
Bidding, competitive, 79, 100, 152, 158; and establishment of compensation requirements, 206; on high technology products and services, 59
Blue Cross, 123, 143, 145n.1, 160-62, 188-89
Boredom, 37, 48
Burnout, 109

California, caseload in, 121n.3. *See also* San Diego
Care. *See* Continuity of care; Home care; Quality of care
Clients: clustering of, 207; custodial vs. medical care of, 39, 104, 108; elderly, 5, 12, 63; family members of, 36; public vs. private, 49-50, 56-57, 60, 158, 188; relationship with aides, 39-40; satisfaction of, and turnover of, 11; self-paying, 63-64; types of, 34-35
Clients, difficult: with Alzheimer's disease/dementia, 12, 14, 35, 36, 109; amount of care needed by, 104, 121n.3; assignment to, 111, 157; bedridden, 34-35, 38; behavior problems in, 35-36, 109, 120; continuity of care for, 113-17, 151, 175-77; definition of, 109; medically complex, 120; pay increments for care of, 109, 111, 120, 159; training in care of, 109, 159
Competition (among agencies), 64, 151-52, 158; for funding of proposals, 206; and high technology home care, 59

Consultants, outside, 155, 188
Continuity of care, 113-17, 151, 175-77, 189
Cost control measures. *See* Financial considerations

Dementia. *See* Alzheimer's disease/dementia, clients with
Dinkins, David, 120, 153
Dropouts, 99, 130, 138; from full-time work requirement, 170-71; among new workers, 190-91; from training programs, 169
Drug, Hospital and Health Care Employees Union, 104, 105, 118, 120

Educational status, 25, 50, 76, 185
Elderly: chronic illness in, 5, 6; emotional problems of, 12; financial status of, 207-8; increased population of, 5; needs of, 209
Equipment, deficient, 38

Family members: behavior problems of, 36; provision of care by, 5-6
Field support liaisons, 120, 203
Financial considerations: competitive bidding, 79, 100, 152, 158; cost control measures, 6, 15n.3, 65, 81, 92, 101n.10; health care cost escalation, 6, 19; and home care industry, 55-67, 187, 191n.1, 208-9; and private insurance reimbursement, 160; and unions, 80-81; and work life improvements, 158-59, 188. *See also* Wages
Ford Foundation, 4, 72
Full-time work, guaranteed, 200-202. *See also* Work schedules

Gender issues: home care as "women's work," 8, 26; and labor market segregation, 17-18, 20-23, 76, 185; male-female income differentials, 22; origin of stereotypes, 22-23; and part-time employment, 20; and service sector, 19
Grand Metropolitan PLC (GrandMet), 125

Health care costs, escalation of, 6, 19
Health Care Financing Administration (HCFA), 15n.3, 65
Health Delivery Systems, 125
High technology products and services, 58, 59
Home aides/home attendants: advancement opportunities for, 9-10, 18, 120, 202-3; age of, 48, 52; attitudes of, 41-53, 84, 106, 107, 126, 127; benefits for, 9, 104-7, 126, 135, 144; categorization of, and task definition, 158-59; certified, 108; characteristics of, 25, 76-78; commitment to clients, 39; daily routine of, 30-34; disadvantaged status of, 26, 76; dropout rate of, 99, 130, 138, 169-71, 190-91; and field support liaisons, 120; immigrants as, 76, 105-6; inactive, 115, 116; individual providers, 8, 79, 81-82, 104, 205; isolation of, 9, 29, 39; job description of, 104; new, 178-80, 190-91; numbers of, 7-8; part-time status of, 9, 12; and performance gap, 151; as primary wage earner, 26, 76; productivity demands on, 12; reason for changing clients by, 113, 115, 175-77; recruitment of, 10-11, 105-6, 124, 128, 194-95; relationship with client, 39-40; replacement or weekend, 37, 38, 129, 135; screening of, 195; "senior" home attendants, 108, 158, 202; services provided by, 3, 30-38, 104, 108; "shared," 206-7; SHARP, 110, 119; shortage of, 11, 151; sleep-in, 37, 38; and staff aides, 128-29, 136-42; stress on, 12; and supervisor, 29, 48; support services for, 12, 85, 90-91, 120, 155-56, 197-98; survey of, 4, 15n.2, 24-25, 186, 211-15; terms for, 15n.1; transitional pay for, 177, 200; turnover of, 10, 11, 21, 114-17; and unionization, 12-13, 104-6; workweek of, 76, 77, 83, 91, 131-33; younger vs. older, 186. *See also* Benefits; Job problems; Job satisfaction; Training; Wages; Working conditions; Work life demonstrations; Work schedules

Home care: and AIDS, 6-7; Blue Cross coverage of, 123, 145n.1, 188-89; continuity of care in, 113-17; of elderly, 5; and health care costs, 6; increased demand for, 4-7, 56; medical care services, 39, 108; personal care services, 104, 108; provision by family, 5-6, 56; state regulation of, 108, 188, 205
Home care agencies: caseload of, 103, 123; certified vs. noncertified, 7, 123; clients of, 34-38; competition among, 151-52; and consultants, 155, 188; expansion of, 7; for-profit/proprietary, 7, 48, 57, 61-63, 72, 150; goals of directors of, 153-54; and implementation of work life changes, 154-57; management capacity, 155; management concerns, 10-13, 124; and Medicare/Medicaid, 6, 7, 56-67, 108, 118; motives for adopting work life changes, 149-54; not-for-profit, 48, 72, 73; and performance gaps, 151; political considerations affecting, 152-53, 158-59; and public vs. private clients, 158, 188; revenues of, 80, 103, 123; supervision of, 40n.1; and survey results, 212-13; and unions, 105-6, 118; unlicensed, 7; and wage agreements, 118-20. *See also* Management; Work life demonstrations
Home Care Council, 105, 118
Home care industry: demand characteristics of, 56; financial conditions in, 55-67, 187; high technology segment of, 59; labor market trends affecting, 17-27, 118; and public bureaucracy, 149-50; supply characteristics of, 56-57; unskilled services in, 55, 57, 60-61. *See also* Home care agencies; Profitability
Home Care Services for Independent Living, Inc. (Independent Living), 103, 153-59, 161, 162; work force characteristics, 76, 77; work life demonstration at, 106-21, 167-70, 172-176
Home health aides. *See* Home aides/home attendants
Homemakers. *See* Home aides/home attendants
Hospital aides. *See* Nursing aides, pay differential vs. home aides
Hospitals: fixed levels of employment in, 19; voluntary, and home care provision, 7
Hours, work. *See* Work schedules
Human Resources Administration (HRA), 72, 106-9, 118, 119, 149-51

Illness, chronic, in elderly, 5, 6
Immigrants, 76, 151
Immigration Reform and Control Act (1986), 105, 118, 151
Income. *See* Wages
Independent Living. *See* Home Care Services for Independent Living, Inc. (Independent Living)
Individual providers (IPs): in California, 121n.3; and contract with counties, 101nn.4,5; number of, 8, 79, 101n.1; and unions, 81-82; vs. "vendorization," 104, 205
In-Home Supportive Services (IHSS), 4, 79-81, 100, 158
Instructions, deficient, 38
Insurance. *See* Benefits; Blue Cross; Third-party coverage
Isolation, 9, 29, 39; and inadequate training, 9; reduction of, 120

Job attachment, 177-78, 190
Job description, 104
Job motivation, 39
Job problems: boredom, 37, 48; burnout, 109; comprehensive programs addressing, 180-81; deficient equipment and supplies, 38; difficulty with bedridden clients, 38; difficulty with client behavior, 35-36; difficulty with family members, 36; difficulty with replacement aides, 38; inadequate information or instructions, 38; inadequate training, 9, 11; isolation, 9, 29, 39, 107, 186; lack of benefits, 9, 20, 26, 106, 107, 186; lack of opportunity for advancement, 9-10, 106; loneliness, 46-47, 52-53, 106, 127, 186; low wages, 8-9, 14, 18, 24, 33, 46, 48, 82, 83, 106, 107, 126, 186; racial factors in, 48,

52; sexual harassment, 36-37; sleep-in situations, 37, 38; transportation difficulties, 26, 38; unsafe neighborhoods, 38-39; work schedule/part-time status, 9, 12, 19-20, 106
Jobs: low-status, 14, 18; supplementary, 25. *See also* Part-time employment
Job satisfaction, 83-84, 106, 107, 126-27; effect of race on, 48, 52; factors affecting, 186-87; as indicator of quality of work life, 13; and productivity, 41; and quality of service, 12; and relationship with client, 39; research about, 41-42; role of benefits and pay in, 48; sources of, 39-40; survey of, 213-14; and task variety, 48; and turnover, 44-45; and work life programs, 140-43
Job tenure, 127. *See also* Turnover

Kimberly Home Care, 125
Kimberly Quality Care, 123. *See also* Quality Care, Inc.

Labor market: gender segregation of, 17-18, 20-23; primary vs. secondary, 14, 18, 23, 24, 185; and racial stereotyping, 23; service sector, 18-19; women in, 8, 17-18
Labor shortage, 11, 151
Level 3 care: definition of tasks in, 108, 121n.3, 158-59; implementation of, 119; and medically complex clients, 120
Life Time Industries, 125
Local 1199 (Drug, Hospital and Health Care Employees Union), 104, 105, 118, 120
Loneliness, 46-47, 52-53, 106, 127
Long Life Home Care Services, Inc. (Long Life), 103, 153-59, 161, 162; work force characteristics of, 76, 77; work life demonstration at, 106-21, 167-70, 172-76

Management: concern for volume, 124; constraints on, 155; perspective on work life demonstration, 111-12, 134-36, 153-54; and productivity, 12; and quality of service, 12; recommendations for, 194-204; training improvements by, 195-96; and turnover, 11; union pressures on, 12-13; and worker recruitment, 10-11, 124, 194-95
Massachusetts: turnover in, 11; worker recruitment in, 10-11
Medicaid: amounts paid out by, 204; and Blue Cross cutbacks, 143; and cost increases, 6; for home aides, 9, 57, 65, 107, 208-9; rate increases, 11, 118. *See also* Medicare
Medical equipment and supplies: deficient, 38; high technology, 58, 59; standard, 58-60
Medical procedures, by home aides, 39, 108, 158. *See also* Level 3 care
Medicare: and agency certification, 7, 57, 144-45; amount paid by, 65, 205; and cost increases, 6, 15n.3; and medical equipment, 59, 60; and need for additional services, 56, 63; prospective payment system, 6, 56. *See also* Medicaid
Michigan Organizational Assessment Questionnaire (MOAQ), 211
Milwaukee, 14, 76, 77; work life programs in, 75, 123-45, 188
Multistate firms, 57

National Association for Home Care, 7, 65
National Homecare Systems, 100
National Long-Term Care Survey, 5
New York City: AIDS cases in, 7; home care program, 4, 6, 152-53; and Medicaid, 4, 6, 107; moratorium on nursing home beds, 106; "vendorization" of home care, 103, 104; work life programs in, 14, 74-75, 106-21, 188-90
New York State: Department of Social Services, and definition of level of care, 108; worker shortage in, 11
Nursing aides, pay differential vs. home aides, 9, 15n.4, 82, 104, 126
Nursing homes: vs. home care, 6, 106-7; waiting lists for, 118

Part-time employment, 9, 12; vs. full-time, 104, 155; and service sector, 19-20. *See also* Work schedules
Political factors: and increased reimbursement rates, 203-4; regulatory policies, 108, 188, 205; and wage/benefit agreement, 118-19; and work life changes, 152-53, 158-59, 188-89
Poverty, and secondary labor market, 18
Productivity, 12; and job satisfaction, 41; and part-time workers, 20; in service vs. industrial sector, 19; and turnover, 11; in women's vs. men's jobs, 21
Profitability, 57-63, 124-25, 150, 155, 191n.1; factors interfering with, 63-67; of publicly held agencies, 61-63
Prospective Payment System (PPS), 6, 56
Psychiatric cases, 35, 36. *See also* Clients, difficult
Public transportation, 26, 38, 171

Quality Care, Inc., 4, 123, 150; conditions in, 125-27; corporate history of, 125; dropouts from full-time work requirement, 170-71; and labor shortage, 151; local agencies of, 124; and Medicare certification, 144, 145; and turnover, 172-75, 190; work force characteristics, 76, 77; work life programs at, 128-45, 152-61, 167-68, 188-91
Quality of care: and commitment to clients, 39-40; expectation of, 193; and independent providers, 205; and performance gap, 151; upgrading of, 108; and worker satisfaction, 12
Quality of work life. *See* Working conditions; Work life demonstrations

Racial issues: and job satisfaction, 48, 52; and labor market segregation, 21, 23, 185; work force characteristics, 76, 77
Recruitment, 10-11, 105-6, 124, 128, 134; proposed improvements in, 194-95
Referrals, 152
Reliability, worker, 12
Remedy Home and Health Care, Inc., 4; corporate management, 80; dropouts from full-time work requirement, 170-71; sales, 80; staff and budget of, 79; and turnover, 151, 178-80; and union, 80-83; work force characteristics, 76, 77; working conditions at, 82-84; and work life programs, 85-100, 150, 152-53, 155-59, 167-82, 189, 190
Remedy Temporary Services, 80
Replacement aides, 37; problems with, 38; staff aides as, 129, 135
"Request for proposal" (RFP) process, 206

Safety problems, 38-39
Sales volume, 80, 124, 135
San Bernardino County, 81, 101n.4
San Diego: turnover in, 11, 151; work force characteristics, 76, 77; work life programs in, 14, 74, 85-102, 188-90
San Diego County Board of Supervisors, 79, 80, 100
San Diego County Department of Social Services: and competitive bidding, 100, 158; and participation in work life programs, 74, 86
Scheduling practices. *See* Work schedules
Screening mechanisms, 195
Service. *See* Quality of care
Service Employees International Union, 104, 105
Service sector employment, 18-19; and part-time workers, 20
Sexual harassment, 36-37
"Shared aide" programs, 206-7
Sick leave, 135, 144. *See also* Benefits
Sleep-in situations, 37, 38
Spanish-speakers, 89-90, 179
Special Home Attendant Research Project (SHARP), 110, 119
Staff aides, 128-29, 136-42, 171, 202
States: regulatory policies of, 108, 188, 205; and work life improvements, 206
Stress, reduction of, 12
Supervisor(s), 29, 40n.1, 48; support from, and loneliness, 47
Supplies, deficient, 38
Support services, 12, 85, 90-91, 120, 155-56, 180, 182n.9, 197-98

Syracuse, 14, 76, 77; work life programs in, 75, 123-45, 188, 189

Task variety, 48
Television watching, 37
Third-party coverage, 57, 203; of high technology products and services, 59; innovative forms of, 207-9. *See also* Blue Cross; Medicaid; Medicare
Training: and agency operations, 155-56; basic, 166, 182n.1, 195; in care of difficult clients, 109, 110, 159; dropouts from, 169; improved programs for, 13, 14, 88-90; inadequate, 82; in medical care, 108; of new workers, 178-80; and quality of service, 12; requirements, 9; specialized, 109, 110, 159, 196; and turnover, 11, 178-80, 190
Transitional pay, 177, 200
Transportation problems, 26, 38, 171
Travel pay, 12, 15n.6, 26, 82, 182n.7
Turnover, 10, 11, 83; and age factor, 46, 52; analysis of, 44, 216; and continuity of care, 175-77; definition of, 216; effect of schedule on, 96; effect of work life demonstration on, 93-94, 114-17, 120, 137-40, 172-77, 189, 190; and job satisfaction, 43-53; in new workers, 97, 98; rates of, 11, 151; in women's jobs, 21

Unemployment, 152; and worker recruitment, 10
Unions, 12-13, 125; and individual provider system, 81; in New York, 104-6, 118-19; in San Diego, 80-81; and wage/benefit packages, 80-82, 118-19
United Domestic Workers (UDW), 74, 80-83, 85

Vacation pay, 80, 126, 129, 135. *See also* Benefits
Visiting nurse associations (VNAs), 7, 101n.7, 144, 152, 154

Wages, 8-9, 33, 76, 77, 82, 104-5, 126; of black women, 21, 23; comparative, 66; differential for difficult clients, 109, 111, 157, 159; differential for work life programs, 128-29, 136, 142, 188; dissatisfaction with, 8-9, 14, 18, 24, 33, 82, 106, 107, 126, 186; of home- vs. institution-based workers, 9, 15n.7, 82, 104, 126, 199, 206; increases in, 118-19, 198-99; of independent providers, 81; for live-in work, 40n.4, 104, 106; of males vs. females, 21, 22; median, in survey, 25; minimum, 100; and recruitment problems, 10; and reward for performance, 199; in secondary vs. primary labor market, 14, 18, 24; starting, 104; transitional pay, 177, 200; and travel costs, 15n.6; and unions, 80-82, 118-19; for weekend work, 104, 106, 201
Weekend work, 38, 104, 106, 201
Wheelchair-bound clients, 35
Wisconsin Blue Cross. *See* Blue Cross
Women, employment of. *See* Gender issues
Worker recognition demonstration, 121
Workers. *See* Home aides/home attendants
Working conditions: improvement of, 10; problem areas, 8-10, 35-39, 82-84, 105-6, 125-26, 186-87; and quality of service, 12. *See also* Job problems; Job satisfaction
Work life demonstrations, 4, 13-14; administrative time consumed by, 135; and agency goals, 154-56; competitive advantage of, 151-52; components of, 85, 109, 128-29; comprehensive programs, 180-82; and continuity of care, 172-77; costs of, 92, 112, 136, 150, 189; differences among, 168; difficulties in implementing, 149-50; dropouts from, 130, 138, 168-71; effects of, 92-99, 112-17, 136-42, 189; evaluation of, 215-16; feasibility of, 187-89; implementation of, 85-92, 109-12, 129-36, 154-63; at Long Life and Independent Living, 106-21; management perspective on, 111-12, 134-36, 153-54; participation in, 86-89, 129-31,

166-68; and performance gaps, 151; and political factors, 152-53, 158-59; at Quality Care, 128-45; at Remedy, 85-92; site selection, 72-74; targets of programs, 177-82; and turnover, 93-94, 114-15, 120, 172-77; and unbillable hours, 132-33; wage increments in, 111, 129
Work schedules: guaranteed hours, 91-92, 100, 131-33, 144, 156-57, 167-68, 200-202; and health insurance, 83; and job attachment, 177-78; for live-in situations, 104; of new workers, 180; part-time vs. full-time, 9, 12, 19-20, 76, 78, 83, 104, 129, 131-33, 155, 200-202; and program dropouts, 170-71, 191; and turnover, 96; unexpected changes in, 26; weekend/replacement work, 37, 38, 104; and work life changes, 155

ABOUT THE AUTHORS

PENNY HOLLANDER FELDMAN is Lecturer in Political Science in the Department of Health Policy and Management, Harvard School of Public Health. Among her recent publications are *Recruiting an Elite: Admission to Harvard College* (1987) and, with Alice M. Sapienza, "Strategic Management of Quality of Worklife in the Home Care Industry" in *Human Resource Management in the Health Care Sector: A Guide for Administrators and Professionals* (Greenwood Press, 1989).

ALICE M. SAPIENZA is Assistant Professor of Management in the Department of Health Policy and Management, Harvard School of Public Health. In addition to her work in home care, she has published several recent articles on the management and diffusion of biotechnology in the United States and abroad.

NANCY M. KANE is Assistant Professor of Management in the Department of Health Policy and Management, Harvard School of Public Health. Her recent publications include "Home Care Crisis of the Nineties," which appeared in *The Gerontologist* (1989).